T0361344

Farming Simulator Modding with Blender

This is a comprehensive guide to creating and customizing mods for the popular video game Farming Simulator within Blender. This book covers all aspects needed to create your own vehicle mods from start to finish.

The book begins with a basic introduction in Blender before showing you how to prepare your hierarchy and set up pivots. You'll then learn to create physics components and how to set up your ModDesc and Vehicle XML files. The book then covers all you need to know about implementing vehicle functions before applying LOD meshes ahead of testing and finally publishing your mod on the official GIANTS ModHub.

This book will appeal to all Farming Simulator modders, as well as those looking to learn game development concepts within Blender.

Jason van Gumster does a lot of things. Mostly he makes stuff up. He writes, animates, and occasionally teaches. He has heavy entrepreneurial tendencies that run nearly as deep as his creative ones, so he has a constant fascination with producing creative content with as much control and independence as possible. Naturally, he's a big proponent of open source software; very nearly everything that he produces is made using free and open source tools.

Stefan Maurus serves as the Lead Integrator at GIANTS Software, overseeing the integration of vehicles and assets into the Farming Simulator game series. Prior to entering the gaming industry, Stefan initiated his career as a modder, gaining recognition for the detailed mods he crafted. At GIANTS FarmCon and other industry events, he conducts workshops and presentations to assist modders in enhancing their mod creation skills.

Farming Simulator Modding with Blender

A Step-by-step Guide to Creating, Optimizing and Publishing Mods

Jason van Gumster and Stefan Maurus

CRC Press
Taylor & Francis Group
Boca Raton London New York

CRC Press is an imprint of the
Taylor & Francis Group, an **informa** business

Designed cover image: GIANTS Software

First edition published 2025
by CRC Press
2385 NW Executive Center Drive, Suite 320, Boca Raton FL 33431

and by CRC Press
4 Park Square, Milton Park, Abingdon, Oxon, OX14 4RN

CRC Press is an imprint of Taylor & Francis Group, LLC

© 2025 GIANTS Software

ISBN: 9781032659480 (hbk)
ISBN: 9781032639697 (pbk)
ISBN: 9781032659497 (ebk)

DOI: 10.1201/9781032659497

Typeset in Minion
by codeMantra

Contents

Foreword, xii

CHAPTER 1 ▪ Introduction to Farming Simulator Modding   1

  TECHNICAL REQUIREMENTS   2

  GETTING FAMILIAR WITH THE GIANTS DEVELOPER NETWORK (GDN)   2

    Creating a GDN Account   3

    Discovering What's Available on the GDN   4

  EXPLORING THE FARMING SIMULATOR MODHUB   4

    Creating a ModHub Account   5

    Using ModHub as a Mod Research Tool   7

  DISCOVERING VIDEO TUTORIALS ON MODDING AND 3D   7

    Taking Advantage of Video Tutorials on GDN   7

    Getting the Most Out of Blender with Tutorials by CG Cookie   8

  SHARING WITH THE COMMUNITY ON THE GIANTS SOFTWARE FORUM   10

  DIGGING INTO THE TOOLS USED FOR MODDING   12

    Using Blender as Your DCC   13

    Exporting 3D Assets with the GIANTS I3D Exporter   16

    GIANTS Editor: Your Last Stop before Going to Farming Simulator   17

    Getting into the Details with GIANTS Studio/Debugger   18

  SUMMARY   20

CHAPTER 2 ▪ Working with Blender   21

  TECHNICAL REQUIREMENTS   22

  GETTING STARTED WITH BLENDER   22

    A Quick Primer on Blender's Interface   22

    Navigating 3D Space   23

    Working with Modes   24

    Using the Toolbar and Hotkeys to Edit   25

Some Recommended Settings to Make Your Life Easier   26

What You Really Need to Know for the Purposes of Modding   29

USING THE GIANTS I3D EXPORTER   42

TIPS AND TRICKS FOR WORKING WITHIN BLENDER   44

General Purpose Hotkeys   45

Editing Hotkeys   45

SUMMARY   46

CHAPTER 3 ■ Defining Surface Materials   47

TECHNICAL REQUIREMENTS   48

SETTING UP MATERIALS IN BLENDER   48

Understanding the Differences between Blender Materials
and Farming Simulator Materials   48

Creating Your Placeholder Material in Blender   49

Configuring GIANTS I3D Exporter to See Farming Simulator
Shaders   50

ASSIGNING MATERIALS TO YOUR VEHICLE   51

Using Prefabricated Materials   51

Customizing Your Material Colors with Color Materials   53

Applying Vehicle Masks (vmasks) and Normal Maps   54

ADDING DECALS TO YOUR MOD   57

Setting up Your Decal Material   57

Positioning and Unwrapping Your Decal Geometry   60

Cleaning Up   62

TESTING YOUR MATERIAL IN THE GIANTS EDITOR   64

Confirming Your Colorized Material Shaders   65

Checking Variable Shader Properties   65

CONVERTING TEXTURES TO DDS   67

Getting and Installing the GIANTS Texture Tool   68

Using the GIANTS Texture Tool   68

UNDERSTANDING THE MATERIAL SYSTEM IN FARMING
SIMULATOR 25 AND BEYOND   69

Updates to Names on Shader Variations and Parameters   69

Adding Shaders and Materials in the New Material System   70

Working with the New StaticLight Shader Variation   74

SUMMARY   76

CHAPTER 4 ▪ Preparing Your Hierarchy and Setting up Pivots   77

  TECHNICAL REQUIREMENTS   77

  SEPARATING YOUR VEHICLE MESH INTO PARTS   78

  ADJUSTING THE POSITION OF OBJECT ORIGINS (PIVOTS)   83

  PREPARING YOUR VEHICLE HIERARCHY   84

  SUMMARY   85

CHAPTER 5 ▪ Creating Physics Components and Function Nodes   86

  TECHNICAL REQUIREMENTS   87

  DEFINING NONPHYSICS COMPONENTS   87

  BUILDING COLLISION MESHES   88

  SETTING UP YOUR MAIN COLLISION COMPONENT   89

  CONFIGURING COMPOUND CHILDREN   91

  SPECIFYING ATTACHMENT POINTS AND CONNECTION HOSES   93

    Adding an Attachment Point   93

    Handling Connection Hoses   95

  SUMMARY   98

CHAPTER 6 ▪ Setting up ModDesc-XML and Vehicle-XML   99

  TECHNICAL REQUIREMENTS   99

  GIVING YOUR MOD A HOME   100

  BUILDING YOUR MODDESC.XML FILE   101

    The Basics: Understanding the Essential Parts of the modDesc.xml File   102

    Understanding Additional Information Provided by modDesc.xml   104

  SETTING UP YOUR VEHICLE-XML FILE   109

    Enabling Developer Mode in Farming Simulator   109

    Understanding Vehicle-XML   110

    Getting Help with Your Vehicle-XML   116

    Testing Vehicle-XML (and Your Mod) in Farming Simulator 116

  GETTING BLENDER TO SEE YOUR XML FILES   117

  SUMMARY   118

CHAPTER 7 ▪ Implementing Vehicle Functions   119

  TECHNICAL REQUIREMENTS   119

  DEFINING WHEELS   120

    Configuring Simple Wheels   120

    Setting Up Wheel <speedRotatingParts>   124

Adding Wheel Chocks   128

Improving Performance with Merge Children   130

SETTING UP WORK AREAS   133

Configuring Work Areas   133

Defining Your Ground Reference Node   135

Helping Your Vehicle Know the Distance to the Ground with
Ground Adjusted Nodes   135

Setting up AI Areas and the AI Collision Node   137

PUSHING AWAY YOUR CROPS WITH FOLIAGE BENDING NODES   141

CREATING VISUAL EFFECTS FOR YOUR VEHICLE   142

Adding a Particle System   142

Adding Soil Effects   144

SUMMARY   148

CHAPTER 8 ■ Animating Your Vehicle   150

TECHNICAL REQUIREMENTS   150

SETTING UP BASIC ANIMATION   151

CONTROLLING THE FOLDING PROCESS   153

DEFINING MOVING PARTS   156

Setting Up Hydraulics   156

Setting Up Moving Arms   159

INCLUDING SOUNDS WITH YOUR ANIMATIONS   161

PREVISUALIZING ANIMATIONS BY ANIMATING IN BLENDER   162

Setting up for Animating   163

Animating in Blender   168

SUMMARY   170

CHAPTER 9 ■ Adding Extra Vehicle Features   171

TECHNICAL REQUIREMENTS   171

IMPLEMENTING LIGHT SOURCES   172

Referencing Shared Lights from Farming Simulator   172

Working with Real Light Sources   173

ADDING A LICENSE PLATE   176

VALIDATING YOUR VEHICLE-XML   177

SUMMARY   179

CHAPTER 10 ■ Creating Merge Groups | 180
TECHNICAL REQUIREMENTS | 180
UNDERSTANDING MERGE GROUPS | 181
ASSIGNING OBJECTS TO YOUR MERGE GROUP | 182
Defining a Merge Group Root | 182
Adding other Objects to Your Merge Group | 183
CREATING A CUSTOM BOUNDING VOLUME | 184
SUMMARY | 186

CHAPTER 11 ■ Building Level of Detail (LOD) Meshes | 187
TECHNICAL REQUIREMENTS | 187
UNDERSTANDING LOD | 188
MODELING YOUR LOD MESHES | 189
SETTING UP A MERGE GROUP TO MANAGE YOUR LOD | 191
ADJUSTING YOUR VEHICLE HIERARCHY AND SETTING ATTRIBUTES TO CONTROL LOD MESHES | 192
SUMMARY | 194

CHAPTER 12 ■ Constructing Hydraulic Hoses | 195
TECHNICAL REQUIREMENTS | 195
UNDERSTANDING ARMATURE OBJECTS IN BLENDER | 196
ADDING ARMATURE BONES THAT MOVE WITH YOUR VEHICLE | 197
Adding Bones to Your Armature | 198
Setting Constraints on Your Armature Bones | 199
ASSIGNING VERTEX WEIGHTS TO CONTROL DEFORMATIONS | 200
Assigning Weights to Your Root Bone | 201
Defining Weights for Other Vertex Groups | 202
SUMMARY | 204

CHAPTER 13 ■ Generating Icons | 205
TECHNICAL REQUIREMENTS | 205
GETTING THE FARMING SIMULATOR ICON GENERATOR | 206
BUILDING A STORE ICON FOR INDIVIDUAL VEHICLES | 208
CREATING AN ICON FOR YOUR MOD | 209
SUMMARY | 210

Chapter 14 ■ Tips and Tricks for Testing Your Vehicle In-Game   211

   TECHNICAL REQUIREMENTS   212

   SETTING UP FARMING SIMULATOR FOR TESTING   212

   POPULATING FIELDS QUICKLY   214

     gsFieldSetGround   214

     gsFieldSetFruit   217

     gsTipAnywhereAdd   219

     gsPalletAdd and gsBaleAdd   220

     gsTreeAdd   222

     gsMoneyAdd   222

   MODIFYING YOUR VEHICLE FROM THE IN-GAME CONSOLE   223

     gsFillUnitAdd   223

     Testing the Dirtiness and Wear on Your Vehicle   224

     Adjusting Fuel and Temperature Levels   224

     gsCameraFovSet   225

   RELOADING YOUR VEHICLE WITHOUT RESTARTING THE GAME   226

   DEBUGGING YOUR VEHICLE MOD   226

     gsVehicleDebug   226

     gsVehicleDebugLOD   230

     gsRenderingDebugMode   231

   SUMMARY   232

Chapter 15 ■ Publishing Your Mod   233

   TECHNICAL REQUIREMENTS   234

   DISCOVERING THE MODHUB   234

   PREPARING YOUR MOD FOR PUBLISHING   235

     Giving Your Mod a Description   235

     Capturing Good in-Game Screenshots   236

     Preparing Your Mod for Console Play   237

     Pre-Verifying Your Mod with TestRunner   238

   PUBLISHING YOUR MOD TO THE MODHUB   240

     Uploading Your Mod   240

     Getting Feedback and Updating Your Mod   243

   UNDERSTANDING MONETIZATION FOR MODS   244

WHERE TO GO FROM HERE   245

    Attending FarmCon   245

    Mod Contests!   247

    Scripting Farming Simulator with Lua   247

    CG Cookie   249

SUMMARY   249

APPENDIX: CODE/FILE EXAMPLES, 251

INDEX, 277

Foreword

WELCOME TO THE DYNAMIC world of *Farming Simulator Modding with Blender*! In this exciting journey, you are about to embark on a creative exploration of the intersection between virtual agriculture and digital craftsmanship. Farming Simulator has grown into a thriving community where enthusiasts and developers converge to enhance the gaming experience through the magic of modding.

This book serves as your comprehensive guide to mastering the art of modding using Blender, a versatile and powerful 3D modeling tool. Whether you're a seasoned modder or a newcomer to the field, the knowledge contained within these pages will empower you to bring your virtual farming dreams to life.

This book provides step-by-step tutorials, insider tips, and hands-on exercises to improve your skills. By the end of this journey, you'll be equipped with the expertise to design and implement your own mods, adding a personal touch to the expansive world of Farming Simulator.

So, buckle up and prepare to sow the seeds of creativity. Your virtual farm awaits, and with the knowledge gained from this book, you'll be cultivating a modding legacy that extends far beyond the fields of your digital homestead.

Happy Modding!
Stefan Geiger
Co-Founder and CTO GIANTS Software

CHAPTER 1

Introduction to Farming Simulator Modding

W ELCOME TO THE WORLD of Farming Simulator Modding! It's wild and wooly and a ton of fun. (Well, it's really only wooly if you happen to be farming sheep, but I digress.) If you're reading this then you probably already know what Farming Simulator is, but in the event that you're entirely new to all of this, allow me to explain. Farming Simulator is the incredibly popular video game that gives you the experience of the work and business of farming without spending your days working in the hot sun or pouring rain. It's available on nearly every available gaming platform and in the last 15 years the series has sold over 30 million copies and had 145 million downloads on mobile devices. That's a huge community of virtual farmers!

And not only is playing the game itself popular, but so is customizing, or *modding*, the game. The creators of Farming Simulator, GIANTS Software, have designed the game to be incredibly easy to extend and update with your own customizations. That's what this whole book is about! You can create your own vehicles, buildings, game maps, or even complete gameplay customizations. And then you can put them into Farming Simulator and use them in your own games, share them with friends, or put them up on the GIANTS Software ModHub for other people to use. It's worth noting that the main focus of this book is on creating a vehicle mod. However, the knowledge that you gain from that process can be extended to make any of the other mods I just listed.

Being the first chapter of this book, this is where you get started. We'll introduce you to the GIANTS Developer Network (GDN), the home of the GIANTS Engine (the game engine that's at the core of Farming Simulator). You'll explore the Farming Simulator ModHub where you can see the mods that other people in the community have created, and perhaps your own mods in the future. We'll direct you to where you can watch video tutorials that have been produced by GIANTS Software and others to help you on your

DOI: 10.1201/9781032659497-1

modding journey. You'll also learn about the community over at the GDN Forum, where you can share works in progress and get feedback from other modders. And last, we'll cover some of the specific tools that you'll use to create your mods. In a way, this chapter is really laying the groundwork for having a really great time. Let's get started!

In this chapter:

- Getting familiar with the GIANTS Developer Network (GDN)

- Exploring the Farming Simulator ModHub

- Discovering video tutorials on modding and 3D

- Sharing with the community on the GDN Forum

- Digging into the tools used for modding

TECHNICAL REQUIREMENTS

For this chapter, there aren't very many technical requirements other than a computer (or a phone) with a web browser. In each section of this chapter, you'll see one of the resources that's available online to help you with creating your mods for Farming Simulator. The addresses for those websites are covered in each section.

GETTING FAMILIAR WITH THE GIANTS DEVELOPER NETWORK (GDN)

As you start creating mods for Farming Simulator, you'll probably find that your primary home base is going to be the GDN, the *GIANTS Developer Network*. This is a website that GIANTS Software has specifically put together to help modders get their work done. To access the GDN, fire up your favorite web browser and point it at the following URL:

https://gdn.giants-software.com

You should be greeted with a page that looks like the image in Figure 1.1.

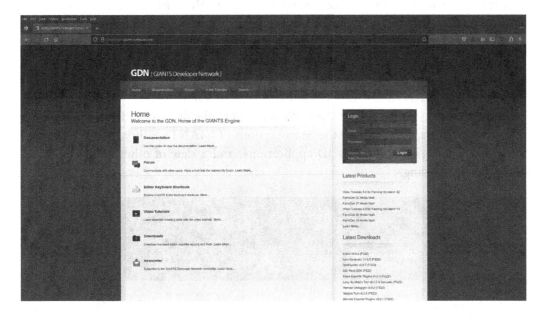

FIGURE 1.1   Welcome to the GIANTS Developer Network! You're a modder now.

When you get to the GDN, it's a good idea to log in. Being logged in to the GDN gives you the ability to download files as well as make threads and comment on the forum. In fact, quite a bit of the GDN's content is hidden unless you are logged in. Of course, logging requires that you have an account for the site, so that's the next thing you need to do.

Creating a GDN Account

Fortunately, registering on the GDN is absolutely free. If you look at the bottom of the blue Login box on the right of the GDN's home page, there's a link labeled *Register Here*. Click that link and you'll get a registration form where you enter a little bit of information, particularly the username you want and your email address so you can receive occasional notifications from the website. There's also a check box that you can enable if you'd like to receive the newsletter from GIANTS Software. The newsletter is pretty low-traffic, only coming out for new updates or major announcements, so your inbox won't get filled with a bunch of unnecessary emails.

After filling out all of the required information click the Register button. Within a minute or two, you should receive an email from the GDN to let you know that your registration has gone through and that you can log in with the provided password. Keep that password safe. If you lose it, you'll need to go through the password reset process. That process is pretty painless—just an email confirmation to reset—but it's always nicer if you don't have to do it all.

Discovering What's Available on the GDN

Once you log in to the GDN, you have complete access to all of the resources that GIANTS Software makes available for modders. One especially helpful section of the GDN is the Documentation page. This book should give you everything you need to create your own mods, but there's some really great technical information in there about Farming Simulator's scripting API (application programming interface) and specifications for the I3D format that GIANTS Software created for Farming Simulator.

The other really helpful part of the GDN is the Downloads section. Here, as the image in Figure 1.2 shows, you can find the latest versions of GIANTS Editor, GIANTS Studio/Debugger, exporters for different 3D applications, and a slew of other handy tools and resources for modding.

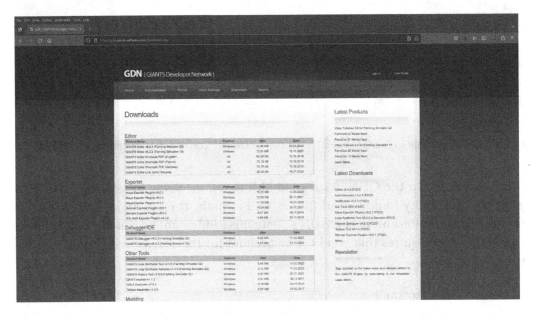

FIGURE 1.2   The Downloads section of the GDN is where you can get the latest version of GIANTS Editor and a bunch of other handy resources for making mods.

The GDN is also the home of the GDN Community Forum and a variety of video tutorials, but those are covered later in this chapter.

EXPLORING THE FARMING SIMULATOR MODHUB

One other heavily-trafficked location for a Farming Simulator modder is the Farming Simulator ModHub. The ModHub is where the community shares their mods for other people to download and use. Mods are free to download. Even better, if your mod is on ModHub and users start downloading it, GIANTS Software pays you a little for every download (see Chapter 15, for more on this)! To see what ModHub is all about, point your web browser to the following URL:

https://farming-simulator.com/mods

When you load the page, you should see something like in Figure 1.3.

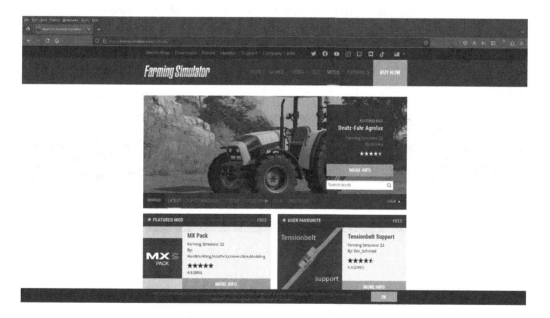

FIGURE 1.3   ModHub is where you go to get and share mods.

Creating a ModHub Account

Like the GDN, in order to take full advantage of ModHub, you need to log in, and logging in requires an account. With an account, you're able to upload your own mods to ModHub. We don't cover that process in detail until Chapter 15, but it's a good idea to go ahead and get your account created now.

Unfortunately, you can't just re-use the same account that you created over at the GDN, so you'll need to create a separate account for ModHub. Fortunately, the process for registering is almost as easy as it is on the GDN:

1. Click the Login button on the ModHub page. It's in green text on the right side of the ModHub menu. You don't yet have an account, so it may be a bit confusing to click "Login" if you want to create an account, but bear with me.

2. On the ModHub login page, click the *Register new account here* link beneath the login form. This link is the one that brings you to the page where you can create a new account.

3. Fill out the required fields on the registration form. Be sure to enable the *terms of use* check box at the bottom of the form. If you're curious about what the terms of use are, you're welcome to click the link and read them.

4. Click the Register button and your ModHub account is created. You should get an email at the address you entered that gives you your login credentials. As with the GDN account, definitely make it a point to keep track of your password and keep it safe.

Once you're logged in to ModHub, you should be greeted with a page that looks like Figure 1.4.

FIGURE 1.4   You're logged in to ModHub. Woohoo!

Since you haven't created any mods yet, the page looks rather empty. Now worries, though. I'm sure you'll be filling that page with all your awesome mods before too long.

In the meantime, you should take this opportunity to have a look through the mods that other people in the community have created.

Using ModHub as a Mod Research Tool

One of the great things about ModHub is that it gives you the ability to check out the work of other Farming Simulator modders. Of course you can see their mods and test them out just like any other person who plays Farming Simulator, but you're not just a player anymore. You're a modder. You can have a look at these mods with a more critical eye now. What mods are already out there? Is your mod idea already done? Could you collaborate with the person making that mod? How are other mods put together? Are there any tricks they use that you could also use in your own mod?

The answers to these questions are the things you should keep in mind as you build out your own mod. This way you can emulate what other people are doing well while you avoid doing things that aren't working. So take some time and scroll through the mods in ModHub. Check out all the categories of mods that people have put out. Download and play with the ones you like to see how they feel. Run them in Developer Mode and check their debugging information with the commands covered in Chapter 14. Take notes on them and think about how you might improve them. Now you're thinking like a modder!

DISCOVERING VIDEO TUTORIALS ON MODDING AND 3D

This book is [hopefully] a great resource for helping you along in your modding journey. However, not everyone resonates with text and images. Sometimes it's really helpful to follow along and learn from watching video of people doing the work you're trying to do. That's why video tutorials are so popular. And the best thing is that you're not limited to using one or the other. You can keep this book with you as a handy reference while also watching video tutorials to get a better sense of the "flow" of what's described in text.

There's a lot of tutorials out on YouTube that would be helpful to modders, but many of them are only really useful if you already know what you want. Sometimes it's best to have a more directed and curated selection of tutorials to get yourself started. That's what I'm describing in this section: the modding tutorials that are available to you on GDN and the modeling, rigging, and animation tutorials that are available over on CG Cookie.

Taking Advantage of Video Tutorials on GDN

Heading back over to the GDN (https://gdn.giants-software.com), there's a section of the site that we didn't cover earlier. It's the section labeled Video Tutorials. Click on that link in the menu at the top of the GDN and you should get a page that looks like the image in Figure 1.5.

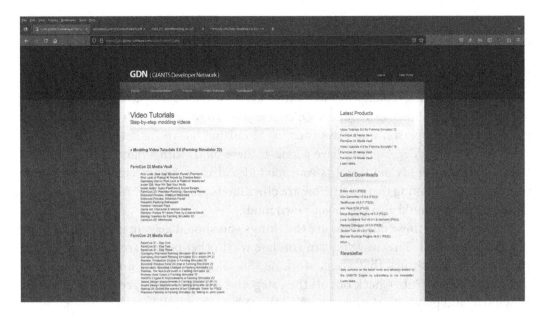

FIGURE 1.5 The Video Tutorials section of the GDN gives you access to all kinds of helpful video content.

Right at the top of this page is a link to the latest modding video tutorials. These tutorials cover the process of modding for the latest version of Farming Simulator. All of the older tutorials are available for free while newer video tutorials are available for purchase and they're well worth it.

Of course, there's other helpful video content available on the GDN. If you scroll down the page, you can find the previous series of video tutorials that were produced for earlier versions of Farming Simulator. Some of the information in those tutorials is out of date, but the general workflow should still apply for current versions of Farming Simulator.

Also on the Video Tutorials page of the GDN are the media vaults for each of the annual FarmCon events that are hosted by GIANTS Software. Not only do these videos give you a sense of how cool the community is around Farming Simulator, there are also some really interesting presentations that you may find helpful and inspirational when creating your own mods.

Getting the Most Out of Blender with Tutorials by CG Cookie

You can use just about any 3D digital content creation (DCC) tool for building the 3D assets in your mods. However, **Blender** is the tool that's used by the vast majority of Farming Simulator modders. Blender is a free modeling and animation suite that's used to make all kinds of incredible things in 3D, even beyond games and mods. If you're not familiar with Blender yet, don't worry. We cover enough to get you started in Chapter 2 of this book.

Of course, since this book is primarily focused on the process of modding, we cover enough to get you started and get comfortable working in Blender. However, the pages of this book can't cover all of the things you can do in Blender (there are other books for that… some of them written by me!). And Blender is such a visual tool, a lot of 3D work-flows are best captured in the form of video tutorials.

It just so happens that CG Cookie is a fantastic platform that hosts whole courses on using Blender. With these courses, you can up your skills in modeling, texturing, rigging, and animation with all of the tools and features available to you in Blender. You can get to CG Cookie by pointing your web browser to the following URL:

https://cgcookie.com
You should see something like the image in Figure 1.6.

FIGURE 1.6   CG Cookie is your home for learning Blender.

There's a large number of free courses on CG Cookie (particularly ones for beginners who are just getting started with Blender), but the real value of CG Cookie comes when you sign up for their membership. And since you have this book, CG Cookie is actually offering a promotional price for Farming Simulator modders. Just go through this special URL:

https://cgcookie.com/farmingsimulator

My recommendation is that, in addition to this book, you work your way through the Blender Basics course for the latest version of Blender (which is free) and then, with your membership, check out the Tread course. That course walks you through the process of making a game-ready 3D model that is a great primer for modding. If you choose not to get a membership, the Press Start course is free and also serves as a decent primer, although it's not specifically focused on game assets.

SHARING WITH THE COMMUNITY ON THE GIANTS SOFTWARE FORUM

One of the most useful things you can do as a modder is get yourself involved with the community. The community that's grown around Farming Simulator is incredible. And it's not just about the game. There's also a lot of great community energy among Farming Simulator modders. There's a reason why there's a two-day FarmCon event every year where players, devs, and modders get together.

Of course, not everyone can make it to that conference and even if you can, what about the other 363 days of the year when the event isn't happening? That's why the Community Forum exists. To get to the GIANTS Software Community Forum, point your browser to the following URL:

https://forum.giants-software.com
You'll arrive at a page like the one in Figure 1.7.

FIGURE 1.7   The Community Forum is where you can connect with other modders.

Like the GDN and ModHub, the forum requires that you register an account, but once you've done that, you have the ability to make posts on the Community Forum and connect with other modders. You can get help on specific issues you're running into, share your works in progress, or just kick back and just socialize with your fellow modders. The folks on the forum are friendly, welcoming, and always willing to help. Pop on in and say hello!

DIGGING INTO THE TOOLS USED FOR MODDING

We're about to get started on our modding journey. Before we get into it, though, we should really review what the basic workflow looks like and the kinds of tools that you'll need. Each chapter in this book has a **Technical requirements** section that covers what you'll need for that chapter. However, it's useful to know ahead of time all of the different tools that you'll need as a Farming Simulator modder. Fortunately, the list is not that long. You really just need four things:

- **3D digital content creation (DCC) tool** like Blender to create 3D models that you want in your mod
- **GIANTS I3D Exporter** to get your 3D data from the DCC ready for your mod
- **GIANTS Editor** to preview and debug your mod
- **GIANTS Studio/Debugger** to modify the various XML files that control the behavior of vehicles in your mod

In terms of workflow, your typical creation pipeline uses the following sequence:

1. Create your 3D assets in your DCC. Depending on the nature of your mod, these assets don't have to be fully finalized. They just need all of the relevant parts and have the rough dimensions for your mod. This way you can test functionality even with a rough model and then, if you'd like, go back and refine the model with more details.

2. Export your 3D assets using the correct GIANTS I3D exporter for your chosen DCC.

3. Pull your exported I3D file into GIANTS Editor for preview and testing.

4. Use the GIANTS Studio/Debugger to edit your mod's XML and your vehicle-XML files to control the behavior of vehicles and your mod overall.

5. Continue testing in GIANTS Editor.

6. Test in-game with Farming Simulator.

That's the basic flow. Of course, the actual work isn't always that linear. You'll find yourself going back a step (or three!) to modify or fix something based on the results of your testing. So really, it's best to think of this workflow as a sequence of loops where you test at every step in the process, jump back to previous steps to make adjustments, and then move forward to test again. This kind of iterative approach helps you get something working early. The whole thing might be ugly at each step until you're done, but at least your mod is functional and you can then put your energy into refining it.

The next few sub-sections cover each of the specific tools used in this workflow

Using Blender as Your DCC

When it comes to 3D DCC tools, there are a lot of choices available to modders. However, the vast majority of modders in the Farming Simulator modding community choose to use Blender to get their work done. And really, it's a great choice. Blender is a fully-featured 3D application that you can use to make 3D models, texture them, rig them, and even animate them. It works on Windows, macOS, and Linux and even functions well on relatively modest hardware. On top of all of that, it's absolutely *free*. Anyone can download Blender and get to work making whatever they want.

At this point, if you haven't already, you'll want to go ahead and get a copy of Blender for yourself. Open your web browser and point it to the following URL:

https://blender.org

When the page loads, you should be greeted with a page that looks like Figure 1.8.

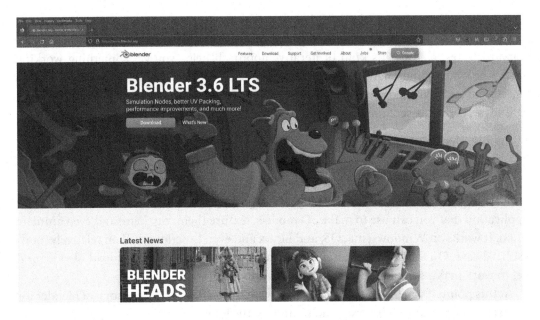

FIGURE 1.8   Blender.org is where you go to get the latest version of Blender.

From the Blender home page, you can click the **Download** button to get the version of Blender that matches the operating system on your computer. If you use Steam, Blender is also available there if you prefer to get your 3D tools that way.

NOTE

As for which version of Blender to get, my recommendation is to get the latest *long term support* or LTS version of Blender. LTS versions are supported for 2 years after release. They tend to be the most stable and most of the available documentation and tutorials tend to focus on those versions. Don't get me wrong, the latest and greatest version of Blender has all the fantastic new toys to work with and is also pretty stable. However, if you're just starting out, my opinion is that the LTS versions are a better way to go.

Once you download Blender, the installation process is pretty straight-forward. You just use the standard tools for your computer's operating system and you should be up and running without issue. After you have Blender installed, you can launch it and you should see something like the screenshot in Figure 1.9.

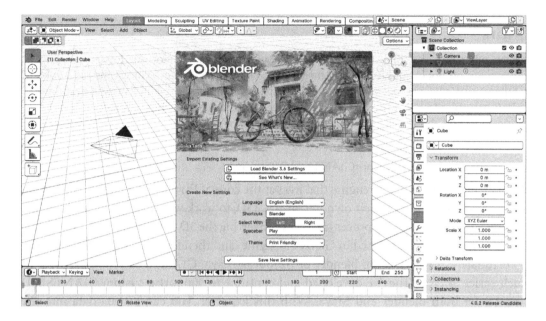

FIGURE 1.9   This is what Blender looks like when you launch it.

NOTE

You might notice when you see screenshots of Blender in this book, the colors may not exactly match what you see on your computer monitor. The difference is because I'm using a different theme than Blender's darker default so the screenshot looks better when printed on paper. If you want to use the exact same theme, you can do so by going to **Edit ▶ Preferences** and navigating to the **Themes** section. From there you can load the *Print Friendly* theme preset from the dropdown menu at the top of that section.

Chapter 2: Working with Blender serves as this book's primer on Blender to get you familiar with its interface and tools so you can get started using it for your mods. We also reference Blender frequently in other chapters because if you're using the iterative workflow described in the preceding section, you'll find yourself going back to Blender to make adjustments to your models.

It is worth mentioning that you can certainly use other 3D DCC tools if you prefer not to use Blender. The biggest challenge is getting data out of that DCC tool and into the GIANTS I3D format. GIANTS Software maintains current versions of their GIANTS I3D Exporter add-on (covered in the next section) for Blender and a similar exporter for Autodesk Maya. However, if you're using any other DCC, you're probably going to need to figure out how to export from that tool and into Blender or Maya.

> **NOTE**
>
> One other tool you may find yourself using is a good application for texture painting. Blender is no slouch in this area, but there are some specially designed programs like Adobe Substance 3D Painter that you may find have a more comfortable texture painting workflow. That particular task is a bit outside of the scope of this book, but there is plenty of instructional material about using this tool with Blender and other DCCs.

Exporting 3D Assets with the GIANTS I3D Exporter

GIANTS Engine is the game engine that lives at the core of Farming Simulator. The folks at GIANTS Software created their own file format, I3D, to work with their game engine. That means part of your modding process involves converting the 3D data in your DCC to the I3D format so it can actually be used in GIANTS Engine (and therefore in Farming Simulator).

Fortunately, if you're using Blender or Autodesk Maya, GIANTS Software has made it much easier for you. They've developed and continue to support a custom GIANTS I3D exporter for both Blender and Maya. With this exporter, you can get 3D data into the GIANTS I3D format, while also setting some important parameters on export in order to ensure that everything looks and behaves properly.

To get the latest version of the GIANTS I3D exporter for your preferred DCC, go to the **Downloads** section of the GDN. This book is written using the 9.1.0 release of the Blender exporter. The add-on is bundled in a self-extracting EXE file for automated installation in Windows. If you're on Linux or macOS, you should be able to manually extract the add-on as if it were a normal compressed ZIP file.

> **IMPORTANT**
>
> Even though it's possible to get the GIANTS I3D Exporter installed on a non-Windows computer, that's about as far as you'll be able to go. The GIANTS I3D Exporter has its own EXE file and expects that you have the GIANTS Editor installed, which only runs in Windows. So even though you can activate the GIANTS I3D Exporter add-on on a non-Windows computer, you won't be able to export.

Once you have the GIANTS I3D Exporter installed, you need to enable it. Use the following steps:

1. Open Blender and navigate to **Edit ▸ Preferences** in the top menu.

2. Within the Preferences window, go to the **Add-ons** section.

3. Use the search field on the right (you can type i3d as an easy way to search) to find the **GIANTS I3D Exporter Tools** add-on. You can also find it in the Game Engine category.

4. Enable the add-on by clicking the check box to the left of its name.

Once you have the add-on enabled, it's ready to be used. One thing to note is that unlike most other exporters in Blender, you don't export I3D files from the **File ▶ Export** menu. Instead, there's a new tab added to the 3D Viewport's sidebar called **GIANTS I3D Exporter**. This is where you do the work of preparing your Blender assets for going to the GIANTS Editor. Figure 1.10 shows what this tab on the sidebar looks like, along with where to activate the GIANTS I3D Exporter add-on in Preferences.

FIGURE 1.10   Enabling the GIANTS I3D Exporter in Blender.

As far as using this add-on we cover it a lot in this book, but the best place to start is in Chapter 2 in the section titled **Using the GIANTS I3D Exporter**.

GIANTS Editor: Your Last Stop before Going to Farming Simulator

The tool that you use for previewing and debugging the I3D data that is exported from Blender is the GIANTS Editor. Blender is where you create cool vehicles and buildings to use in your mod, and it's really the place where you're doing all of the creation activity for your mod. GIANTS Editor is where you test what you've created and, perhaps more importantly, debug your file if something exports incorrectly. This tool is also a must for adjustments on maps. You can also use GIANTS Editor to tweak existing vehicles or make a custom version of any vehicles available in the base game. In fact, there's a function in GIANTS Editor that allows you to create a mod from a base game vehicle with just one click (see Chapter 6 for more on this feature).

In order to get GIANTS Editor, you need to log in to the GDN and go to the **Downloads** page. There you can download the installer for the latest version of GIANTS Editor. This book was written using version 9.0.4, but even if you're using a more recent version, the same principles covered in the pages of this book should still hold true.

Once you have the installer downloaded, go ahead and launch it to install GIANTS Editor. When it's done, the installer will give you the option of immediately launching GIANTS Editor. If you do, you should see something like what's shown in Figure 1.11.

FIGURE 1.11   GIANTS Editor is installed and running. Now you're ready to go!

When GIANTS Editor launches, there's a Getting Started window with links to documentation, the community forum, keyboard shortcuts, and video tutorials. In fact, since you've already gotten yourself an account on the GDN, you already know where these things live. However, these links give you a nice, quick way to access them without requiring you to type anything in a web browser.

As you might imagine, since GIANTS Editor is your main hub for modding, we use it in a bunch of chapters within this book.

Getting into the Details with GIANTS Studio/Debugger

The process of modding doesn't necessarily involve a lot of coding—or any coding at all if you don't want—but you do still need to edit text files. In particular, your mod and the vehicles in your mod are all configured using XML text files. While it's certainly possible to just do all of your work in Notepad, there are much better tools for the job... and most of them are free!

If you don't already have a preferred text editor, I have a few recommendations. However, there are (in my opinion) two features that any text editor you choose should have:

- **Tabbed editing.** Basically, you want to be able to open more than one text file at the same time. Just like browser tabs, tabs in a text editor give you the ability to quickly switch between files without cluttering your screen with extra windows.

- **Syntax highlighting.** The files that you edit for your mods are in a structured mark-up language called XML. Because it's a language with rules about how it's supposed to be set up, a text editor with syntax highlighting can easily color code different parts of the text to make them more easy to read. Really good text editors can even let you know when part of that structure is missing (like a closed tag… don't worry if you don't understand what that means, we'll get to it later in the book).

So what text editor should you choose? For some people, that's a very deep and personal question. However, it's best not to get too emotional about it. My recommendation is that you use the official GIANTS Studio/Debugger. It's actually more than just a text editor. It's more like an *integrated development environment* (IDE) for GIANTS Engine. Because it's developed and maintained by GIANTS Software, it already understands the XML files that you'll be editing for your mods (see Chapters 6 through 9). Not only that, but it also can provide useful debugging information to more easily track down any errors in your mod while it's running in Farming Simulator.

Like GIANTS Editor, GIANTS Studio/Debugger is available for free in the **Downloads** page of the GDN. This book was written using version 9.1.0 of GIANTS Studio/Debugger. However, if you have a more recent version, the principles in this book should still apply. Once you download the installer for GIANTS Studio/Debugger, launch the installer. When that's finished, you can launch GIANTS Studio/Debugger and you should see something similar to what's shown in Figure 1.12.

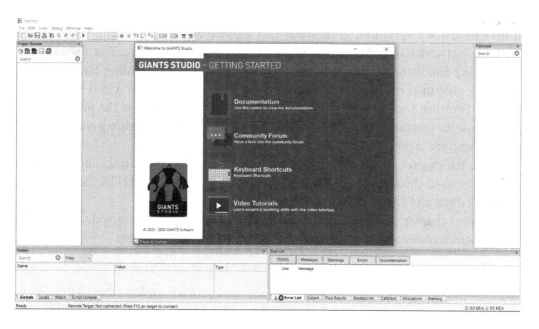

FIGURE 1.12   What you see when first launch GIANTS Studio/Debugger.

Of course, GIANTS Studio/Debugger isn't the only choice out there. If you try it and decide you don't like it, you might enjoy any of these other tools more:

- **Notepad++** (https://notepad-plus-plus.org)—Before GIANTS Studio/Debugger got to be as fully featured as it is now, Notepad++ was the go-to text editor for modding. It's actually what's featured in the official Farming Simulator modding video tutorials described earlier in this chapter. It's a lightweight text editor that gives you most of the functionality that you need for modding.

- **Visual Studio Code** (https://code.visualstudio.com)—This is a Microsoft product that's more commonly used as a full-blown software development tool. If you're already coding, chances are good that you already have it installed. If you're not, this may be a little heavy-handed for tweaking a few XML files.

- **Brackets** (https://brackets.io)—Originally developed by Adobe, this tool was primarily created for people who do web design, but it can easily work well for editing files for your mod. After all, HTML is basically a subset of XML, so syntax highlighting should work just fine.

- **Sublime Text** (https://www.sublimetext.com)—Unlike the other choices listed in this section, Sublime Text isn't free, but the people who love to use it consider it to be well worth the price. You can evaluate it for free, though, so download it and see what the buzz is all about.

SUMMARY

So here we go! We're off to a great start. This chapter began by covering the GIANTS Developer Network (GDN) and all the fantastic goodies available there. You also explored the Farming Simulator ModHub, where you can get mods for Farming Simulator and eventually publish your own mods. You also got some resources for video tutorials on modding Farming Simulator as well as working with Blender, one of the primary tools modders use for creating assets. You also saw that the GDN has an engaging community of modders who are eager to help each other make excellent mods.

Finally, the chapter closed by getting into details, covering the various different tools that will be used throughout the book, including Blender, the GIANTS I3D Exporter, GIANTS Editor, and GIANTS Studio/Debugger.

In the next chapter, you'll get started on the asset creation process for your mod by giving you a quick introduction to Blender and the GIANTS I3D Exporter.

Working with Blender

ALRIGHT. TIME TO GET to work. When it comes to modding, it all starts with building the assets that are going to be a part of your mod. Those assets are 3D models, a pile of points in space connected by edges and faces, then wrapped with an image. In a lot of ways, it's like a three-dimensional game of "connect the dots", only it's a lot more fun, and the finished thing that you create tends to look a whole lot cooler.

But you need a tool to control the placement of those points in space (*vertices*) and all of the connections between them. The general name for this kind of tool is a 3D digital content creation tool, or 3D DDC. The most commonly used 3D DCC among Farming Simulator modders (and arguably all modders) is Blender.

Blender has all the tools you need as a modder to create the 3D assets you need. You can sculpt, model, UV unwrap, texture, rig, and animate. You can even render movies and do visual effects work with it if you'd like. And on top of that, Blender is absolutely free. Not only can you get it without paying any money, it's also open source. That means that if Blender doesn't have a feature you need, you can change Blender yourself (or pay someone to do it) so you can get that feature. Even the team of artists and developers within GIANTS Software has started using it more frequently in the creation of their games. It really is that good.

We'll use the pages in this chapter to get you familiar with Blender, its interface, and the basics of what you need to know in order to make your mods. This chapter is by no means comprehensive. Blender is a complex tool with a metric ton of features. There aren't very many people who know everything there is to know about Blender. However, this chapter should arm you with enough information to get started. At the very least, you'll know the right questions to ask in order to increase your skills over time, as well as the right tutorials and courses to look for at places like CG Cookie. We'll also cover the custom GIANTS I3D Exporter tools that GIANTS Software created to help you get your models from Blender to GIANTS Editor. And at the end, I'll share a few handy hotkey combinations that should help you get your work done faster while in Blender. There's a lot to cover, so let's get started.

DOI: 10.1201/9781032659497-2

In this chapter:

- Getting started with Blender

- Using the GIANTS I3D Exporter

- Tips and tricks for working within Blender

TECHNICAL REQUIREMENTS

Technically speaking, the only thing you really need for this chapter is Blender and the GIANTS I3D Exporter add-on. If you don't have either of these, have a look back in **Chapter 1** within the section titled **Digging into the tools used for modding**. There you'll find instructions on downloading and installing both Blender and the GIANTS I3D Exporter add-on.

GETTING STARTED WITH BLENDER

If you followed the steps in Chapter 1, you should have Blender installed and running on your computer. Unless otherwise stated, I'm going to assume that you're running Blender with all of its default settings. There are a few tweaks to those settings that I'm going to recommend a little bit later in this chapter in the sub-section titled **Some recommended settings to make your life easier**, but for now, let's assume the defaults.

Blender is a complex tool, and it can be a little bit intimidating when you first start using it. Although it's improved quite a bit over the years, its interface is still quite different from almost any other application you might be familiar with, including other 3D DCCs. However, if you take your time and ease yourself into using it, you may start to find yourself wondering why other programs don't do things "the Blender way".

A Quick Primer on Blender's Interface

If you launch Blender and move past the splash screen that appears when it first launches, you should see something like the screenshot in Figure 2.1.

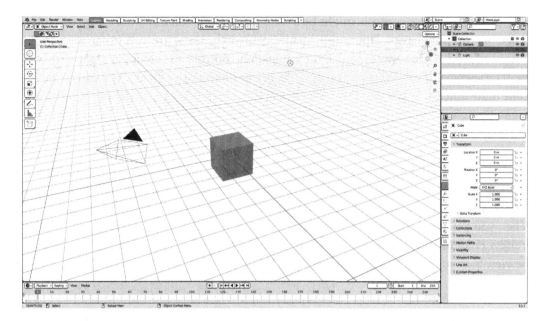

FIGURE 2.1 This is what Blender looks like when you first launch it.

By default, Blender first launches in what's called the **General** workflow template, and you start in the **Layout** workspace. The General template is a great one to get started with because it has the most versatile set of default workspaces for you to work in. A *workspace* is a particular arrangement of areas and editors within Blender's interface in such a way that they help you complete a particular task more quickly. You don't have to use them, but they're pretty handy to have available. For modding, the workspaces that you'll find yourself using the most are the Modeling, UV Editing, and Shading workspaces. If you end up painting textures in Blender, then the Texture Paint workspace is also pretty useful.

Navigating 3D Space

In each of the workspaces described in the previous section, there's a fairly large amount of screen real estate that's dedicated to the 3D Viewport. That's the big area with the cube in the figure above. The 3D Viewport is where you're likely to spend the majority of your time. This editor is where you can navigate around your scene in three dimensions. It's also where you actually build your 3D models.

The most common way to move around in the 3D Viewport is with your mouse, primarily using the middle mouse button and the following controls:

- **Rotate**—click and drag the middle mouse button to orbit around the scene.

- **Pan**—Hold *Shift* while clicking and dragging the middle mouse button to move around the scene without rotating.

- **Zoom**—Use the mouse's scroll wheel or hold *Ctrl* while clicking and dragging to move your view in or out of the scene.

As I mentioned, these controls might be a bit frustrating if you don't have a three-button mouse or you only have a laptop touchpad. Fortunately, there are two other ways to get around the space. One way is to use the navigation controls on the upper right corner of the 3D Viewport. If you left click and drag the orientation control gizmo, you can rotate the scene quite quickly. Likewise, if you left click and the magnifying glass icon just below the orientation gizmo, you'll get zoom control of your scene. The icon of the hand just below that gives you panning control of the 3D Viewport.

And since we're coming from a gaming background, there's one other way to navigate the scene that you might find very comfortable. In the 3D Viewport's header, go to **View ▶ Navigation ▶ Walk Navigation**. Right when you choose that menu item, you get standard WASD controls with mouselook, just like you might expect from most modern PC games. When you get the 3D Viewport positioned and oriented the way you like, either left click or press *Enter* to set the view. Right click or press *Esc* to get out of Walk Navigation and put the view back to how it was before you started.

Working with Modes

Another important concept to think about when working in Blender is the fact that you can choose different modes for interacting with your selected objects. By default, Blender has you working in Object Mode. In this mode, you work with things in your 3D scene as whole objects rather than the component parts that make up those objects. However, if you want to drill down to actually manipulate the vertices, edges, and faces that make up your object, you'll need to switch to Edit Mode.

You can switch modes in the 3D Viewport by clicking the Mode dropdown menu in the 3D Viewport's header. Depending on the type of object you have selected, you'll have a few different choices for the kind of mode you want to switch to. Most of the assets that you'll be using in your mod are mesh objects, so with a mesh selected, you have the ability to choose between Object Mode, Edit Mode, Sculpt Mode, Vertex Paint, Weight Paint, and Texture Paint. The modes that you're going to be using most frequently are Object Mode and Edit Mode Because you'll be switching between these modes so frequently, there's a hotkey you'll want to burn into your mind. *Tab*. Press the *Tab* key on your keyboard to toggle between Object Mode and Edit Mode. Blender users do this so frequently; they've turned *Tab* into a verb. On Blender forums, it's common to talk about *Tabbing* into Edit Mode or back out to Object Mode.

NOTE

Pay attention to the location of your mouse cursor when using hotkeys. In Blender, each of the areas in a workspace can be considered a different editor—almost an entirely separate sub-application within Blender—each one potentially with its own set of hotkeys. Blender infers which editor you are working in based on the location of your mouse cursor. So if you want to use a hotkey that does something in the 3D Viewport, be sure that your mouse is hovering over that area.

Using the Toolbar and Hotkeys to Edit

If the right side of the 3D Viewport is for navigating the space of your 3D scene, then the left side is for editing your selected object. The Toolbar along the left side of the 3D Viewport provides you with a relatively familiar interface for modifying the selected objects in your scene. And when you *Tab* into Edit Mode, the Toolbar expands with a wide assortment of tools that are specific to working in that mode. Figure 2.2 shows a screenshot of Blender in Edit Mode with an example 3D model.

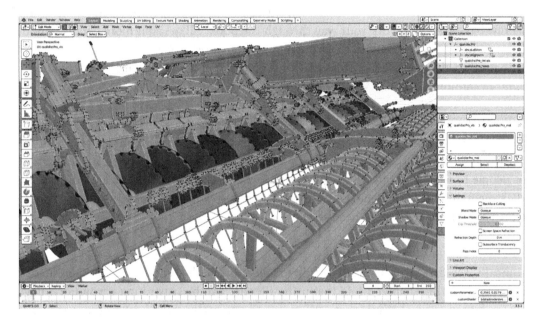

FIGURE 2.2   Tab into Edit Mode and the Toolbar in the 3D Viewport expands with more tools for you to use.

Depending on the tool that you choose from the Toolbar, Blender will provide you with a control widget on your selection that you can use to make whatever modification you're interested in, whether you're adding more geometry or just moving vertices around.

As familiar as the workflow of using tools from a Toolbar might be, it can still be pretty time-consuming to move your mouse cursor all the way to the left side of the 3D Viewport each time you want to do anything. Fortunately, Blender has an incredibly broad set of hotkeys and hotkey combinations associated with each tool. To get a sense of what I'm talking about, hover your mouse cursor over any of the tools in the 3D Viewport's Toolbar. The tooltip that appears after about a second will include the hotkey for instantly activating that tool without the need for any additional clicks or even a control widget. It's just a raw operation.

That said, there is a bit of a trick to using hotkeys in Blender. However, once you figure out the pattern, you'll find that you're working quite a bit faster. The pattern basically works like this:

1. Press and release the hotkey to activate the operator (tool) you want to use.

2. Move your mouse to adjust the influence of that operator. You may sometimes modify how you make your adjustment by pressing an additional key like *Shift* or *Ctrl* (see the status bar at the bottom of the Blender window for clues on what's available).

3. Left click or press *Enter* to confirm and finalize the operation. If you want to cancel, right click or press *Esc*.

Once you nail that pattern, you'll be off to the races!

There's so much more we can cover when it comes to working in Blender, but these are the raw basics. As you work your way through the book, I'll get a bit more detailed about the specific steps you'll want to go through to get your work done.

That said, I do have a few settings that you can make in Blender to make working in it a lot more comfortable.

Some Recommended Settings to Make Your Life Easier

Whenever I first start helping anyone get their feet wet in Blender, there are a handful of settings that I tell them to go through and make. These settings often make it easier for people to work without tripping over somewhat common pitfalls. Nearly all of these adjustments are made in Blender's Preferences editor, so it's a good idea to go ahead and go to **Edit ▸ Preferences** to get a head start.

Emulate 3 Button Mouse (Optional)

Ironically, the first recommended setting to adjust is one that I'm calling optional. Recall how earlier in this chapter I said that using Blender can be frustrating if you don't have a three-button mouse? While that's still true and you really should get a proper mouse if you're doing 3D work, there's a setting in Blender's Preferences that can still help. Go to the **Input** section of Preferences and look in the **Mouse** panel. In that panel, there's a check box labeled **Emulate 3 Button Mouse**. Enable that check box, and now you can use *Alt+left mouse* in the 3D Viewport to do any of the navigation behaviors I described in the preceding section using the middle mouse button.

I call this an optional setting because if you use a three-button mouse, you shouldn't have to enable this feature. That said, there are some other 3D DCC tools out there that use *Alt+left mouse* for navigation. So if you're more familiar with that navigation style, enabling this check box might make you feel a little bit more at home.

Orbit around Selection

Speaking of navigation, Blender's navigation style can sometimes feel a bit unwieldy to some folks when they first start using it. This is because Blender's defaults don't really take the position of the mouse cursor into account when navigating. Everything basically happens relative to the center of the 3D Viewport. This behavior can be a bit disorienting for new users, so there are a few settings I recommend changing to alleviate this issue. The first of which is the way Blender handles orbiting (rotating) around the scene.

A lot of people feel like they have a better sense of the space if the 3D Viewport orbited around their selected object (or objects) rather than the center of the 3D Viewport. Blender's Preferences has a setting to help you with that. Go to the Navigation section of Preferences and look in the **Orbit & Pan** panel. In that panel, enable the **Orbit Around Selection** check box. Now your scene rotations will be centered on whatever you have selected.

Auto Depth

There's a funky thing that sometimes happens when viewing your scene from a perspective view (as opposed to an orthographic view). Every now and again, you will be zoomed in on something, and it will feel like no matter how much you try to orbit or pan, the scene doesn't seem to move. This relates to the depth of the scene being set, somewhat arbitrarily, to a central point. And when you get closer to that point, movement around it gets to be very slight.

You can avoid running into this issue by enabling **Auto Depth**. Basically, instead of choosing that center point, Blender can automatically adjust where it thinks the center should be based on what's visible in the 3D Viewport. This prevents you from running into the problem of getting "stuck" when zoomed in close.

Like the Orbit Around Selection feature, the control for Auto Depth is also in the Navigation section of Preferences. Go there, and within the Orbit & Pan panel, there's a **Depth** check box beneath Auto Perspective. Enable that check box, and you're good to go with automatic depthy goodness.

Zoom to Mouse Position

For the last navigation-related recommendation, I'm going to suggest you change how Blender does it's zooming. Like with orbiting around the scene, Blender's default behavior is to zoom towards the center of the 3D Viewport. A lot of people prefer that the zooming behavior be directed at wherever the location of the mouse cursor is. It helps give the feeling that you're in the scene, much like the Walk Navigation described earlier in this chapter.

To enable zooming towards the mouse cursor, go to the Navigation section of Preferences and look down in the Zoom panel. Within that panel, enable the **Zoom to Mouse Position** check box, and Blender will instantly change the way that it zooms in the 3D Viewport to this more comfortable setting.

Set the Spacebar Action to Search

When you have a program that's as feature-packed as Blender, it can be tough to find exactly where a particular operator is hidden in all of the different buttons and menus. Fortunately, Blender has an integrated search feature that allows you to type in the name of the operation that you want to perform, and it'll give you the ability to run that operator immediately or tell you where it can be found in Blender's interface.

Unfortunately, the default keymap for Blender has that search functionality assigned to the *F3* button all the way at the top of the keyboard. When you're in the flow of working, that's not necessarily an easily accessible part of the keyboard. Add in the fact that some keyboards have removed those function keys altogether; the *F3* key is a pretty inconvenient place to put such a useful feature.

The good news is that this mapping is pretty easy to fix and doesn't require a deep dive into custom keymaps. Just go to the **Keymap** section of Preferences and look for the set of buttons next to the **Spacebar Action** label. By default, the *Spacebar* is set to activate playback from the timeline. That may be a familiar interface for anyone who does video or audio editing, but for all the other things you can do in Blender, I personally feel it's the wrong fit. If you click the **Search** button to the right of **Spacebar Action**, you'll remedy this situation. Now when you don't know where to find a particular operator in Blender, you can just smash *Spacebar* and start typing the name of the operator you want.

Tab for Pie Menu

While we're on the subject of keymaps, there's another setting in the Keymap section of Preferences that I recommend you enable. A lot of menus in Blender are the standard linear sort that have a vertical list of things that you can choose from. However, these menus can sometimes be slow to navigate and don't really take advantage of muscle memory for fast gestures.

The solution for that problem is pie menus. Pie menus are menus with options that are arrayed in a rough circle around the mouse cursor. You get a much larger click target, and because the menu items are always in the same place relative to the mouse cursor, you can use gestural movements to make your selection. They're a really fast way to work.

Blender has quite a few pie menus already by default, but one of the menus that's disabled by default is the one for switching modes. As I covered earlier in this chapter, you can press *Tab* to quickly toggle between Object Mode and Edit Mode. However, if you happen to switch through a bunch of different modes more frequently, this simple toggle, while fast, may not be versatile enough. So we have a pie menu as an optional alternative.

In the **Keymap** section of Preferences, enable the **Tab for Pie Menu** check box, and once you do that, if you press *Tab* while in the 3D Viewport, you'll get a nice little pie menu that will let you quickly choose any of the available modes for your selected object.

GPU Rendering

I hesitated to add this option here since, as a modder, you're not likely to be all that concerned with rendering your model with Blender's built-in ray trace render engine, Cycles. However, there's still a possibility that you may want to do that at some point, and I definitely make this recommendation to every new Blender user that I help. So I've included it. Basically, Cycles can take advantage of general computation features in modern GPUs to render images faster. However, you need to tell Blender how you prefer that it talk to your GPUs.

The place where you do that "telling Blender about your GPU" stuff is in the **System** section of Preferences. The first panel in that section is labeled **Cycles Render Devices**. By default, this is set to **None**. However, if you have a modern NVIDIA video card, you may choose OptiX or CUDA in this section. If your card is made by AMD, then you'll want to use HIP. For other GPUs, like the high-performance ones made by Intel, you could choose one API.

Once you choose the device type, if Blender recognizes any compatible devices of that type, you have the ability to select which one (or ones) that you want to use for rendering. Now, if you ever find yourself rendering with Cycles, you can use GPU Compute as your device, and your render jobs should complete in a much shorter amount of time than if you just rendered with your CPU.

Add-ons to Enable

The last recommendations that I have are add-ons that you should enable. Blender has a programming interface where you can use the Python programming language to extend Blender and give it more features. These extensions are called *add-ons*. A lot of people have created add-ons for Blender, including the core Blender development team. Quite a few of these add-ons ship with Blender, but they're disabled by default. The reason is that the core development team believes that those add-ons (the ones disabled by default) are for more specialized use and not necessarily something that every Blender user would want or need to take advantage of.

For the most part, I agree with them. However, there are a couple of add-ons that I strongly recommend that you go and enable. The process for enabling these add-ons is very straight-forward since they already come with Blender. You don't have to install anything. You just go to the **Add-ons** section of Preferences, search for the add-on you want, and click the check box next to its name to enable it.

The two add-ons I suggest you go ahead and enable are these:

- **Copy Attributes Menu.** When you're working with a lot of objects in Blender (and since you're building complex farm machinery for your mod, you likely will be), there's a lot of occasions where you want to copy a value or a modifier or some other property on one object to a bunch of other objects in that same scene. While it's possible to do that copy operation without this menu, the process is way faster with this add-on. You just select all the objects you want to get the copied property; select the one that you want to copy, and then press *Ctrl+C*. This add-on will then show you a menu of all the stuff that's available to be copied, and you just need to choose the one you want.

- **F2**. This is an add-on that can help speed up your modeling workflow. In a lot of ways, it works similarly to Blender's native Poly Build tool, but in my opinion, the workflow is just a little bit faster once you get used to it.

What You Really Need to Know for the Purposes of Modding

Blender is a fully featured DCC with a metric boatload of things it can do. In fact, it can do way more than you actually need for creating your mod. So rather than try to give you an exhaustive rundown on all of Blender's capabilities, let's focus on the critical things you need to know in order to build your mod. Not only will that make this book more useful to you, it also gives you the right terms to search for when trying to look for other tutorials to improve your skills.

When building assets for your mods, there are three categories of work that you do the most in Blender: modeling, organizing, and surfacing. **Chapter 3: Defining Surface Materials** is dedicated to the work of surfacing your assets for your mod, so this section is going to focus primarily on modeling and organizing the objects in your Blender scene. And we're going to further break down modeling into two more categories: 3D modeling and UV editing.

> **NOTE**
>
> While UV editing isn't *exactly* modeling, you're still working directly with a 3D mesh's component parts—vertices, edges, and faces—and the topology of your modeled mesh can directly affect how your UV coordinates lie, so it's worthwhile to think about them in the same context.

Modeling in Blender

Modeling is the process of digitally building a 3D object, typically composed of multiple points in space (*vertices*) that are connected to one another by *edges*, which in turn form polygons, or *faces*. Without a mature suite of tools, this process can be extremely time-consuming and downright annoying. However, modern modeling workflows have made the process much more efficient… I daresay it's even fun.

Depending on what you're creating, there are a bunch of different approaches to take when 3D modeling. For the most part, the models that you create for a Farming Simulator mod fall under the category of **hard surface modeling**. That is, most models for Farming Simulator mods are vehicles or buildings. These objects are made of steel or wood, materials that don't bend, stretch, or easily deform. While it's certainly possible to do hard surface modeling with sculpting tools and retopologize afterwards, most modders are using a more traditional approach to modeling. That is, they're typically either box modeling or moving vertices around and manually building edges and faces between them. You can accelerate this workflow by making use of Blender's modifier system (more on that later in this section). And in more advanced cases, you can build your model in a more procedural way using Geometry Nodes.

> **TIP**
>
> There are some great third-party add-ons that are specifically geared for hard surface modeling. These add-ons cost a little bit of money since they're for purchase on Blender Market (https://blendermarket.com), but they can quickly make up for that in the amount of time they save you when modeling. In particular, you should have a look at Boxcutter, Hard Ops, and Meshmachine.

Regardless of whether you're sculpting, box modeling, or working with Geometry Nodes, most mods are built based on some kind of reference. The key is to have good *orthographic* reference images, that is, images of the object from the front, side, top, and so on with as little perspective distortion as possible. The absolute best resource for these kinds of reference images is CAD (*computer-aided design*) drawings, but it's often pretty difficult to come by those. Of course, if the object is something you've designed yourself, you could create that drawing as a sketch. Without either of those, your next best option is to use photographs. For modeling like we're describing in this chapter, it's best to have a view of the object from at least the side and the front, but the top and the rear are also good to have if you can find them. With this kind of reference drawing, you can more quickly get a sense of scale for your object and better understand what parts you actually have to model.

TIP

Another approach that's gaining popularity is using *photogrammetry*, the process of automatically generating a 3D model based on a sequence of photographs of a specific object. It's often difficult to find orthographic photos of what you want to model, but it's usually quite easy to find photos from a bunch of interesting angles. Using a tool like Meshroom (https://alicevision. org/#meshroom), you can use a bunch of these photos to generate a rough model that you can either use as a 3D reference or perhaps even directly retopologize to create your model.

Assuming that you have your reference images and you've already cropped them in an external image editor like GIMP or Photoshop, you can get those reference images loaded into Blender with the following steps:

1. In the 3D Viewport, align the view to the front so you're looking down the Y-axis by choosing **View ▶ Viewpoint ▶ Front** or pressing *Numpad 1*.

2. Still in the 3D Viewport, choose **Add ▶ Image ▶ Reference**. You can also use *Shift+A* to bring up the add menu without going all the way up to the 3D Viewport's header.

3. In the File Browser that appears, navigate to the location on your hard drive where your front-view reference image lives, select that image, and click the **Load Reference Image** button. Blender will load your reference image into the 3D Viewport, but it will still need to have its scale and position adjusted.

4. In the Properties Editor, go to the Object Data Properties tab and, in the Empty panel, change the **Offset Y** value to **0.00**. Doing this step puts the origin of your reference image at its bottom. This way, when you start modeling, your object is sitting on the ground plane rather than having the ground run through it.

5. Still in the Empty panel of Object Data Properties, adjust the **Size** value to match the realistic size of your object. This may require a bit of research on your end. Also note that Blender defaults to being in meters for units; if you prefer to work in imperial units, you'll need to make those changes in the Scene Properties tab of the Properties Editor.

NOTE

The size for reference images is a little bit funky. There's only one value, and that's the length of the longest edge of your image. So if you have an image that's more tall than it is wide and the size is set to 5 meters, then your reference has a height of 5 meters and a width that's proportionate to that value. If your image is more wide than tall, then 5 meters would be the width, and the height would be some proportion smaller than that.

6. (Optional) Also in the Empty panel of Object Data Properties, enable the **Opacity** check box and set its value to something semi-transparent. I find that a value of **0.600** works as a good starting point. This helps prevent your reference image from obscuring your model too much.

7. Back in the 3D Viewport, align the view to the right side (**View ▶ Viewpoint ▶ Right** or *Numpad 3*) and work your way through steps 1–6 for the side view of your model.

8. Repeat these steps for any other views you have of your object.

When you've completed adding your reference images, your Blender scene should look something like what's shown in Figure 2.3.

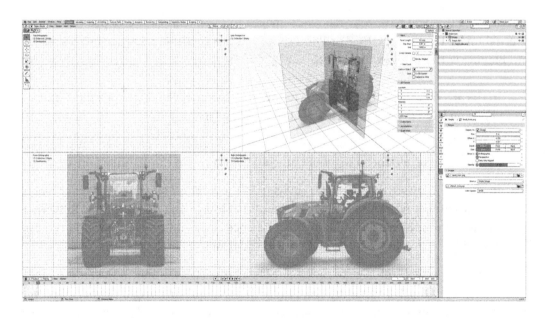

FIGURE 2.3   Adding reference images in Blender's 3D Viewport.

As an extra tip, if you happen to have front and back views of your object, you can use the **Side** setting in the Empty panel of Object Data Properties to only show the image from the front or back of the reference object in Blender. Also, as the image above shows, the 3D Viewport can look pretty cluttered from the perspective view, so you can enable the

Only Axis Aligned check box, and the reference image will only appear when looking down a specific axis in orthographic view.

Now that you have your reference in the 3D Viewport, you can begin modeling in earnest. There's not enough room in this book to give detailed, step-by-step instruction on modeling, but fortunately, there are some great video tutorials you can use to get going. The place that I always recommend that you start is the Blender Basics course on CG Cookie. That course, plus the Press Start course, are really good introductions to modeling in Blender as well as general Blender workflows. Both of them (plus a few other handy resources) are available here: https://cgcookie.com/farmingsimulator (you can also scan the QR code after this paragraph).

https://cgcookie.com/farmingsimulator

That said, there are a few handy tips to keep in mind as you work:

- **Work from big to small**—It's incredibly easy to get caught in the weeds of putting details on your model early on. Resist this temptation! Start rough and big, being sure to get the rough shape and dimensions of your model correct before you dive into details. In fact, you can even do early exports of this rough model for testing in your mod. Then you can refine and add details as you go. Working this way allows you to spot errors or other challenges early on.

- **Use the Modeling workspace**—This workspace is not that different from the Layout workspace, but it saves you a little bit of space by removing the Timeline from the bottom of the window, and when you switch to the Modeling workspace, Blender automatically switches to Edit Mode on your selected object.

- **Take advantage of modifiers**—Blender's modifier stack is one of the best ways to get your work done faster. In particular, the Mirror, Array, and Solidify modifiers are really handy for hard surface modeling because they procedurally generate geometry for you, saving you time. The Boolean modifier is also really helpful for machine parts.

- **Pay attention to your stats**—You're building a mod for a game, a *real-time* environment that has to be able to render your model to screen 60 times every second. That means you can't have objects in your mod made up of millions of vertices. So it's a good idea to always have those numbers in mind while you work. Go to the **Viewport Overlays** rollout in the 3D Viewport's header and enable the *Statistics* check box to get a more clear understanding of the number of vertices and faces that make up your object.

- **Take advantage of random colors**—On the far right of the 3D Viewport's header is a button that gives you a rollout for controlling the viewport's shading. In the **Color** section, switch from the default *Material* color to *Random* color, and all of the individual objects in your scene become a lot easier to distinguish from one another, as shown in Figure 2.4.

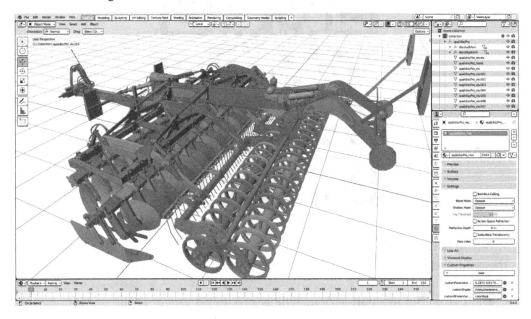

FIGURE 2.4 Use random object coloring to make it easier to see the different parts of your model.

Working with UVs

The other critical 3D workflow that you should have a firm understanding of is the process of working with UV coordinates so you can properly apply textures to your objects. Have you ever broken down a cardboard shipping box so it's completely flat? *UV unwrapping* is like the digital equivalent of that process. You're taking the X, Y, and Z coordinates of the vertices in your mesh and rearranging them to fit on a flat plane of just two coordinates, U and V.

And when it specifically comes to making mods for Farming Simulator, the UV coordinates serve an additional role because that's how the game engine decides which material to use on your object. We'll get into that process a bit more in the next chapter. For now, let's focus on getting familiar with the UV editing tools that Blender provides.

The best place to work with UVs in Blender is the UV Editing workspace. Click the UV Editing tab at the top of the Blender window to switch to this workspace. When you do so, Blender automatically switches your selected object into Edit Mode so you can see how your UVs are mapped. Figure 2.5 shows an example model in the UV Editing workspace with part of the model already unwrapped.

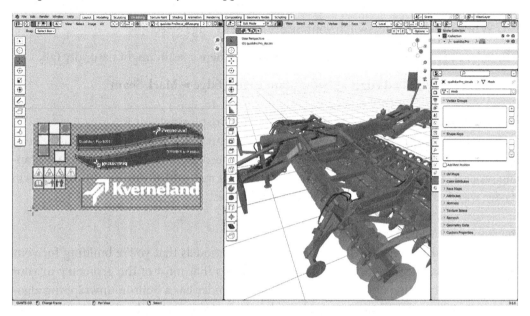

FIGURE 2.5   The UV Editing workspace in Blender is where you can define and edit the UV mapping of vertices, edges, and faces in your mesh.

In the UV Editing workspace, the right-hand side of the Blender window should look pretty familiar; it's not that different from the Layout or Modeling workspaces. The main difference is the editor taking up the left half of the window, the UV Editor. Vertices, edges, and faces that show up here (only while your object is in Edit Mode) correspond to the same components in the 3D space of your mesh.

Now, in the image above, the mesh is already *unwrapped*. That is, the components of the mesh have already been flattened to fit the UV coordinate system. If you're starting from scratch with your own model, chances are good that UV mapping isn't nearly as well defined. That's because you haven't unwrapped the model yet.

Traditional UV Unwrapping

Fortunately, the process for unwrapping meshes in Blender is pretty straight-forward:

1. While in Edit Mode, select all the vertices of your mesh (**Select ▶ All** or press *A*).

2. Unwrap your mesh (**UV ▶ Unwrap**).

Of course, the first time you do this, expect the results to be pretty unimpressive. These results are because the default unwrapping algorithm in Blender expects you to mark seams on your mesh. Think back to the example of the cardboard box. To truly flatten that cardboard box, you need to cut anywhere where it's taped closed, and you also need to cut through part of the box where it's glued to itself. These are your seams. In 3D meshes, seams live along edges, the connections between vertices.

To mark a seam, use the following steps:

1. While in Edit Mode, switch your Select Mode to Edge Select.

2. Select a series of edges on your mesh, usually where a seam might naturally fall.

3. Mark your selected edges as being seam edges (**Edge ▶ Mark Seam**).

Now, when you unwrap, the result should be a lot more pleasant.

Of course, there are sometimes faster ways to get this done. Because you're mostly dealing with mechanical objects here, you don't always need to mark seams for your unwrapping process. There are two other ways to unwrap that may possibly get you good results in a faster way: Smart UV Project and Project from View.

Unwrapping with Smart UV Project

You can take advantage of the fact that most of the models that you're building for your Farming Simulator mod are mechanical. This means that most of the geometry in your mesh is probably facing either the X, Y, or Z axis. Blender has a built-in unwrapping algorithm called Smart UV Project that takes advantage of this fact and automatically tries to define seams for you while unwrapping. As an added bonus, this unwrapping algorithm also does a reasonably good job of *packing* your UVs so they make the best use of your available texture space.

To use Smart UV Project unwrapping, the process is almost the same as unwrapping the traditional way:

1. Select all the vertices in your mesh (**Select ▶ All**).

2. Unwrap with Smart UV Project (**UV ▶ Smart UV Project**).

3. Adjust values in the pop-up that appears.

4. Click **OK**.

Figure 2.6 shows the result of an unwrap using Smart UV Project.

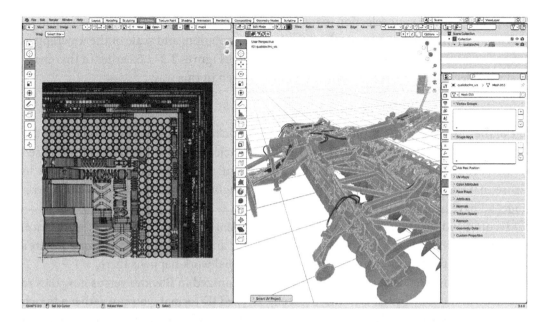

FIGURE 2.6 The Smart UV Project algorithm for UV unwrapping automatically generates seams and packs your UVs to nicely fill the texture space.

Unwrapping with Project from View

There's another unwrapping method that's specifically useful when you're making decals on your model. Because of the way that GIANTS Engine works, decals aren't textures applied to the main model with UV mapping. They're actually 3D meshes that have their own UV maps. Of course, you have to define those maps.

While it's certainly possible to use the traditional unwrapping workflow or even Smart UV Project, there's a way that works a little bit better: Project from View. The idea here is that Blender takes whatever you have visible in the 3D Viewport from the specific angle you're viewing and flattens that to UV space. No seams. No extra work. The process looks something like this:

1. In the 3D Viewport, select what you want to unwrap in Edit Mode. Typically, for decals, this is a simple four-sided polygon, so you'd select the four vertices that make up that polygon, or if you're in the Face Select selection mode, the face that those vertices make.

2. Align the 3D Viewport to your selection (**View ▶ Align View ▶ Align View to Active ▶ Top**). The result in the 3D Viewport might be rotated 90° from what you'd prefer, but don't sweat that at the moment; you'll fix that shortly.

3. Make sure the 3D Viewport is in *orthographic view* (**View ▶ Perspective/Orthographic**). You can tell which view (orthographic or perspective) you're in by looking at the text overlay in the upper left corner of the 3D Viewport.

4. Unwrap with Project from View (**UV ▶ Project from View**).

Blender will unwrap your selection to match what you have in the 3D Viewport. From here, you can go to the UV Editor and adjust the location, rotation, and scale of the unwrapped face so it conforms to your decal image. For reference, Figures 2.2–2.5 earlier in this chapter show a decal with coordinates that were unwrapped in this way.

Organizing Your Blender Scene for Exporting to I3D

One of the most important things you can do while you're working on your mod in Blender is properly prepare your model so it can be exported cleanly to the I3D format that's used by GIANTS Editor and Farming Simulator. In particular, you should spend some time to ensure that the hierarchy of your model is well thought-out and that the objects in your model all have meaningful names.

I recommend that you do this kind of organizational work from the Layout workspace, perhaps adjusting the division between the Outliner and the Properties Editor so there's more room for the Outliner since a lot of organizational work happens there.

The biggest difference between how things are organized in Blender versus how they're organized in the I3D format is in the hierarchy. In the I3D format, you can gather a bunch of objects into a *transform group*. In GIANTS Editor, transform groups are selectable and moveable as if they are a single object. Blender doesn't quite have behavior that's equivalent to that. You can create *collections* in Blender, but because objects can be members of multiple collections, you don't have the same hierarchical structure that the I3D format requires.

Fortunately, we have a way around that by making use of Blender's Empty objects and parenting. Let's say you have a simple model like the one shown in Figure 2.7 (remember what I said about not getting buried in details too early?).

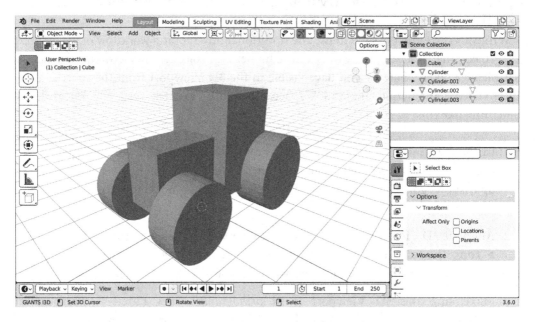

FIGURE 2.7   A rough model of a tractor that is not at all organized enough to export to I3D.

NOTE

If you'd like to follow along, you can get this simple model among the downloads for this book at https://gdn.giants-software.com/blenderBook. You can scan the QR code after this note to jump right to that URL.

https://gdn.giants-software.com/blenderBook

Looking at this image, there are a few things that show that it's not ready for exporting. The first thing to notice is that the naming for all of the objects is incredibly generic and not all reflective of what is in the scene. In fact, they just have the original names of the primitives that were used to construct them.

So your first step is giving each object a meaningful name. To change the name of an object in Blender, double-click its name in the Outliner. Then you'll be able to rename it. In the case of this example, you might rename the **Cube** object to **tractorBody** and then change the names of **Cylinder, Cylinder.001, Cylinder.002, Cylinder.003** to **wheelFrontLeft, wheelBackLeft, wheelFrontRight**, and **wheelBackRight**, respectively.

Now that you have some sensible naming, the next thing to do is build our scene hierarchy. To do this, though, the process is much easier if you change the Outliner from its default **View Layer** display mode to **Scenes**. The Scenes view mode has controls that are more friendly for parenting objects to one another.

In this example, we'll use Empties to make transform groups for all of the wheels, and then we'll wrap everything into a transform group for the whole vehicle. It's possible to set individual transform groups for just the front or back wheels, but the convention in Farming Simulator is that all wheels are in a single group with an Empty that lives at the world origin. Use the following steps:

1. In the 3D Viewport, make sure nothing is selected (*Alt+A*) and use the **Create Empty** operator that's built into the GIANTS I3D Exporter to add an Empty at the world origin (**3D Viewport sidebar ▶ GIANTS I3D Exporter ▶ Tools ▶ Create Empty**).

NOTE

The **Create Empty** operator is really just a convenience function. You could do the same by setting the 3D cursor to the world origin and adding any of Blender's Empty objects. It's important to mention that if you have any object selected, the **Create Empty** operator will put the Empty at the location of your active object, so be sure that you have nothing selected for this step. As an additional bonus note, you can actually access this operator outside of the GIANTS I3D Exporter tab in the sidebar by using Blender's search feature. It will be listed as **i3d.createempty ▶ CreateEmpty**.

2. From the Outliner, rename your new Empty from **EmptyGroup** to **wheels**.

3. Parent all of your wheels to your **wheels** Empty in the Outliner (again, from the Scenes display mode) by clicking their names and dragging them over the **wheels** name. When you release your mouse button, the wheels will be children of the **wheels** object.

4. In the 3D Viewport deselect everything (**Select ▶ None** or *Alt+A*).

5. From the GIANTS I3D Exporter tab, use the **Create Empty** operator to add a new Empty for the whole vehicle (**3D Viewport sidebar ▶ GIANTS I3D Exporter ▶ Tools ▶ Create Empty**).

6. (optional) From the Object Data Properties tab of the Properties Editor, change the **Size** value to **2 m**. This step isn't really necessary, but it does make it easier to select your vehicle Empty instead of the **wheels** Empty.

7. In the Outliner, rename your Empty from **EmptyGroup** to **tractor**.

8. Still in the Outliner, make your **tractor** Empty the parent of the **tractorBody** object, as well as your **wheel** Empty that you created by clicking and dragging as you had before.

Now you have a sensible hierarchy that you should be able to export and test in GIANTS Editor. Your Blender session should look something like Figure 2.8.

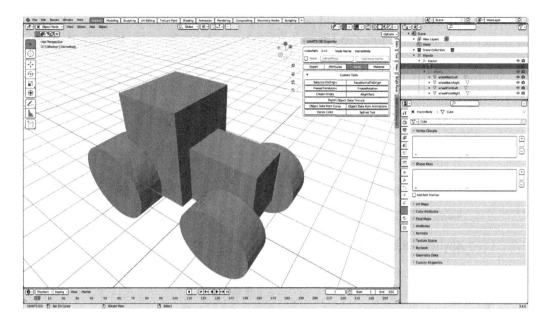

FIGURE 2.8 A simple model with a sensible hierarchy for exporting to I3D.

Each of the Empties that you created in the scene represents a transform group that gets created when you export from Blender to the I3D format. In case the hierarchy isn't clear in the image, your Outliner should show something like the following:

- tractor
  - tractorBody
  - wheels
    - wheelBackLeft
    - wheelBackRight
    - wheelFrontLeft
    - wheelFrontRight

As an additional tip, you might find that you're not fond of the way that Blender's Outliner organizes the objects in your scene. As of this writing, there are no simple, drag-and-drop solutions for re-structuring how those objects are ordered. At this point, you're limited to using alphabetical ordering. However, there is a nice feature of the GIANTS I3D Exporter. It recognizes prefixes on object names if you choose to use those for re-ordering. A prefix is defined by putting a number and a colon at the front of the object name. Taking the example above, let's assume that we'd prefer to have the front wheel objects re-ordered so the front wheels are listed first. You can use prefixes to adjust the order, like this:

- tractor

  - tractorBody

  - wheels

    - 1:wheelFrontLeft

    - 2:wheelFrontRight

    - 3:wheelBackLeft

    - 4:wheelBackRight

When you export (as covered in the next section), the prefix is removed, but the order is preserved in the resulting I3D file.

USING THE GIANTS I3D EXPORTER

The GIANTS I3D Exporter that GIANTS Software created for Blender is a lot more than just a file exporter. It's really best to think of it as a suite of tools in Blender that are built to help prepare your mod. In fact, you can almost build the whole mod using this exporter and make edits to the associated XML files using GIANTS Studio/Debugger.

> **NOTE**
>
> If you haven't already, make sure that you have the GIANTS I3D Exporter Tools add-on installed and enabled in Blender. See **Chapter 1** for more information on this process.

The GIANTS I3D Exporter does so much with respect to preparing your model to be a mod; you don't access it the same way that you would access other exporters in Blender. Instead, the majority of the functionality lives in a tab labeled **GIANTS I3D Exporter** in the 3D Viewport's sidebar. If it's not visible, you can expand the sidebar by pressing *N* on your keyboard. If you have the add-on enabled and you're still working in the example file from the previous section, your Blender session may look like the screenshot in Figure 2.9.

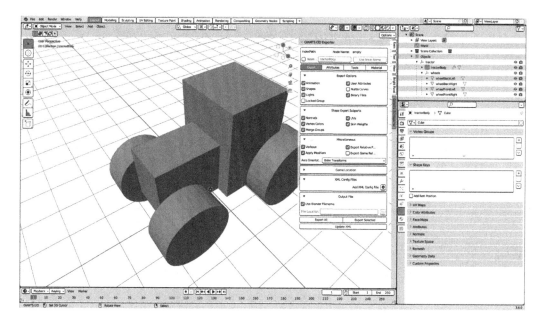

FIGURE 2.9   The controls and settings for the GIANTS I3D Exporter live in their own tab in the 3D Viewport's sidebar.

In the simplest case, such as exporting the rough model in the previous section, you just need to go to the bottom of the sidebar and click the **Export All** button. This builds your I3D file and saves it with the same name as your `.blend` file, in the same folder.

> **NOTE**
>
> If you'd like to use a different file name than what you're using for your `.blend` file, uncheck the **Use Blender Filename** check box in the **Output File** section of the GIANTS I3D Exporter tab and use the **File Location** field to pick a different file name using Blender's File Browser.

Once your model is exported, you can load it in GIANTS Editor to confirm that everything was exported to the I3D format correctly. If you look at Figure 2.10, you should see the same model exported from Figure 2.9 but loaded in GIANTS Editor. Furthermore, you should be able to see that your transform groups from the tractor, its body, and the wheels are all preserved in the GIANTS Editor Outliner.

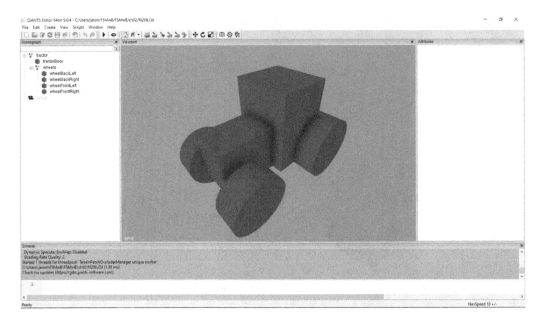

FIGURE 2.10   Your Blender model, exported to I3D and opened in GIANTS Editor.

As you can tell from Figure 2.9, there's a lot more to the GIANTS I3D Exporter add-on than just exporting. It also provides you with a bunch of handy tools that can be quite useful when building models for Farming Simulator. In fact, we covered one earlier in this chapter: the Create Empty operator in the Tools section of the exporter. That Tools section has a bunch of useful convenience operators that can help you while you model. For instance, the **FaceNormalToOrigin** is especially useful for orienting the rotation of an object's origin to match the angle of a selected face in your object. Of course, this can be done manually using Blender's native tools, but this function gives you much faster access to that capability. We cover more of these features later in the book; for now, the most important button is the Export All button at the bottom of the Export section for this add-on.

TIPS AND TRICKS FOR WORKING WITHIN BLENDER

As I said earlier in this chapter, there's a whole bunch of things that you can do within Blender. Quite frankly, with that much functionality, it can get pretty overwhelming. And navigating menus to find the feature or operator that you need can get really tedious and time-consuming. So I'm adding this section with a handful of useful shortcuts that you can use to get your work done faster in Blender. Most of the shortcuts I cover here are meant for use in the 3D Viewport, but quite a few of them also work in Blender's other editors, so be sure to try them out. I'll make a note for some of the more exceptionally helpful hotkeys.

General Purpose Hotkeys

This first set of hotkeys serves a general purpose; they're typically used in Object mode and are often available in multiple editors within Blender. Here we go:

- **Home**: Pulls the camera back in the 3D Viewport to see all visible objects. This hotkey also works in animation editors and 2D editors.

- **Numpad dot (.)**: Frames or focuses the view on whatever you currently have selected. This hotkey is especially useful for finding a selected object in the Outliner.

- **F3** or **Spacebar**: Search (depending on whether you followed my advice earlier in the chapter). If you don't know a hotkey or where to find something in a menu, Blender's search is a huge help.

- **Ctrl+Spacebar**: Maximize the active area. I use this feature the most in the 3D Viewport to get the most screen real estate for modeling.

- **Ctrl**: When you're in the middle of changing a value (this could be a transform or just changing the value on a slider), press *Ctrl*, and that adjustment will be broken into increments. In the 3D Viewport, if you have a different snap setting than Increment, this key is a quick toggle for that kind of snapping.

- **Shift**: A cousin to pressing *Ctrl*, but for precision instead of snaps. Press and hold *Shift* and your movement will be in a smaller, more refined scale. This feature is particularly nice when you need to visually position something with a lot of precision.

- **Z**: Shading pie menu. Use this in the 3D Viewport to quickly switch between shading types. In particular, I like to quickly switch to wireframe mode if I want to select through an object to another one (or a component like a vertex or an edge) through it.

Editing Hotkeys

Whether you're working in Object mode or Edit mode, there are some hotkeys that are really helpful for working through the modeling process. Here's a quick rundown:

- **Ctrl+A**: Apply menu. Use this menu to apply rotation, location, scale, or any combination of these. In other applications, this is similar to "freezing the transform."

- **Ctrl+J**: Join. Use this operation in Object mode to make two separate objects a single object. The vertices aren't linked together, but they're all contained within the same object.

- **L**: In Edit mode, hover your mouse cursor over an element (vertex, edge, face) and press this hotkey to select all other elements that are linked to that one.

- **P**: In Edit mode, use this hotkey to bring up the Separate menu. It's like the reverse of the Join operator just described.

- **Period (.)**: Not to be confused with the Numpad-dot, this hotkey brings up the Pivot Point menu. I most frequently use this to switch between Median (the default) and using the 3D cursor as my temporary pivot point.

- **Shift+R**: Repeat the last operation. Handy if you need to do the same thing multiple times in a row (like smoothing).

- **Shift+S**: Snapping pie menu. In particular, I use this one a lot to snap the 3D cursor to things, or snap things to the location of the 3D cursor.

Of course, there are a lot of other shortcuts and hotkeys that you can discover and make use of in Blender. I encourage you to pay attention to tooltips and extra text when working in Blender. The interface is usually pretty good at helping you figure them out.

SUMMARY

What a ride! Technically speaking, we only covered two topics in this chapter, but they absolutely form the basis for what you'll need to know when building your vehicle mod. The chapter started by briefly going over Blender, its interface, and a quick primer on starting to model in Blender. You also saw how to correctly structure the hierarchy of your Blender scene so it can export cleanly to the I3D format. Of course, this chapter barely scratches the surface on all of the capabilities and modeling tools in Blender, so I highly recommend that you check out more resources on modeling with Blender, such as those by CG Cookie or even other books (I've written a couple!).

After going over Blender, we also covered the GIANTS I3D Exporter add-on for Blender. We went through the basic process of exporting and even covered a few of the handy convenience tools that have been included to make the modeling process a bit easier.

Finally, we closed the chapter by going through a few hotkeys that should help you do your work faster.

In the next section, you start using the add-on even more because you're using it to define the look of shaders and materials on the surface of your object.

CHAPTER 3

Defining Surface Materials

W HETHER YOU'RE BUILDING A mod for a game or creating an object for a still render, one of the things that really brings any 3D object to life is its materials. Your surface materials do an immense amount of visual heavy lifting to add realism to your 3D models and feel like they're part of the scene. Most things in Farming Simulator (and the real world) are made of a variety of materials: metal, rubber, paint, and wood. Very few, if any, are made of the default gray "clay" material that you start with in Blender.

So this chapter is about getting those realistic materials on the models in your mod. As with most of the modding workflow, the process starts in Blender, so you'll start by setting up your base material there. Of course, there are differences between how materials are handled in Blender versus how they work in Farming Simulator, so you'll need to be aware of those as you work. Once you have that understanding, the next thing you'll do is start assigning your Farming Simulator materials to your object. From there, we have a look at the somewhat special case of adding decals to your vehicle mod. With your materials accounted for, the next step is testing your work in the GIANTS Editor to see how it will look in the game. And to ensure the best in-game performance, we cover how to convert the textures in your material to DDS format using the GIANTS Texture Tool. Finally, we close the chapter by going over some of the details on how materials will be handled in future versions of Farming Simulator.

In this chapter:

- Setting up materials in Blender

- Assigning materials on your vehicle

- Adding decals to your mod

- Testing your material in the GIANTS Editor

- Converting Textures to DDS

- Materials in future versions of Farming Simulator

DOI: 10.1201/9781032659497-3

TECHNICAL REQUIREMENTS

For this chapter, you should have a recent version of Blender with the GIANTS I3D Exporter add-on installed and enabled. You should also have GIANTS Editor and Farming Simulator installed; the latter of those is particularly important because the GIANTS I3D Exporter add-on uses material files from the Farming Simulator game; if you don't have the game installed, you can't export with those materials. See Chapter 1 for more information on getting these tools installed on your computer.

In addition, you may want to grab the simple tractor model that's used at the end of Chapter 2. That's available at https://gdn.giants-software.com/blenderBook or by scanning the QR code at the end of this section. You can, of course, choose to use your own model instead, but we made this simple model available in case you wanted to follow along.

https://gdn.giants-software.com/blenderBook

SETTING UP MATERIALS IN BLENDER

There's a specific workflow for setting up surface materials on your mod. That workflow starts in Blender, but it makes use of material definitions provided by Farming Simulator game data. Basically, you're going to set up a material (or multiple materials) for your 3D object, and then, using the tools in the GIANTS I3D Exporter add-on, you're going to associate your Blender material with a corresponding Farming Simulator material. This section covers how you go through that set-up process.

Understanding the Differences between Blender Materials and Farming Simulator Materials

The first thing you need to know in this whole process is that the material system used in Blender is very different from the material system used in Farming Simulator. The custom game engine that Farming Simulator runs on doesn't use the same material properties you would use in Blender to render with Eevee or Cycles. Farming Simulator also has some customized ways in which it uses image textures for mapping (that gets covered later in this chapter in the section titled "Applying vehicle masks"). For that reason, your model's materials rendered in Blender's 3D Viewport will look different—often very different—than what's rendered in Farming Simulator or GIANTS Editor.

> **NOTE**
>
> It's certainly possible to get your model to render in Eevee or Cycles such that it comes pretty close to what's shown in Farming Simulator. However, that effort really only benefits you if you want to make nice still images or animations from Blender. If you want your mod to look good in-game, your effort is probably better spent working with Farming Simulator's material system.

That said, even though you're not using Blender's render engine, the GIANTS I3D Exporter takes advantage of Blender's material system to define which materials are to be used when the model finally makes it to Farming Simulator. So, technically speaking, your object is still going to have material, and it's still going to be renderable using Eevee or Cycles. That material just won't look anything like what you'll see in-game (not without a lot of extra work, at least).

Creating Your Placeholder Material in Blender

The first step in the process is adding a material to your 3D object. The node graph associated with this material, is what the GIANTS I3D Exporter will use to define the look while in-game. Because you're not really using this material as it was originally intended for the Eevee or Cycles render engines, I like to think of this as a "placeholder" material. It gives a reference that the exporter can use when doing its work.

If you already have a Blender file with your scene organization and hierarchy already set up, you can use that. Otherwise, you can use the simple tractor model referenced in the technical requirements section of this chapter. That's the example we'll be using here.

Let's say you want to add your material to the `tractorBody` object in the scene. Use the following steps to add material to that object:

1. Select the **tractorBody** object.

2. **In the Properties editor, go to the Material tab** (in the default theme, the icon is a red ball).

3. **Near the top of Material Properties, click the New button.** A new material slot is added to the listbox above the New button and in that material slot is a new material named `Material`.

4. Rename your new material to **tractorBody**. You can rename a material by double-clicking its name in the listbox or by using the material datablock that's currently where the New button used to be. Technically, you don't have to use `tractor _ mat` as the name; that's just what we're using for this example.

At this point, your base material is set up. Figure 3.1 shows what your Blender session might look like at this point.

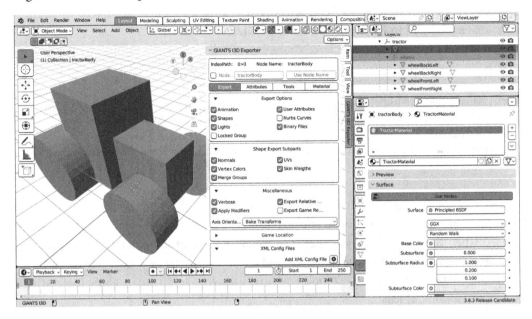

FIGURE 3.1   A simple tractor with the `tractor_mat` placeholder material added to it.

Of course, just setting the material name to `tractor_mat` isn't actually enough to tell the GIANTS I3D Exporter how the material is supposed to look when it gets to Farming Simulator. In fact, if you click the Export All button within the GIANTS I3D Exporter tab in the 3D Viewport, the model will certainly be exported. However, if you open it in the GIANTS Editor, it will look just as gray as it is in Blender.

In order to assign Farming Simulator materials to objects in your mod, you need to let the GIANTS I3D Exporter add-on know where to find those materials. That process is covered in the next section.

Configuring GIANTS I3D Exporter to See Farming Simulator Shaders

You need to get the GIANTS I3D Exporter add-on to know where the Farming Simulator materials (called *shaders*) are located on your hard drive. In particular, for vehicle mods, we need the `vehicleShader` shader. Often, the add-on is capable of finding this path automatically, but if you have Farming Simulator installed in a non-standard location, the add-on may have trouble finding it.

To confirm that the add-on is looking in the right place, go to the Material section within the GIANTS I3D Exporter tab in the 3D Viewport. The first field in that section is labeled **Shader Folder Location**. To the far right of this field is a button labeled Set Game Directory. Click this button and the add-on should automatically find your game folder.

If the add-on can't automatically find your game, click the folder icon that's to the right of the **Shader Folder Location** field and use Blender's File Browser to navigate to where you installed Farming Simulator and find the `shader` folder there (it's typically in the `data` folder).

Once the path to your shader folder is set, you can expand the **Shader File** dropdown menu and choose *vehicleShader.xml* from that list. When you choose that option from the menu, the add-on displays a gigantic list of parameters that you can assign to your material, as shown in Figure 3.2.

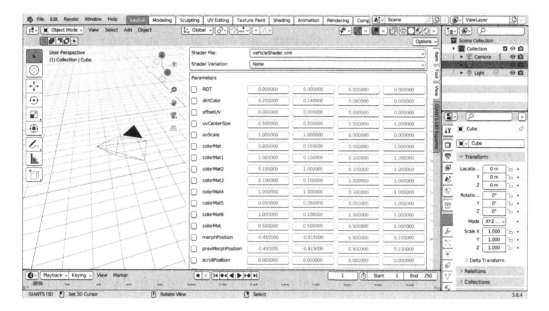

FIGURE 3.2   After you let the GIANTS I3D Exporter add-on know where your Farming Simulator materials live on your hard drive, you have a wide assortment of shader parameters you can use.

Unlike the values in your Blender material, the parameters in the Material section of the GIANTS I3D Exporter *are* recognized by the Farming Simulator game engine and will give you visual results when you export. You just need to set the parameters correctly. That process is covered in the next chapter.

ASSIGNING MATERIALS TO YOUR VEHICLE

Now that you have a placeholder material for your object in Blender and the GIANTS I3D Exporter add-on knows where Farming Simulator is installed, you can finally go about the process of configuring your materials. You'll finally be rid of that dull gray look when you open your exported model in GIANTS Editor!

Using Prefabricated Materials

Continuing the example of making a material for this simple tractor model, your next step in the process is actually defining that material and setting parameters that accurately reflect what the material should look like in Farming Simulator. The work here starts in the Material section of the GIANTS I3D Exporter tab within Blender's 3D Viewport.

If you worked through the preceding section, the add-on should already know where Farming Simulator is installed on your hard drive, and you should have the *vehicleShader. xml* option selected from the **Shader File** list. Now you can adjust your parameters.

As mentioned before, the GIANTS Engine only uses Blender's material system as a mechanism for defining what shaders and material properties should be used when you get in-game. That means it won't make use of any of Blender's more complex material networks. However, that doesn't mean you just have to rely on a bunch of plain, flat colors for your mod. Instead, the folks at GIANTS Software have created a mechanism to have standardized surfaces. This standardization makes it possible for you to define prefabricated materials such as steel, plastic, upholstery, and other surface structures. And because it's built into the GIANTS I3D Exporter add-on, this approach simplifies the modding process and also creates a more consistent quality across different mods.

The process uses a function in the GIANTS I3D Exporter add-on called the UV Vehicle Array. It's a fancy name, but it's really a means of moving your UV map around the UV coordinate system, often *outside* of the base UV square. In a lot of ways, this is similar to the approach that's used for UDIM textures, if you're familiar with that process. However, it doesn't actually use UDIM tiles, so don't worry about doing that if you've never worked with them before.

It's easiest to understand this feature by seeing it in action. With your 3D model selected, use the following steps:

1. **Switch to the UV Editing workspace.** This step automatically puts your selected object in Edit mode and gives you a view of your UV map in the UV Editor. It's important that your model is unwrapped for the rest of this process. See Chapter 2 for more on UV unwrapping.

2. **Expand the sidebar in the UV Editor and choose the GIANTS I3D Exporter tab.** Assuming that you've already configured the GIANTS I3D Exporter add-on to know where Farming Simulator is installed on your computer, you should see a large list of all the possible surfaces supported by the game.

3. **Select all of the vertices in your UV map.** For convenience, you can use the *A* hotkey to select all.

4. Click on one of the materials listed in the UV Vehicle Array, such as `Chrome _ 02 _` . You should see that when you click that material, your selected UVs are moved to a different location in the UV coordinate space.

Using this feature, it's possible to very easily assign multiple materials to the same object. You just select a subset of faces in your UV map, and you can use the UV Vehicle Array feature to assign any of the available materials to that selection.

TIP

If you decide you want to set a different material for a portion of your UV map, you may need to use Blender's Split operator to make those UVs their own island. You can split your selection by going to *UV → Split → Selection* in the UV Editor (or by pressing *Y*).

Customizing Your Material Colors with Color Materials

By default, the color for the faces you're moving around in UV space is defined by whichever prefabricated material is associated with the coordinates you put it in. However, you're not limited to that. You have the ability to customize your colors using Color Materials.

To use color materials, after you choose your prefabricated material in Blender's UV Editor, scroll down to the bottom of the UV Vehicle Array in the sidebar to the section labeled Color Masks. With all of the faces in your UV map selected, click the button for **Color 0**. This lets the GIANTS I3D Exporter know that it should use the values defined by a color material called **colorMat0**. For mixed materials, you can use up to eight color materials on a single object. Of course, if you like the colors provided by the default materials in the UV Vehicle Array, you don't need to use color materials.

The work of customizing your color material happens back in the 3D Viewport. Go to the GIANTS I3D Exporter tab in the Sidebar and switch to the Material section. Then enable the checkbox next to the label, **colorMat0**. You're going to use the parameters next to this label to define the color for your tractor _ mat material.

All of the colorMat parameters are defined by a list of decimal numbers, each separated by a space. The first three numbers are color values for red, green, and blue channels, respectively. Each value is a decimal number, with 0 representing no color influence and 1 representing full color influence. The fourth number in each colorMat parameter is specific to the Farming Simulator game engine and is used to define a material that's loaded from the engine.

> **TECHNICAL NOTE**
>
> It's worth mentioning that the color values for color materials are a specific standardization of red, green, and blue known as sRGB. While most of the time, it's not necessary to know this distinction, it can sometimes be useful if your colors in-game don't quite look as expected. Chances are good that you might be using RGB values instead of sRGB values.

To set the color for your tractor _ mat material to be blue, change the **colorMat0** parameter to read as 0 0 1 0. Setting these values tells the GIANTS engine that you're using no color from the red and green channels but full color on the blue channel. The last value in that parameter is to define which prefabricated shader to use from the UV Vehicle Array; in this example, we have the value set to zero, meaning the material is just color.

Once you've set the parameters for **colorMat0**, scroll down to the dropdown menu labeled **Shader Variation**. Choose *colorMask* from this menu so the shader knows that it will be colored. The *colorMask* option should be set any time you use the Farming Simulator material library as well as when using color materials. After you've set your parameters and defined the shader variation, click the **Add Shader** button at the very bottom to ensure that these parameters are included when you export your model to the I3D format.

This is the basic workflow you use for all materials in your mod. As a summary, the workflow uses the following steps:

1. Ensure that the add-on has the correct location for your Farming Simulator shaders.

2. Choose your desired shader file (in this case, vehicleShader.xml).

3. Set the Shader Variation menu to colorMask, as described in the preceding paragraph.

4. Use the UV Vehicle Array in the UV Editor to pick a prefabricated material.

5. In the 3D Viewport, go to the Material section of the GIANTS I3D Exporter tab in the Sidebar to enable and adjust any parameters you need for your material.

6. Set the shader variation that relates to your chosen parameters (in this example, colorMask).

7. Click the Add Shader button to apply your parameters to your selected object's material.

Figure 3.3 shows what your GIANTS I3D Exporter tab might look like for this example.

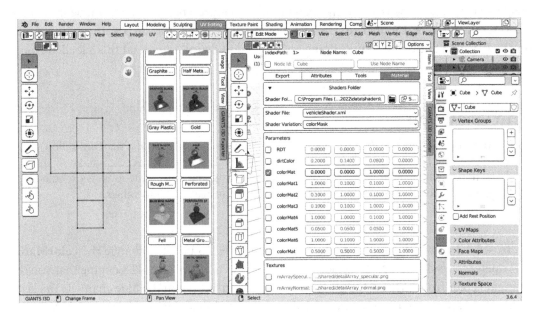

FIGURE 3.3   The Material section of the GIANTS I3D Exporter, configured to set a blue color on colorMat0.

Applying Vehicle Masks (vmasks) and Normal Maps

Before you export, there's another step you need to take in order to have your vehicle shader work without errors. You need to add a vehicle mask, or *vmask*, to the material. A vmask is an image texture that's applied to your model and takes advantage of your model's UV coordinate system (see Chapter 2). In a way, a vmask is a little similar to a specular map, but the GIANTS Engine expects the color channels in a vmask to be used in a very different way. For vmasks, each color channel is used to define a different texture property. Think of it like having three grayscale masks packed into a single image file. The color channel mappings are as follows:

- **Red**: scratch and wear

- **Green**: shadows and ambient occlusion

- **Blue**: dirt accumulation

To assign a vmask to your model, it first needs to be UV-unwrapped. See Chapter 2 for more on UV unwrapping. Assuming that your model is already unwrapped and you've already created a vmask, you assign your vmask to your material by using Blender's built-in material system. If you don't have a vmask image, there's a handy blank one that comes with Farming Simulator that you can use. It lives in the `data/shared` folder for the game. The file you're looking for is named *default_vmask.png*.

Whether you use the vmask image provided by Farming Simulator or you make your own, you can proceed with connecting it to the specular value on your `tractor_mat` material. Select your object and use the following steps to add a vmask:

1. **Go to the Material tab of the Properties editor and ensure that your material is selected.** In this example, it's the material named `tractor_mat`. By default, Blender should provide this material with a Principled BSDF shader.

2. **Within the Principled BSDF shader, find the Specular value and click the gray circle on the left side of the value.** Blender gives you a huge menu of input choices to feed into this value.

3. **From the input menu, choose Image Texture.** Now underneath the Specular value there are buttons you can use to load an image.

4. **Click the Open button and find your vmask image using Blender's File Browser.**

As with the vmask, your material should also have a normal map. If you don't already have a normal map texture for your model, there's a blank one available with Farming Simulator, just like with the vmask texture. The file that you're looking for is named *default_normal.png*.

If you're testing your normal map in Blender, it's also important to correctly set the color space for your normal map image. Like the vmask, the normal map is not really an image but a representation of data that's packaged in an image. So you want to be sure that there are no additional color transformations in the image. You can do this from the Image tab in the Image Editor's sidebar. Go to the **Color Space** dropdown menu and choose *Non-Color*. Then you can save your placeholder normal map to your hard drive. This step is only really necessary if you're creating or testing your normal map in Blender. Since your ultimate destination is Farming Simulator, the GIANTS I3D Exporter add-on only needs to know the path to the image; the GIANTS Engine will handle rendering it.

Once you have your normal map image created or located on your hard drive, you need to connect it to your material shader. The steps are similar to those used for adding the vmask, but there are a few extra steps:

1. From the Material tab of the Properties editor, ensure you're on your **tractor _ mat** material and scroll to the bottom of the Principled BSDF shader values and find the value labeled *Normal*. The initial setting for this property should just read as Default.

2. **Click the blue circle to the left of the Normal value and choose *Normal Map* from the large menu that appears.** The Normal Map option should be in the third column, labeled *Vector*. When you choose this option, Blender provides a set of additional values associated with your normal map. You only need to adjust one of them.

3. **From your new Normal Map properties, click the yellow circle next to the Color value and choose *Image Texture* from the menu that appears.** The *Image Texture* option should be in the second column, labeled *Texture*. When you choose this option, you get buttons for loading an image, just like with the vmask.

4. **Click the Open button to find your normal map image on your hard drive.** Or, if you created a placeholder within Blender, you can choose it from the Image datablock widget. Whichever way you choose to go, be sure that the Color Space for your normal map is set to *Non-Color*.

Now you have a vmask image and a normal map image connected to your Blender material. If you're familiar with how Blender's node graph works for materials, Figure 3.4 gives a

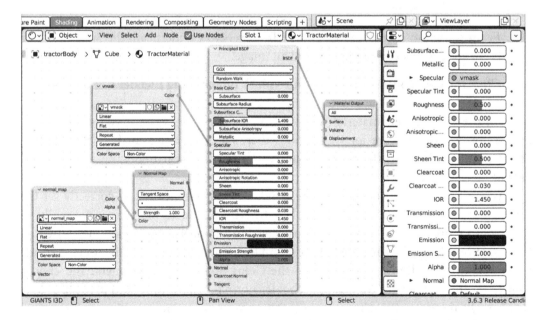

FIGURE 3.4 The node graph on a Blender material with a vmask image and a normal map image correctly connected to the Principled BSDF shader.

more clear view of how the material node graph looks after you've correctly assigned a vmask and a normal map to your model.

Now when you export your vehicle mod to the I3D format and load that file into GIANTS Editor, you should experience no errors.

ADDING DECALS TO YOUR MOD

There's one small exception to what I said earlier in the chapter about your materials not looking the same in Blender and in Farming Simulator, and that's with decals. Typically speaking, vehicle decals are not part of your main vehicle material. They're usually separate meshes that are part of the vehicle hierarchy as children of the object that they're applied to. The reason for this structure is to ensure that when that part of the vehicle moves (like a folding arm on a cultivator), the decals move with it.

Now, there are a few guidelines about how to do decals correctly in your mod. They are as follows:

- **Try to pack all of your decals on a single image texture.** This approach keeps you efficient and helps with in-game performance. Loading a bunch of individual texture images tends to be more taxing than loading one image and mapping UV coordinates to it.

- **Take advantage of the alpha channel on your decal image.** If you can avoid modeling the shape of a decal and can instead just use a rectangle that's mostly transparent except for the decal, do that. Generally speaking, transparency in a game engine is less computationally expensive than geometry.

- **Don't make your decal mesh unnecessarily bigger than the visible part it's applied to.** This seems like a bit of a contradiction to the previous point, I know, but although it's good to use transparency, you don't want to abuse it. Basically, you don't want to have too much *overdraw* where the game engine has to calculate transparency intersections with more than just your vehicle.

- **Convert your textures to the DDS format using the GIANTS Texture Tool.** The DDS image format offers fantastic compression for games and is the preferred format for Farming Simulator. While the DDS format has been standardized, all of your conversions to this format for your mod should be done with the GIANTS Texture Tool. Details on using this tool can be found later in this chapter in the section titled, "Converting Textures to DDS."

Setting up Your Decal Material

Normally, I'd suggest using Blender's built-in Images as Planes add-on to get your decals loaded in Blender. However, since all of the decals should be in a single image, this approach doesn't work so well. Instead, you'll need to use a somewhat more manual approach.

Everything starts with making sure you have a mesh for your decals, properly set up with the UV maps that the game engine is expecting. Use the following steps:

1. Create a mesh object for your first decal. A plane is a good way to start; use **Add ▶ Mesh ▶ Plane**.

2. Name your plane something sensible by double-clicking its name in the Outliner. For example, in our cultivator example, one of our decal meshes is named `armRightDecals`.

3. Switch to the UV Editing workspace using the tab at the top of the Blender window. Blender should automatically switch your new decal plane into Edit mode.

4. Rename the base UV map from its default name of *UVMap* to something sensible (like *map1*) by going to the UV Maps panel in the Object Data tab of the Properties editor and double-clicking the UV map's name. This is the UV map you use for your decals. You can use any name you want. The important thing is that this is the first UV map in the list.

5. Still in the Properties editor, add a second UV map and name this one *map2*. This second UV map is what you use for the vmask on your decals. Again, the name can be whatever you'd like. It's the order that's important.

6. Click *map1* in the UV Maps panel to make sure that it's the active UV map.

At this point, you have your mesh data all set up properly, but you need to set up your materials on your mesh so you can see what's going on. Use the following steps:

1. Switch to the Shading workspace using the tab at the top of the Blender window. Your plane should now be back in Object mode.

2. If your decal mesh doesn't already have material on it, go ahead and add one by clicking the **New** button in the header of the Shader Editor, and name your material something that makes sense, like `tractorDecal_mat`. The default Blender material is a single Principled BSDF node wired to a Material Output node. You need to connect some Image Texture nodes to the correct sockets on the Principled BSDF node.

3. Add a new Image Texture node (**Add ▶ Texture ▶ Image Texture**) and place it to the left of the Principled BSDF node.

4. In the Image Texture Node, click the **Open** button and use the File Browser that appears to find the image that holds your decal images.

5. Connect the Color socket of the Image Texture node to the Base Color socket of the Principled BSDF. This connection gets the color data of your decal to your shader.

6. Connect the Alpha socket of the Image Texture node to the Alpha socket of the Principled BSDF. With this connection, you ensure that the transparency in your decal image is used. Now you just need to add your vmask.

7. Add another Image Texture node (**Add ▶ Texture ▶ Image Texture**) and also place this node to the left of the Principled BSDF node.

8. Click the **Open** button in the Image Texture node to find your vmask image.

9. Wire the Color socket on your vmask's Image Texture node to the Specular socket on the Principled BSDF node.

At this point, all of the basics for your decal material are set. Your node graph in Blender should look something like what's shown in Figure 3.5.

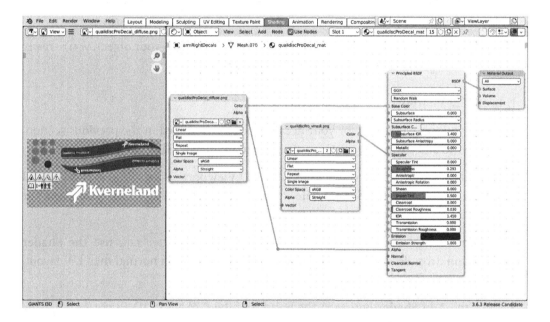

FIGURE 3.5 Setting up the shader network for your decal mesh.

With your plane created and material added, you need to make sure it has the correct shader variation when exported to the I3D format. You've already done some of the pre-work necessary to make sure everything plays nicely with the shader. It's part of the reason why you used a specific order for the UV maps on your decal object.

There are actually two different shader variations for decals that you have available, depending on your needs. Those needs are actually defined by how many UV maps you require. At the minimum, you need one UV map for the diffuse (color) texture of your decals and one UV map for your vmask. If you have a need for a custom normal map UV layout, then you would have to create a third UV map. Regardless of the shader variation you choose, your UV maps in Blender should have this order:

- Diffuse texture UV map (*map1* in our example)

- Vmask texture UV map (*map2* in our example)

- Normal map texture UV map (we might call this one *map3*, and it's only needed for the *Decal_normalThirdUV* shader variation)

> **NOTE**
>
> For versions of Farming Simulator 25 and beyond, the shader variation that you need has been renamed. For those versions, *Decal* has been renamed to *vmaskUV2* and *Decal_ normalThirdUV* has been renamed to *vmaskUV2_normalUV3*.

Once you have your UV maps created and your material added to your object, you're ready to set up your shader variation. Use the following steps:

1. In the 3D Viewport, select your decal object.

2. Set up your base material for your decal object, as described in the previous section. In order to add a shader variation, you need to first have a shader.

3. From the GIANTS I3D Exporter tab in the 3D Viewport's Sidebar, go to the Material section and choose the **Shader File** drop-down to select the *vehicleShader.xml* for your object.

4. Still in the Material section of the GIANTS I3D Exporter tab, use the **Shader Variation** drop-down to choose *Decal*. If you need a custom normal map UV layout, you can instead choose *Decal_normalThirdUV*.

5. Click the **Add Shader** button at the bottom of the GIANTS I3D Exporter tab. Now you have the correct shader assigned to your decal mesh.

Positioning and Unwrapping Your Decal Geometry

Now you have a mesh that's mostly prepared, but you still need to properly position your plane and do the actual work of mapping that geometry to the image in your decal image. For the simple example of a decal that will fit on a rectangular plane, the process is pretty straight-forward. In Object mode, use Blender's transform tools to adjust your plane to the desired size and position it on your vehicle mesh.

TIP

You can take advantage of Blender's snapping tools to help ensure that your decal mesh is in-plane with the faces on your mod's model. That said, your decal mesh shouldn't be in *exactly* the same location as the vehicle mesh, or you'll end up with a z-fighting issue, where the game engine renderer doesn't quite know which mesh to display. To avoid this problem, you should have your decal placed slightly above the surface of the part it's supposed to be applied to.

Now you need to unwrap your plane. Technically speaking, the plane is already unwrapped, but chances are good that your proportions in the UV Editor don't match the proportions that you've adjusted your plane to match. You could edit the UVs manually in the UV Editor, but that's time-consuming and inaccurate. There's a faster way. Use these steps:

1. Switch to the UV Editing workspace using the tab at the top of the Blender window. Your mesh should automatically switch to Edit mode.

2. Select the face of your plane. Since, at this point, the plane is the only geometry in your decal mesh, you can use **Select ▶ All**.

3. Choose **View ▶ Align View ▶ Align View to Active ▶ Top** from the 3D Viewport to align the scene view to look at your plane along its local normal.

4. Ensure that your decal map is your active UV map by clicking it in the UV Maps panel in the Object Data tab of the Properties editor.

5. In the UV Editor, use the image datablock widget in the header to choose your decal image.

6. In the 3D Viewport, choose **UV ▶ Project from View**. This operator unwraps your plane using the view from the scene camera, maintaining the proportions of your geometry (ideally, your decal texture is square).

From this point, you can make further adjustments to your UV map in the UV Editor to rotate and position the unwrapped geometry over the correct part of your decal texture.

That situation works well for the simple example of a plane. However, what if you need your decal on shaped geometry? You could technically still use a rectangular plane and let it overhang, but that's ugly, and it likely doesn't make the best use of space on your decal texture. In that situation, your best solution is to select the desired faces on your vehicle model, duplicate them, and separate them into their own mesh. The process looks like this:

1. Get your vehicle mesh in Edit mode and select the faces where you want to place your decal.

2. Duplicate selected faces (**Mesh ▶ Duplicate**) and immediately right-click to ensure that the faces stay in the correct location.

3. Choose **Mesh ▶ Separate ▶ Selection** to split your newly duplicated faces into their own objects.

4. Tab back to Object mode and then select your newly separated object.

5. From the Materials tab of the Properties editor, remove any existing materials on your new object and add your decal material to it.

6. Unwrap this mesh using the same steps covered earlier in this section to correctly map your new faces onto your decal texture.

If you look at the integrated cultivator example that this book is built around (you can find it on the GDN), the decals on the outer part of each arm were created using this technique (or one very much like it). Figure 3.6 shows a screenshot of this part.

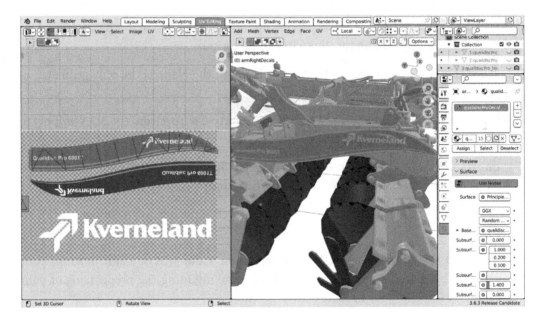

FIGURE 3.6   You can use existing geometry in your vehicle mesh to build your decal mesh.

Cleaning Up

If you worked through the steps in the preceding section, it's likely that you have a bunch of different decal meshes. Each one has its own geometry and origin, but they are all sharing the same material and mapped to the same image. It's time for a bit of consolidation. Your mod will certainly work with all of these meshes, but from an organization and performance standpoint, it's a little bit nicer to collect them into fewer objects. How many objects is up to you, but my recommendation would be to have a "decal object" for each independently moving part in your mod. If your mod has no moving parts, then you only need a single decal object. If your mod is a tool with folding arms, then maybe you need one decal object per arm.

Figure out the organization you need, and then consolidate your objects as necessary. The cool thing is that the consolidation process is rather painless. You need to join objects, make sure your decal object is correctly placed in the hierarchy in the Outliner, and then adjust the consolidated object's origin. Use the following steps:

1. **Join your decal objects.** The process of joining multiple decal objects into a single object is really a process of adding the mesh data of one object to the mesh data of another. Each time you want to do it, use the same basic steps:

   a. Select the object that you want to add.

   b. *Shift*+select the target object, the one you want to have data added to.

   c. Choose **Object ▸ Join** from the menu in the 3D Viewport's header (or use the *Ctrl+J* hotkey combination) to join your selected meshes together. Blender is smart enough to merge the UV maps and materials correctly, assuming they all have the same names. If material or UV map naming is different between objects, I suggest you fix that prior to joining.

2. **Fix your vehicle hierarchy.** Basically, if your decal object is associated with a moving part on your mod (like a folding arm), you want to make sure that decal object is a child of the moving part. You can build this parent-child relationship either in the Outliner or by selecting the decal object, *Shift*+selecting the moving part, and using **Object ▸ Parent ▸ Object** from the 3D Viewport's header menu. Details of these processes are covered in more detail in Chapter 2. And for more on setting up your vehicle hierarchy in general, have a look at the next chapter.

3. **Adjust the origin of your consolidated decal object.** After you've joined your individual decal objects into a single one, chances are good that the origin of your consolidated object is not where you want it to be. Ideally, you'd want to have the origin for this object either at the same location as its parent (defined in the preceding step) or at the median point of the decal mesh. Assuming that you want to do the former, use these steps:

   a. Select the parent object.

   b. Choose **Object ▸ Snap ▸ Cursor to Selected** to move the 3D cursor to the location of the parent object's origin.

   c. Select your decal object.

   d. Choose **Object ▸ Set Origin ▸ Origin to 3D Cursor** to set your decal object's origin at the location of the 3D cursor.

TIP

The preceding steps describe how you would set up your origin in "vanilla" Blender. However, since you already have the GIANTS I3D Exporter add-on installed, you can take advantage of some convenience tools that come with it. If you go to the GIANTS I3D Exporter tab in the 3D Viewport's Sidebar and switch to the Tools section, there are two operators there that are quite helpful, **FreezeTranslation** and **FreezeRotation**. If you select your decal object and click these two buttons, the origin of that decal object is shifted to match the origin of its parent. You can do those four steps just described in just two button clicks!

And with that, you should have a properly put-together decal object that exports cleanly to the I3D format.

TESTING YOUR MATERIAL IN THE GIANTS EDITOR

Now that you have everything in place for the GIANTS I3D Exporter, you can finally export your vehicle mod and open it in the GIANTS Editor for testing. Assuming you have the file that's been worked on throughout this chapter with the `tractor_mat` material with a correctly-assigned vmask and normal map, as well as the UV Vehicle Array set to use Color 0, you're ready to export. Go to the GIANTS I3D tab in the 3D Viewport's sidebar and click the Export All button at the bottom. Blender should generate an I3D file that you can open in the GIANTS Editor.

If you open that exported file in the GIANTS Editor, your screen should look similar to what's shown in Figure 3.7.

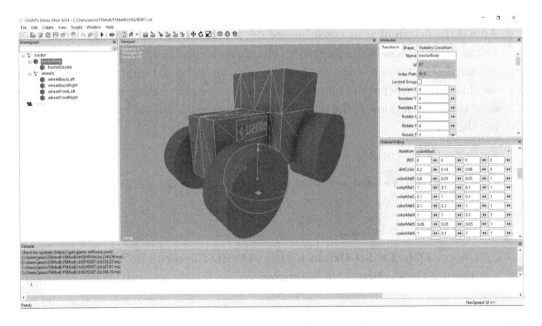

FIGURE 3.7 Your exported model with correct material settings for `tractor_mat`, opened in the GIANTS Editor.

Inspecting this file in the GIANTS Editor, you should note that the hierarchy has been preserved, just like at the end of Chapter 2. However, if you navigate to **Window ▶ Material Editing** and select your model on the panel to the right, you should see your `tractor_mat` material with all the correct parameters you defined in Blender. From here, it's possible to make further tweaks to the materials in your mod. However, the best practice is to make those changes in Blender before you export, so you can keep all of your changes in one place.

Confirming Your Colorized Material Shaders

That said, there is one topic worth covering while looking at your model in the GIANTS Editor. Recall earlier in this chapter that we covered the four values that can be assigned to a color material. The first three values are sRGB values to define the color, while the last value defines a material that's specific to the GIANTS Engine. If you scroll to the Custom Shader section in the side panel of the GIANTS Editor, you should see the values for **colorMat0**, just as you defined them in Blender. However, the difference now is that if you change those values while in the GIANTS Editor, you can immediately see the result of those changes in the 3D Viewport.

As a test, change the fourth value for **colorMat0** to *37*. That number relates to a material texture that looks like a perforated surface. That material number also corresponds to the material defined in the UV Vehicle Array within the GIANTS I3D Exporter in Blender. In this case, it's the material named `PERFORATED 02 _ 37 _`. If you chose that material from the UV Vehicle Array, the exporter would use that material and its default coloring. However, by using the colorMat slots, you're able to colorize that material. If you want to export the colorized material from Blender, then you just need to replace the *0* at the end of your **colorMat0** value with the number *37*, so it would read `0 0 1 37`. In fact, if you do that now from Blender and re-export your I3D file, you should be able to reload it in the GIANTS Editor and see your perforated surface, colored blue.

> **TIP**
>
> You can use the thumbnail images in the UV Vehicle Array to get a preview of these materials while you're in Blender. However, since those thumbnails are so small, it's sometimes easier to have a simple model (or a plane) exported from Blender, where you can play with color and material settings in real time in the GIANTS Editor. Then once you find settings you like, pull those values back over into Blender.

Checking Variable Shader Properties

Using shaders and materials, you have a lot of control over the look of your mod when it's in the game. Some of those things, like dirt coverage, vary as you play the game. Now, you could load your mod in the game and test these properties using the commands covered in Chapter 14, but there is a faster way right from within GIANTS Editor. As with the preceding section, navigate to **Window ▶ Material Editing** and select your model. Now, from the Custom Shader panel, you have the familiar attributes for your vehicle's shader. In particular, look at the values next to the **RDT** label. These values control the dirt shader on your vehicle, mapped in accordance with your vmask. Recall that in Blender, it's difficult to visualize how your dirt texture is going to appear on your vehicle. That's not the case with the GIANTS Editor.

> **NOTE**
>
> The use and naming for the RDT parameter are a bit outdated. In releases of Farming Simulator after FS22, the RDT parameter has been renamed to *scratches_dirt_snow_wetness*.

The first value in the set of attributes next to the **RDT** label is used to see scratches from wear on your vehicle. The second value, however, is more relevant to dirt. That value controls the amount of dirt that appears on your model. If you click on it, GIANTS Editor provides you with a handy slider that you can use to interactively adjust dirt levels on your vehicle, as shown in Figure 3.8. As you adjust the slider, the Viewport should update in real time.

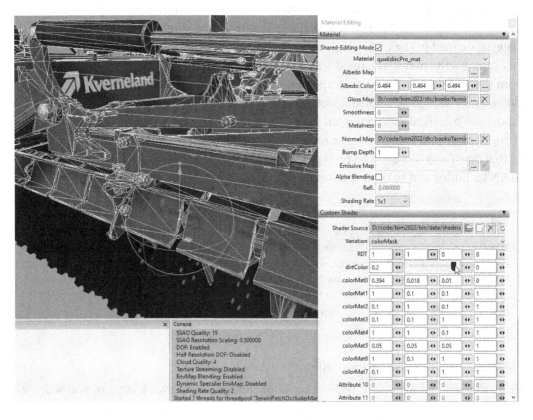

FIGURE 3.8 The Custom Shader panel gives you sliders to control interactive shader values, like the amount of dirt on your vehicle.

Similarly, you can also check the behavior of moving parts that are controlled with shaders. For instance, the example cultivator that we use throughout this book is a disc harrow and the discs have a shader that rotates as the tool is being towed. Like with dirt, it's certainly possible to test this in-game, but you can do a faster spot-check using the attributes in the Custom Shader panel. In the example of the aforementioned cultivator, you can select one of the discs and look at the **rotationAngle** attribute. The discs in this example use the **vtxRotate** shader variation, so they rotate about their local X-axis. That means if you click on the first value of the **rotationAngle** parameter, you can use the provided slider to watch the shader rotate interactively, as shown in Figure 3.9.

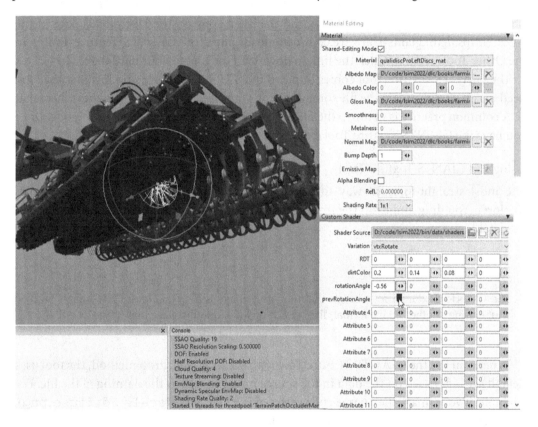

FIGURE 3.9   Use the Custom Shader panel to test the rotation of shaders on moving parts.

CONVERTING TEXTURES TO DDS

To get the best performance on image textures used in your materials (like with decals), the source images that you use need to be converted to **DDS**, or DirectDraw Surface format. This image format is optimized for real-time game engines to give you the best performance in-game. There are numerous tools out there for converting images to DDS format, but for your mod, it's important for you to use the GIANTS Texture Tool that's available in the Download section of the GDN. The DDS images produced by the GIANTS Texture Tool overcome some technical limitations of the standard. This means that those DDS files have additional features like alpha blending and parallax mapping, in addition to having better performance.

> **NOTE**
>
> When you're building your mod, it's best to stick with high-quality PNG images for textures while you're working in Blender. However, Blender reads DDS images just fine. So once you get a little farther along in your mod-creating process, it's OK to switch to your DDS textures in your Blender materials.

Getting and Installing the GIANTS Texture Tool

In order to make use of the GIANTS Texture Tool to convert your images to DDS, you first need to get a copy of it. You can find the latest copy on the Downloads page of the GDN (https://gdn.giants-software.com/downloads.php). The GIANTS Texture Tool is in the Other Tools section. Click the link to download the tool to your hard drive.

The GIANTS Texture Tool comes bundled in a ZIP file, so there's no installer that you need to run. Simply unzip the file somewhere on your hard drive and remember where that is. A common practice is to unzip the file to the folder that's holding all of your mods. Once you have the GIANTS Texture Tool extracted, you're ready to use it.

Using the GIANTS Texture Tool

The most straight-forward way to use the GIANTS Texture Tool is from Windows Explorer. You drag and drop the image you want to convert to the `textureTool.exe` executable.

> **NOTE**
>
> The GIANTS Texture Tool expects that the input image is a .gim file or PNG image. So if you're using another image format, like JPEG, you'll need to first save that image as a PNG.

When you use the GIANTS Texture Tool with the drag-and-drop method, the tool uses default settings based on the data in the source image as well as the naming of the file. For example, if your image file's name ends with _diffuse (like `decals_diffuse.png`), then the converter assumes that the image data is stored in sRGB color format and needs mipmaps.

If you want more control over what settings are used in conversion, you can generate a .gim file with the same name as your PNG. For reference, there are some sample and template .gim files that come within the GIANTS Texture Tool ZIP file that you can inspect to see how to properly create a valid .gim file. The format is based on XML, so it's quite similar to modifying your `modDesc.xml` and vehicle-XML (see Chapter 6 to get started with XML). So using the previous example, a .gim file with custom settings would be named `decals_diffuse.gim`. The .gim files are also useful for converting multiple images in a texture array (like for certain terrain textures) because you specify all the source file names for those PNGs in the .gim file You can just drag the .gim file over the GIANTS Texture Tool executable, and everything gets handled for you.

In addition to the base executable, the GIANTS Texture Tool also includes a few handy helper scripts that you can use:

- **textureToolRecursive.cmd**—If you drag and drop a folder on this script, it runs the GIANTS Texture Tool on every PNG or .gim file with that folder (and the subfolders within it).

- **textureToolLowQuality.cmd**—Use this script to convert a single image in low-quality mode. Typically, you use this when doing multiple iterations on a large texture, and it's more important to have a converted file than one of high quality.

- **textureToolInfo.cmd**—Drag and drop a folder on this script and you'll get a print-out of every DDS file in that folder that wasn't created using the GIANTS Texture Tool. This script is particularly useful for helping find potentially problematic image textures.

UNDERSTANDING THE MATERIAL SYSTEM IN FARMING SIMULATOR 25 AND BEYOND

The bulk of the content in this chapter will work for mods targeting any version of Farming Simulator. However, for versions of Farming Simulator 25 and beyond, there are some improvements to the material system that can affect how you set up your model in Blender. This section walks you through those changes so you can be better prepared for building your mods with the new system.

Updates to Names on Shader Variations and Parameters

One noticeable change in the new material system is in naming. A lot of the parameters and attributes from the material system in Farming Simulator 22 have been renamed in the new system. Some of these changes have been noted earlier in this chapter, but this section is intended to give you a quick reference to all of them.

When it comes to shader variations, new naming comes from improved use of UVs and more generalized handling of color masks. For decals, you're no longer using the *Decal* and *Decal_normalThirdUV* variations. Instead, use *vmaskUV2* and *vmaskUV2_normalUV3*. Furthermore, for color masks, you no longer need to use the *_colorMask* suffix since they're no longer required. And the *uvScroll*, *uvRotate*, and *uvScale* variations have been combined into a single *uvTransform* variation.

For textures, *mTrackArray* has been renamed to be a bit simpler by calling it *trackArray*.

In terms of parameters, there's been quite a bit of shuffling around and renaming. The *RDT* parameter is now *scratches_dirt_snow_wetness*. The *morphPosition*, *scrollPosition*, and *lightControl* parameters have each been shortened to *morphPos*, *scrollPos*, and *lightIds*, respectively. And finally, the *alphaBlendingClipThreshold* parameter now replaces the functionality of the Decal shader variations. Any part with an alpha value that's below the threshold defined by this parameter is completely hidden.

Table 3.1 gives a more simple view of these changes.

TABLE 3.1   Shader Variations, Textures, and Parameters Renamed in the New Material System

FS22	After FS22
Shader variations	
Decal	vmaskUV2
Decal_normalThirdUV	vmaskUV2_normalUV3
XX_colormask	_colormask suffix removed; not required any more
uvScroll, uvRotate, uvScale	uvTransform
Textures	
mTrackArray	trackArray
Parameters	
RDT	scratches_dirt_snow_wetness
morphPosition	morphPos
scrollPosition	scrollPos
lightControl	lightIds
Decal	alphaBlendingClipThreshold

Adding Shaders and Materials in the New Material System

Before you start worrying yourself over trying to wrap your brain around a whole new material system, there's good news. The newest version of the GIANTS I3D Exporter add-on for Blender has a convenient tool to help you convert your Farming Simulator 22 materials to materials for Farming Simulator 25 and beyond. You just need to click the **Convert FS22 -> FS25** button at the bottom of the tab. Figure 3.10 shows a screenshot of the new GIANTS I3D Exporter tab in Blender.

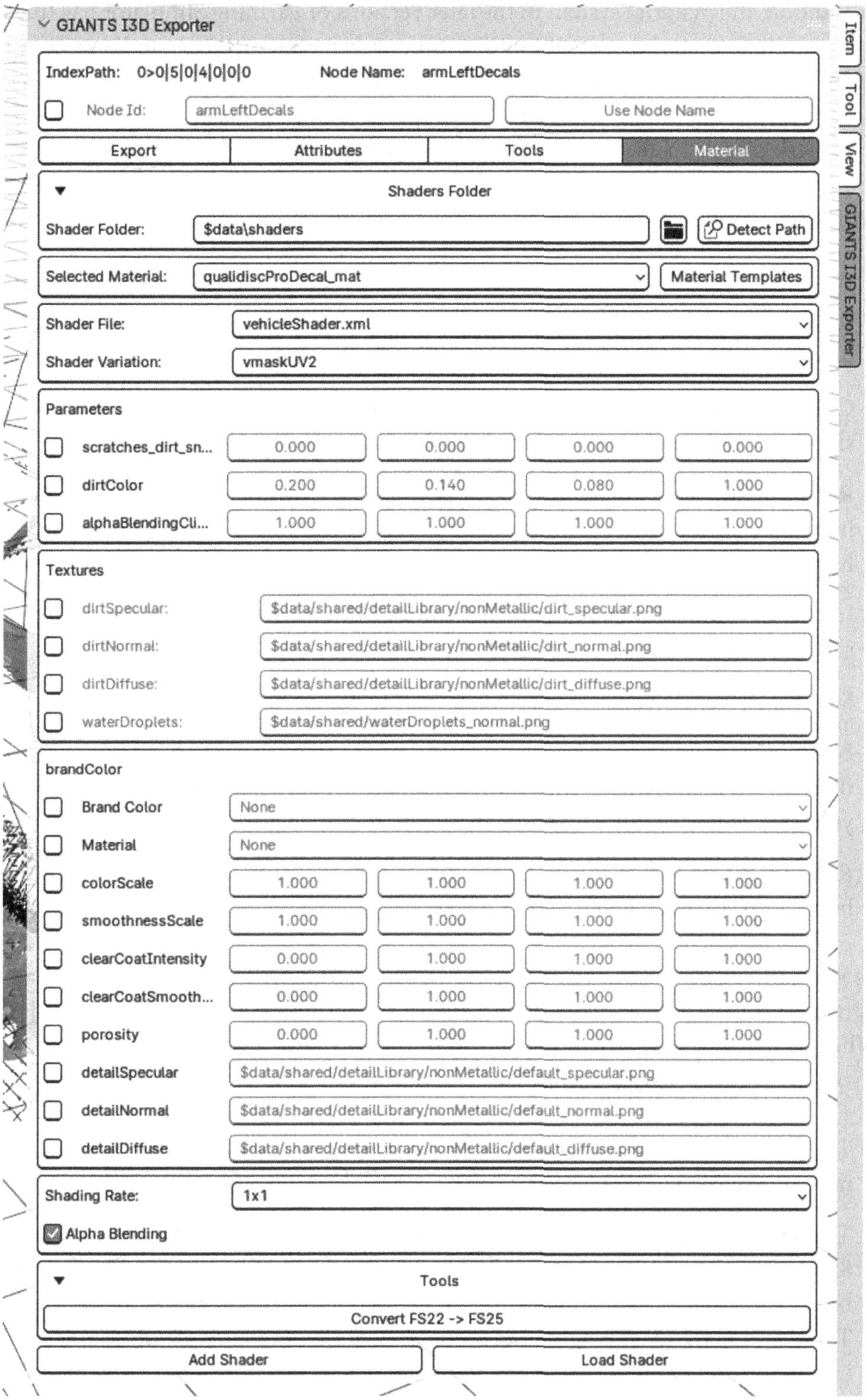

FIGURE 3.10   The new GIANTS I3D Exporter tab in Blender gives you tools for supporting the new material system in versions of Farming Simulator 25 and beyond.

In addition, the material system in the later versions of Farming Simulator has full support for multiple materials per object and takes advantage of the material system provided by Blender's material slots. This means that the UV shifting mechanism and the UV Vehicle Array are no longer necessary for assigning different materials to different parts of your mesh object. Instead, you're able to use Blender's standard material slots to assign different materials to different faces. If you're not familiar with that workflow in Blender, you just need to follow these steps:

1. Select your object and go to the Material tab in the Properties editor. At the top of this tab is a list box. This list box is an index of all the materials associated with your object.

2. Click the Plus (+) button to the right of the material list box, to add a new material slot. You can name the material by double-clicking its name.

3. Repeat Step 2 for as many materials as you have in your object. Materials don't all have to be added in advance, though, so if you need to add more later, you can absolutely do that.

4. In the 3D Viewport, switch into Edit mode (*Tab*) on your object and change your selection mode to Face Selection (*3*).

5. Select the faces on your mesh that you want to assign to a specific material.

6. Back in Material Properties, click the name of the material you want to use in the material list box and then click the **Assign** button below the list box. This step assigns your selected faces to your chosen material.

7. Repeat steps 5 and 6 for each material in your object, being aware that a face can only be assigned to one material; you can't assign multiple materials to a single face.

Once you complete that process, the newer versions of GIANTS I3D Exporter are able to recognize your material assignments and export them to Farming Simulator accordingly.

When it comes to handling multiple materials in the new system, there are a few things that you need to keep yourself aware of:

- The objects with multiple materials need to have the same base attributes (diffuse, normal, vmask, and shader variation).

- The multiple materials feature can only be used with the *vehicleShader* option in the **Shader File** drop-down in the GIANTS I3D Exporter add-on. And to repeat the last bullet (because it's that important), all of the base attributes need to be the same. This way, the GIANTS Engine can merge your different materials while loading your I3D file in the game. If you don't keep these attributes the same, it would lead to multiple draw calls for each material on your object, contributing to poor in-game performance.

- The difference in the material can be additional detail textures plus some shader parameters, such as these:

  - colorScale

  - smoothnessScale

  - clearCoatIntensity

  - clearCoatSmoothness

  - porosity

- The aim of this new system is to be more flexible with fewer limitations. For instance, you can color all of your materials, not just those with colorMat 0 through 7.

In addition to support for multiple materials, the newer versions of Farming Simulator include a material template library. Not only does this library have a lot of pre-defined materials, but those materials are templates. This means that you can assign the material to your model, but you're not totally locked into its appearance. You have the ability to further customize the material after you've added it. As an additional bonus, the next release of the GIANTS I3D Exporter add-on for Blender also includes a browser to let you look through all of the templates that are available directly within Blender. A preview of this material template browser is in Figure 3.11.

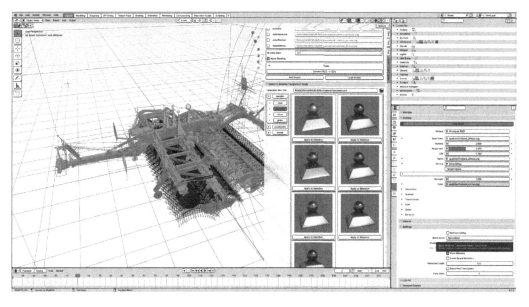

FIGURE 3.11 A preview of the new material templates browser in the upcoming version of the GIANTS I3D Exporter add-on for Blender.

TIP

If you right-click one of the material previews in the new material templates browser, you have the ability to directly assign that material to your currently selected objects or faces. From there, you can further customize the material from the template browser by selecting the face on your model and clicking the **Load** button in the Material section of the GIANTS I3D Exporter tab in the 3D Viewport. From there, you can view and modify the various attributes of that material.

Working with the New StaticLight Shader Variation

Another significant change introduced in the new material system in Farming Simulator 25 has to do with lighting. Chapter 9 gives you a complete rundown of how to set up real lights on your vehicle mod, but in that chapter I leave out the steps for the "old way" of emitting light using vertex colors on your mesh (particularly for when your mod is used on a lower-end computer). That approach doesn't give particularly great results and the new system that uses a custom emissive map is far better.

The way this system works, you can have a light mesh with an emissive texture, as shown in Figure 3.12, that's enabled when the light is turned on.

FIGURE 3.12   An example of a custom emissive map used for controlling lights on a vehicle.

All of your static lighting, including color and intensity, can be controlled with a texture and a custom UV map. The workflow for setting up this kind of light looks like this:

1. Select the object that has your static lights.

2. Add a second UV map to the object to define the functionality of the light.

3. Paint your light texture on your UV map. You can use Blender's built-in texture painting tools or export your UV map to another application like Substance Painter or Photoshop.

4. In the Material section of the GIANTS I3D Exporter tab of the 3D Viewport, make sure your light object has a vehicle shader as a base.

5. Add a staticLight shader variation.

6. In your new shader variation, set the lightsIntensity texture to be your painted texture.

7. Apply your shader variation.

In addition, you can save on performance by merging all of your static light meshes into a single object and then have them all use the same image texture. These light meshes with multiple functions are referred to as *static light compounds*, and their setup is similar to how material assignments have been handled in the old system. That is, the function of each individual mesh is defined by the position of their UV coordinates. These coordinates are referred to as *UV slots* in the GIANTS Engine documentation and are akin to UDIMs used in Blender's UV Editor. In order to ensure that your lights work properly in this system, there are tags you need to include within the `<lights>` tag in your vehicle-XML (for more on lights and your vehicle-XML, have a look at Chapter 9).

Specifically, you need to include a `<staticLightCompounds>` tag, and within its content, you need a `<staticLightCompound>` tag to define your multi-function lights. For example, you might include the following mark-up:

```
<staticLightCompounds>
    <staticLightCompound>
        <node node="vario700Lights01_static" intensity="25"/>
        <node node="vario700LightsGlass01_static" intensity="1"/>
        <node node="vario700Lights02_static" intensity="25"/>
        <node node="vario700LightsGlass02_static" intensity="1"/>
    </staticLightCompound>
</staticLightCompounds>
```

In this example, there are four nodes in your static light compound. There's no need to define anything further in the vehicle XML. Everything is controlled by the UV coordinates on your object. Figure 3.13 shows the function assignment for each UV slot. The gray bottom left UV slot with label *1* is the base UV coordinate box in Blender.

Back Light	Brake Light	Back & Brake Light	Reverse Light	Work Light Front	Work Light Back	Work Light Additional	Work Light Additional 2
9	10	11	12	13	14	15	16
Default Light	Default Light & High Beam	High Beam	Bottom Light	Top Light	Day Time Running Light	Left Turn Signal	Right Turn Signal
1	2	3	4	5	6	7	8

FIGURE 3.13 Static light compounds use UV slots to define functionality for each light. In this figure, the numbers in the lower left corner of each slot are the UV slot indices, which you have the ability to specify in your vehicle-XML.

SUMMARY

This chapter covered the fundamentals of defining and assigning materials to objects in your mod from Blender. You started by discovering how to set up materials in Blender so they're ready to be exported. This process included understanding how the material system Blender uses for its Eevee and Cycles render engines is different from what's used in the GIANTS Engine for Farming Simulator. Next, you went through the process of assigning materials to your vehicle mod. To complete this process, you chose your Farming Simulator material, applied vmasks and normal maps, and took advantage of the prefabricated materials in the UV Vehicle Array. After that, you explored the process of adding decals to your vehicle mod. Then, you tested your exported mod and its materials in the GIANTS Editor. And since your materials tested so well, you used the GIANTS Texture Tool to convert your image textures to the DDS format for best performance. Finally, you saw a little bit about how materials are expected to be handled in future releases of Farming Simulator.

In the next chapter, we get into more details about setting up your vehicle hierarchy and setting up pivots for the moving parts in your mod.

CHAPTER 4

Preparing Your Hierarchy and Setting up Pivots

I F YOU'RE WORKING ON a vehicle mod, then it's going to have moving parts. Each moving part needs a reference point to define that part's location and axis of orientation. In Farming Simulator as well as other 3D modeling tools, this reference point is called a **pivot**. In Blender, it's referred to as the object's **origin**. This chapter gives you a practical example of how to take a 3D model that's arranged as a single mesh object and break it down into its component pieces based on how they move. Then, after separating your moving parts, you can place the pivot so your part moves and rotates correctly. And finally, after getting all of your pieces properly separated with proper origins, you can start building your vehicle hierarchy.

In this chapter:

- Separating your vehicle mesh into parts

- Setting up pivots

- Preparing your vehicle hierarchy

TECHNICAL REQUIREMENTS

In addition to Blender and the GIANTS I3D Exporter, this chapter uses a finished model of a Kverneland Qualidisc Pro cultivator as an example. This model has all of its parts built along with the necessary UV maps and material assignments. You can download this model from the download page for this book (https://gdn.giants-software.com/blender Book; also available by scanning the QR code at the end of this section) if you want to follow along. Otherwise, you can use the same processes on your own model.

DOI: 10.1201/9781032659497-4

https://gdn.giants-software.com/blenderBook

SEPARATING YOUR VEHICLE MESH INTO PARTS

In this example, we're using a model of a cultivator that has been built mostly as one single object in Blender. The discs, hoses, and decals are separate objects, and there are some empties included to help with organization. However, the majority of this model is a single mesh, as shown in Figure 4.1.

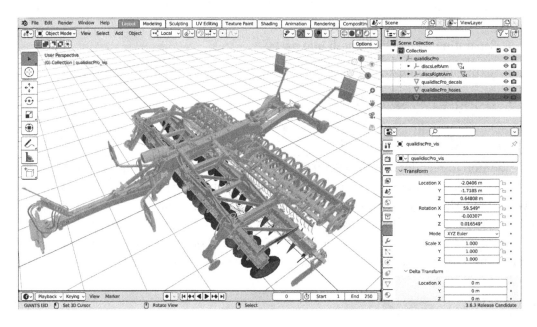

FIGURE 4.1 The provided cultivator model has a few separate parts, but most of it is a single Blender object.

Now, although GIANTS Engine supports deforming parts of an object using an armature-based rig, there is an added computational cost to skinning vertex weights and calculating those deformations. I cover more about skinning and armatures in Chapter 12; however, for simplicity when animating single parts, it's easier to separate different moving parts to their own objects and do transforms like rotation and translation at the object level.

As an example, let's focus on the rollers at the rear of the cultivator. Those parts need to be able to spin around their local axis when the cultivator is engaged and moving. There are four sets of rollers, two on each side. Each of these rollers should be separated from their own objects so they can spin on their own axis while also being able to move with each side's cultivator arm when it's folded.

We'll use the rollers as our example here to give you an idea of the process so you can perform it on your own models. Your first task is to isolate those parts so you can work on them without interference from the rest of the mesh. Use the following steps:

1. Select the mesh you want to work on. In this example, that's the mesh object named `qualidiscPro _ vis`.

2. Isolate your selected object by going into Local View (**View ▶ Local View ▶ Toggle Local View** or press / on your numpad). This makes sure that none of the other objects in your scene are obstructing your view.

3. Switch into Edit mode using the Mode drop-down in the 3D Viewport or by pressing the *Tab* hotkey. Alternatively, you can switch to the Modeling workspace, and Blender will automatically toggle Edit mode for you.

4. Choose Face Select from the Selection Mode buttons in the header (or press the hotkey *3*). By choosing Face Select, you're less likely to select an errant vertex elsewhere in your mesh.

5. Ensure that no geometry is selected by choosing **Select ▶ None** from the header menu or by using the *Alt+A* hotkey combination.

6. Select all of the faces that comprise your roller. There are a *lot* of individual components and pieces in this roller part, so the selection process can be tricky. Fortunately, Blender has a variety of different techniques to help with the process. With a relatively simple object, you could select the parts individually. With something more complex like this example, a better approach is to hide the geometry that you don't want to separate so that all you have left is the geometry you want. The next few steps use a mixture of techniques to achieve this result.

7. Hide the parts of the cultivator that aren't your roller by using the following steps:

   a. Change the view to look from the side (**View ▶ Viewpoint ▶ Right** or press *3* on your numpad if you have one).

   b. Enable the **Toggle X-ray** button in the 3D Viewport's header to ensure that you can select vertices that are obstructed from view by other geometry.

c. Use the Box Select tool to select as many vertices above your roller as you can. Hide the selected geometry (**Mesh ▶ Show/Hide ▶ Hide Selected** or press *H*).

d. Change the view to look from the top (**View ▶ Viewpoint ▶ Top** or *7* on your numpad) and select a bunch of the geometry behind your roller. Then hide those faces. At this point, you should just see the four rollers and some of the mechanical assembly around them. This is where you need to use a bit more care and manual effort.

e. Select the mechanical assembly pieces and hide them as you go. For this, I really love to use Blender's Select Linked operator. If you select one face on a component in your mesh and navigate to **Select ▶ Select Linked ▶ Linked** or use the *Ctrl+L* hotkey combination, Blender will select all faces that are connected (*linked*) to that face as an island of geometry. For an even faster workflow, you can hover your mouse cursor over a part and press *L* on your keyboard. That process selects linked faces without first requiring you to select anything. At this point, everything on your mesh should be hidden other than your rollers. Your Blender session may look like the image in Figure 4.2.

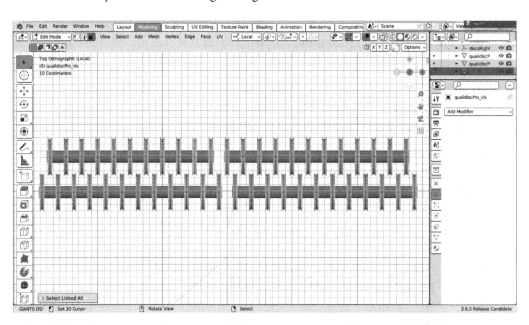

FIGURE 4.2 Everything in your mesh, other than your desired objects, has been hidden, leaving just the rollers in this example.

With your rollers isolated, you can now go through the process of separating your rollers into their own individual objects. Before you start, though, I recommend you make one modification to the display in the 3D Viewport. Make sure you're in Solid viewport shading and click on the Viewport Shading rollout in the header. In the section labeled color, click on the **Random** button to assign a random color to individual objects in your scene. Using this colorizing trick, it's much easier to see when your pieces have been separated into their own objects.

Now you're ready to get to separating. While still in Edit mode, use the following steps:

1. Navigate to **Select ▶ None** (*Alt+A*) to ensure that nothing is currently selected.

2. Select the faces that make up one of your rollers. It should be pretty easy now that the rest of the mesh is hidden. My preferred approach in this example is to make sure X-ray is enabled (*Alt+Z*), box select as much of one roller as possible from the top view, and then use the Select Linked operator (*Ctrl+L*) to ensure that I didn't miss any faces.

3. Separate the roller from its own object by choosing **Mesh ▶ Separate ▶ Selection** or use the *P* hotkey.

4. Repeat these steps on the remaining three rollers. It should get easier as you go because there's less chance of mis-selecting the wrong geometry.

At this point, you can unhide the rest of the geometry in your model (**Mesh ▶ Show/Hide ▶ Reveal Hidden** or *Alt+H*). You now have your rollers separated to their own objects, but if you look in the Outliner, their naming is not clear; they're just `qualidiscPro_vis` with a number tacked on the end. Switch back to Object mode (*Tab*) and rename each of your newly separated objects. You can either do this renaming from the Outliner by double-clicking the name you want to change, or you can do it right in the 3D Viewport by selecting the object and pressing *F2*. In this example, I renamed the rollers to `rollLeft-Front`, `rollLeftBack`, `rollRightFront`, and `rollRightBack`.

Now when you toggle out of Local View (**View ▶ Local View ▶ Toggle Local View** or / on your numpad), your resulting model should look something like what's shown in Figure 4.3.

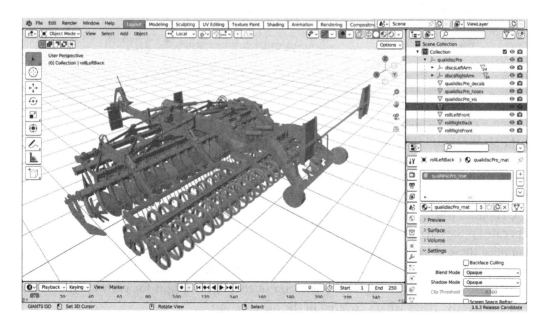

FIGURE 4.3 The example cultivator with nicely separated and renamed rollers.

On the topic of naming, the GIANTS I3D Exporter defaults to using the object's name in Blender as the node name when exporting to the I3D format. However, to be able to refer to your objects in your vehicle-XML file (see Chapter 6), you need to assign a specific node ID to your object. This node ID is also referred to as an *I3D mapping* because it's used to map a reference in your vehicle-XML to the exported object in your I3D file. You can assign a node ID from the GIANTS I3D Exporter tab in the 3D Viewport's sidebar. At the top of this tab is a panel that gives the index path and node name for your active object. Enable the check box labeled **Node Id**, and the field to the right of it uses the same name as the object name in Blender. If you wish, you can customize this node ID to anything you want. You can always reset this value to be the object name by clicking the **Use Node Name** button on the right of the panel. Figure 4.4 shows the GIANTS I3D Exporter tab with a node ID assigned to the `rollLeftBack` object.

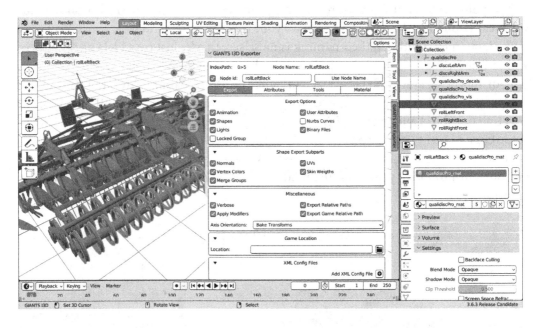

FIGURE 4.4   Assign node IDs to your new objects from the top of the GIANTS I3D Exporter tab in the 3D Viewport's Sidebar.

From here, you can use the same basic process to separate other components from your main mesh object, including naming them and assigning them node IDs.

Of course, when you use this workflow to separate parts from a larger mesh, all of those separated pieces share the same origin point in 3D space. That's not an ideal situation when you need these objects to rotate in place. With the origins in their current position, if you use the Rotate tool and rotate your roller along its local X-axis, the roller is going to move unnaturally. You need to adjust the position of the object origin for each roller so they rotate correctly. That's what's covered in the next section.

ADJUSTING THE POSITION OF OBJECT ORIGINS (PIVOTS)

In order to control the rotational behavior of your separated objects while in Object mode, you need to make sure that the object's origin (or *pivot*, as it's called in other applications) is correctly positioned. For this example, where you've separated the rollers from the rest of the cultivator object, the goal is for each roller to spin about its local X-axis without wobbling or looking like it's lost its connection with the rest of the cultivator assembly. To achieve this result, the origin for each roller needs to be placed in line with an imaginary line that runs the length of the roller's axle.

In "vanilla" Blender, the process of aligning the origin makes use of Blender's 3D cursor. In general, what you do is select one or more pieces of geometry where the median point of that selection is where you want to place the origin. Then you snap the 3D cursor to that location. And finally, you adjust the object's origin to match the location of the 3D cursor. This process can be a bit cumbersome if you have to do it many times, so fortunately, the GIANTS I3D Exporter add-on for Blender has a convenience operator to help with this called SelectedToOrigin.

You can see how it works using our roller example. Select rollLeftBack and use the following steps:

1. Tab into Edit mode and ensure that no geometry is selected (*Alt+A*).

2. Select all the faces on the axle that run the length of the roller. You can make this selection using Blender's Selected Linked feature. Hover your mouse cursor over a part of the axle and press *L*. Alternatively, you can select one face in the axle and choose **Select ▶ Select Linked ▶ Linked** (*Ctrl+L*) from the 3D Viewport's menu.

3. In the GIANTS I3D Exporter tab of the Sidebar, click the **Tools** button to show the Tools section.

4. Click the SelectionToOrigin button and the roller's origin is moved to the median point of your selection.

Now your roller's origin is perfectly placed. You can test it by using the Rotate tool and test rotating the roller about its local X-axis. It should spin cleanly with no wobble or separation from the rest of the cultivator mesh.

TIP

For some simple models, you can sometimes get away with setting the origin *without* using the 3D cursor. If you expand the **Object ▶ Set Origin** menu, you have a few other options, including Origin to Geometry, Origin to Center of Mass (Surface), and Origin to Center of Mass (Volume). For any of the roller objects, because they're mostly symmetric, any of these other three options will work for more quickly repositioning their origins. Just make sure you test afterwards to ensure that there's no wobble in your rotation.

One final step in the process is making sure that your translations and rotations for your newly separated parts are correctly zeroed out. This way, there's no additional transforms added to your parts when they're exported. Because you separated these parts from a mesh object that's already the child of a root Empty (in this case, that's the Empty named `qualidiscPro`), you want to ensure that your object is clear of any additional location or rotation. Use the following steps:

1. Select one of your newly separated parts in the 3D Viewport.

2. Expand the Sidebar on the 3D Viewport by pressing *N* and go to the Item tab to inspect the values for Location and Rotation. If those values are anything other than zero, you should probably apply those rotations so they're zeroed out using the next steps.

3. Choose **Object ▶ Apply ▶ Location to Deltas** from the 3D Viewport's header menu or use the *Ctrl*+A hotkey combination and choose the same option from the menu that appears. Choosing this option takes the parent-child relationship with your root Empty into account, unlike the plain Location option, which actually moves your object origin to the global origin at (0, 0, 0).

4. Choose **Object ▶ Apply ▶ Rotation to Deltas** to do a similar reset on your selected object's rotation. Now when you look at the Item tab in the 3D Viewport's sidebar, the Location and Rotation values should all read zero, while the actual position and rotation of your roller haven't changed at all.

5. Repeat steps 2–4 for all of your other newly separated objects.

Now that you've seen how to adjust the location of the origin for each of the objects in your vehicle mod, you can go through that process on each one, verifying that the rotation is the way you want it each time.

PREPARING YOUR VEHICLE HIERARCHY

All of the work of separating your model into parts and positioning their origins has led to this point. It's likely that the organization in your scene is a little bit of a mess, with either no structure at all to your `.blend` file or something more haphazardly arranged. Whatever the case, it's important to think about how the data of your scene is structured. You want to make sure that this is right because the organization of your model has a pretty substantial influence on the behavior and performance of your mod in-game.

Generally speaking, you want the entirety of your mod asset—whether it's a vehicle, a tool, or a building—to be recognized as a single object by the game engine. To that end, I strongly encourage you to have a look back at Chapter 2 in the section titled "Organizing your Blender scene for exporting to I3D". The entirety of your mod should live under a single root object, most likely an Empty, which gets converted to being a transform group when exported to the I3D format.

Subsequent chapters in this book will go over the specifics of your vehicle hierarchy as you go through them, but things are always easier if you start with a strong structure. In that spirit, here are a few tips and guides:

- Have the root of your vehicle hierarchy be an Empty in Blender that lives at the global origin.

- Any parts that move as a group (like a folding arm on a cultivator) would be best as children of another Empty, and that Empty should be located at the location where any rotation happens, such as a hinge.

- Take advantage of the New Mod from Game feature in GIANTS Editor (see Chapter 6 for more on this) to check existing models in the base game. These models can serve as a great reference for understanding best practices in your own mods.

- Adjust the origins of your objects before organizing them in your vehicle hierarchy. This way, at the very least, the objects will still rotate correctly. The only minor exception to this would be if you need child objects to share the same origin location as their parent (as with decal meshes, described in the preceding chapter). If your hierarchy is built first in those cases, you can take advantage of the FreezeTranslation and FreezeRotation tools in the GIANTS I3D Exporter add-on.

- Use consistent and unique names, especially if the object is going to have a node ID that's referred to in the vehicle-XML file (see Chapter 6). Blender helps with keeping names unique; you can't have two objects with the exact same name in Blender. However, it forces that uniqueness by adding numbers after the name, so it's not an especially descriptive approach.

SUMMARY

This chapter gave you an overview of the necessary steps and tools in Blender to break a unified 3D model into individual pieces that can move on their own. You also got a little bit of information on how to assign a node ID to your newly selected object to make exporting easier later on. Then, you saw that even though those pieces were separate, their object origins, or pivots, were in the wrong location to give correct rotations. So you discovered the process for correctly repositioning those object origins to ensure that their rotations are correct. And finally, you started the process of ensuring that you have a solid hierarchical structure for your vehicle.

In the next chapter, we get into the setup of physics components so GIANTS Engine can do some of the animation work in Farming Simulator for you using its physics engine.

CHAPTER 5

Creating Physics Components and Function Nodes

You're not just creating a cool piece of farming equipment. You're building an asset that you can use in a game. That means your asset needs to be able to interact with the game environment and move realistically according to the laws of physics. The challenge is that simulated physics, such as collisions and falling because of gravity, can be computationally expensive and require a lot of processing power for each element of your model that needs to react to physics.

So instead of setting every single piece of your model to be recognized by the physics system, the most common approach is to build simplified proxy objects for the physics system and transfer their movement to your more complex model. In GIANTS Engine, these proxy objects are called **components**. This chapter is all about creating and configuring those components in Blender, so they're ready to be used when exported. We start by covering how to set up the majority of your model as being a non-physics component, so it's not mistakenly used for physics simulation. From there, we briefly discuss best practices for modeling components. Then we go through the steps of defining your main collision component. After that, we cover compound children, so you can account for moving parts in your vehicle mod. And finally, we finish the chapter by going through the process of defining attachment points and configuring connection hoses on our vehicle.

In this chapter:

- Defining non-physics components

- Building collision components

- Setting up your main collision component

- Configuring compound collision components

- Specifying attachment points and connection hoses

DOI: 10.1201/9781032659497-5

TECHNICAL REQUIREMENTS

In addition to Blender with the GIANTS I3D Exporter add-on installed and enabled, you also need to have some kind of model that you intend on exporting for use in Farming Simulator. If you don't yet have your own model, you're welcome to use the model of the Kverneland Qualidisc Pro cultivator that's available on the downloads page for this book. You can use https://gdn.giants-software.com/blenderBook or scan the QR code at the end of this section. The screenshots and images in this chapter were built using that same model.

https://gdn.giants-software.com/blenderBook

DEFINING NONPHYSICS COMPONENTS

The best place to start is by ensuring that only specific parts of your model are recognized by the physics system in GIANTS Engine. As I mentioned in the introduction, simulated physics can be computationally intensive, so as cool as it might look to have every individual bolt and hose bouncing around when your model is moved by a tractor, that kind of detail is likely to really impact performance in-game and possibly render it unplayable.

To avoid that kind of expensive mistake, it's best practice to start by setting every part of your base model as being a non-physics component. Then you can go through and specifically apply physics properties to only the components that truly need them. Open your vehicle model (or the one mentioned in "Technical requirements") in Blender and use the following steps:

1. In the 3D Viewport select all of the components of your model (**Select ▶ All**).

2. In the 3D Viewport's Sidebar (*N*), go to the GIANTS I3D Exporter tab and click the **Attributes** button at the top to access that section.

3. Within the Attributes section, go to the panel labeled Predefined and choose *Exterior* from the **Non Physics** drop-down menu.

4. Scroll to the bottom of the GIANTS I3D Exporter tab and click the **Apply Selected** button to save your updated physics (well, non-physics) settings on all selected objects.

With this base step complete, you're ready to start creating objects that the physics system is going to use.

BUILDING COLLISION MESHES

Collision meshes are meshes with simple geometry that encapsulate the parts of your actual model's mesh. You want all the parts of your model to be inside your collision mesh, and you want to be really sparse with the amount of geometry that you use. In fact, often you can get away with a collision mesh that is little more than a cube with a few of its faces scaled and moved around. If your mod doesn't have any moving parts, you might be able to model just a single mesh.

That said, most mods (like the cultivator in this example) have moving parts, so you need to make a different collision mesh for each moving part. In this example, you need to create three meshes: the main collision component that accounts for the center body of the cultivator, as well as two compound children, each for an arm on the model.

As you model your collision meshes in Blender, each one should be an individual Blender object. Make sure that their meshes are fully enclosed ("**watertight**") meshes, and check that their normals are all facing outward (**Mesh ▶ Normals ▶ Recalculate Outside**). Also, give each mesh object a sensible name. For this example, I'm using the following naming scheme:

- `qualidiscPro_main_component1`

- `armLeftColPart`

- `armRightColPart`

Also, since your collision meshes enclose your vehicle model, they make it difficult to see and select your model. To fix this, you can change how your components are displayed in the 3D Viewport. Select each of your collision meshes and go to the Object tab in the Properties editor. In the Viewport Display panel, change the **Display As** drop-down menu to *Wire* so you only see the wireframes of your collision meshes, as shown in Figure 5.1. This change makes the visualization in Blender's 3D Viewport match what's ultimately shown if you export your mod and open it in the GIANTS Editor.

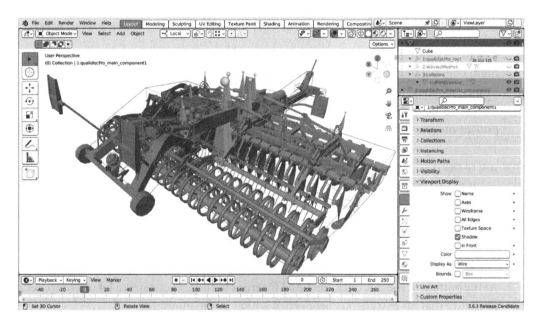

FIGURE 5.1   The cultivator example has collision meshes with their viewport display property set to Wire to avoid obstructing your view.

> **TIP**
>
> To set the Display As property for all selected objects at the same time, hold *Alt* when you click the **Display As** drop-down menu.

SETTING UP YOUR MAIN COLLISION COMPONENT

For the physics system in GIANTS Engine, everything starts with a main collision component. However, before you adjust any physics properties for that component, you need to ensure that your hierarchy is correct. The collision components should be at the top of your vehicle mod's hierarchy. Other collision meshes in your mod should be children of that main component. It is possible to have multiple components, such as in our example cultivator. There's the main component and then there's an additional one for the drawbar, which can freely rotate. This structure ensures that your mod meets the expectations of the game engine. The main component is also where you define things like your vehicle's center of mass in the vehicle XML file (see the next chapter to find out more about the XML files used in your mod). If you have multiple components, the position of each component plus their centers of mass defines the overall center of mass for the vehicle.

The easiest way to put your main component at the top of the hierarchy is to use Blender's Outliner in the Scenes display mode. I'm going to assume that you've followed the steps in the previous chapters and you already have a base hierarchy set up for your mod (or you're using the provided example file). With your file open in Blender, use the following steps:

1. In the Outliner, use the **Display Mode** drop-down and ensure that it's set to *Scenes*.

2. Click the root element in your mod's hierarchy and drag it over the name of your main collision component. In this example, you click and drag the `qualidiscPro` Empty to your recently-created `qualidiscPro_main_component1` object. This action makes the whole hierarchy tree of your mod the child of the main component object.

Now you're ready to begin configuring your physics properties for your main component. Select your main component (in this example, `qualidiscPro_main_component1`) and use the following steps:

1. In the GIANTS I3D Exporter tab of the Sidebar, click on **Attributes** to go to the Attributes section.

2. At the bottom of the tab, click the **Load Current** button. This step is a bit of a self-check to ensure that no extraneous properties are set in the interface.

3. Up in the Predefined panel, click the **Physics** drop-down menu and choose *Vehicle—Compound*.

4. At the bottom of the tab, click **Apply Selected** to save your physics properties to your selected main component object.

The most important settings from the *Vehicle—Compound* preset are found in the Rigid Body panel. Specifically, this preset enables three check-boxes in the Rigid Body panel:

- **Dynamic**—The Dynamic attribute tells GIANTS Engine that this component can move around in-game and is subject to external forces. For example, a player may want to move your cultivator around their farm by pushing it with a tractor.

- **Compound**—The Compound attribute lets the engine know that this component has one or more compound children. As covered in the next section, **compound children** are collision meshes that are within your main component in the hierarchy tree. If you have multiple components, each of them can have their own compound children.

- **Collision**—This attribute is really the one that does the heavy lifting in your configuration. Enabling this check box lets the game engine know that this object is intended to collide with other physics objects.

Figure 5.2 shows the example file with the Vehicle—Compound preset assigned to it.

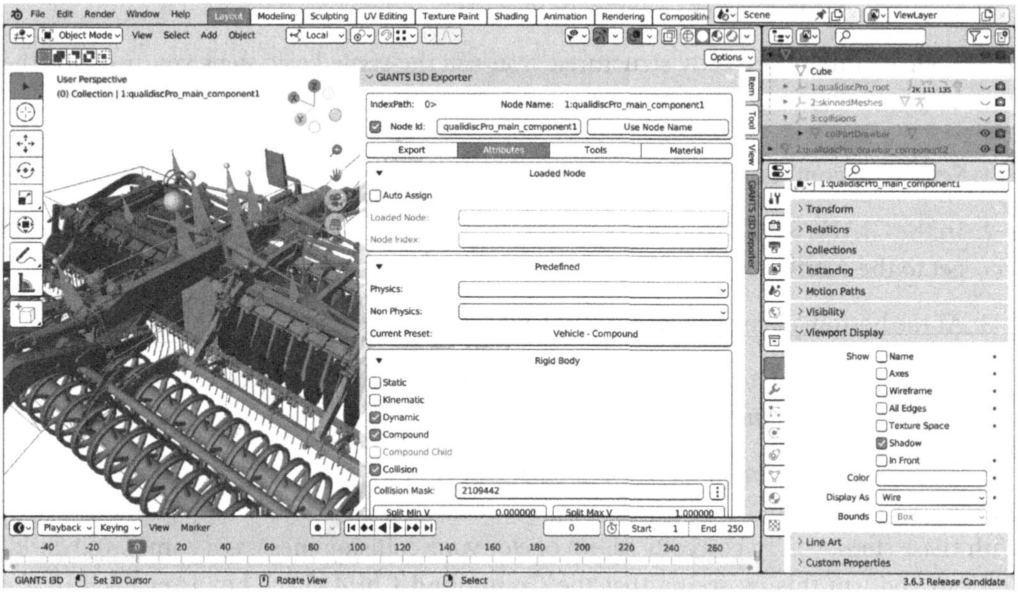

FIGURE 5.2   Use the Vehicle—Compound predefined preset to ensure that your main component is configured to be a dynamic compound collision component.

One further setting that the *Vehicle—Compound* preset enables is in the Rendering panel. In that panel, the **Non Renderable** check box is enabled. With this attribute set, your collision component isn't visible when running in Farming Simulator, but its geometry is still used for physics calculations.

CONFIGURING COMPOUND CHILDREN

On a complex model with moving parts, you're going to have multiple collision meshes as children of your main component, known as **compound children**. Each compound child is associated with a different moving part. As with the main component, you need to make sure that your hierarchy is correctly structured so your compound child moves with its intended part of the mod. The way you accomplish this is by making your collision mesh a child of that moving part or a child of the Empty object that's controlling it.

In this example, the cultivator has an `armLeft` and `armRight` object for each of the sides of the model that rotate. Each of these objects has their origins placed so they rotate correctly. To ensure that each of your collision components moves with its respective part, you make each a child of that part. Ultimately, your hierarchy should look something like this:

- `qualidiscPro_main_component1`
  - `qualidiscPro`
    - `armLeft`
      - `armLeftColPart`

- armRight

  - armRightColPart

With your hierarchy correctly structured, you use the same basic steps you used for the main component, just with a different preset:

1. Select one compound child (e.g. armLeftColPart)

2. In the GIANTS I3D Exporter tab of the 3D Viewport's Sidebar, click on **Attributes** to get to the Attributes section.

3. At the bottom of the tab, click **Load Current** to clear out any previous settings.

4. From the Predefined panel, use the **Physics** drop-down menu to choose *Vehicle—CompoundChild*.

5. Scroll to the bottom of the tab and click **Apply Selected**.

With these steps, you've correctly set up one of your collision mesh as a compound child. You can confirm this by seeing that the **Compound Child** check box is enabled in the Rigid Body panel, as shown in Figure 5.3. Perform these steps on all the other compound children in your mod, and you'll have all of your base physics settings properly configured.

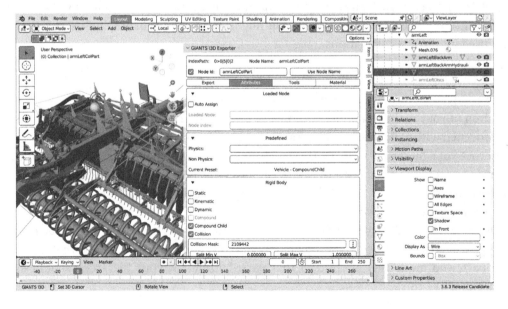

FIGURE 5.3   The Vehicle—CompoundChild preset is the fastest way to set up a compound child.

SPECIFYING ATTACHMENT POINTS AND CONNECTION HOSES

In addition to making your proxy objects in Blender as collision components for use in the game, there's additional work you need to do with your model to facilitate the actual functionality of your vehicle. For example, if you're making a towable vehicle (like the cultivator example we've been working with), you need to let the game engine know where that vehicle is supposed to be attached to the tractor that pulls it. Likewise, your vehicle also has hoses for hydraulics and electric power that need to be connected between it and the vehicle pulling it.

By itself, the game doesn't know where these various attachment points are on your model. You can use your vehicle-XML file (covered in the next chapter) to specify the names of these attachment points and some rough specifications, but the vehicle-XML file has no knowledge of where these points are located and oriented in 3D space relative to your vehicle. The reference points, called **functional nodes**, are stored in your vehicle's I3D file as transform groups. This means that in Blender, you need to place some Empty objects in your scene within your vehicle's hierarchy. Chapter 7 has a lot more detail on the various different functional nodes you can add to your mod. This section deals specifically with attachment points and connection hoses. Having these set up in advance makes it easier to test your vehicle mod in-game.

Adding an Attachment Point

Using our cultivator example, it connects to a tractor using a 3-point hitch. We need to include a few Empty objects to identify the connection points on that hitch. Add these points by using the following steps:

- Select the root Empty for your vehicle. In our example, that Empty is named `qualidiscPro`.

- In the GIANTS I3D Exporter tab within the 3D Viewport's Sidebar, click the **Tools** button to get to the Tools section and click the **Create Empty** button. The Create Empty operator is a convenience function that comes with the GIANTS I3D Exporter add-on. It adds a new Empty at the location and rotation of your currently selected object.

- Name your new Empty `attachable`. You can rename by double-clicking the object name in the Outliner or using the *F2* hotkey. This Empty serves as kind of a container transform group for all the rest of your reference Empties that you're adding.

- Add two more Empties and name them `attacherJoint` and `topReferenceNode`.

- (optional) In the Object Data Properties tab of the Properties editor, use the **Display As** drop-down menu to change the display type of your two new Empties to *Arrows*. You can use any visualization for the Empty that you want. I find that the Arrows display type is particularly nice for quickly letting you know which direction the Empty's axes are pointing

- Make `attacherJoint` and `topReferenceNode` both children of your `attachable` Empty. At this point, your vehicle hierarchy should have the following structure (in addition to the other objects in the scene):

  - `qualidiscPro`

    - `attachable`

      - `attacherJoint`

      - `topReferenceNode`

You've added your reference objects to your vehicle and they're organized in the correct hierarchical structure. However, all three of these Empties are still located at the global origin. You now need to position them in space relative to the actual attachment points on your vehicle.

Start first with the `attacherJoint` Empty. For our cultivator example, the ideal location to put it is centered between the catch hooks of the lower link. Use Blender's Move tool to move attacherJoint along the global Y and Z axes so it stays centered on your vehicle. As a faster way to work, instead of creating the `attacherJoint` Empty and moving it into place, you could select the two catch hooks and use the Create Empty operator that comes with the GIANTS I3D Exporter add-on to add your `attacherJoint` Empty at the correct position. Whichever way you choose, once you've positioned the Empty, you need to rotate it 90 degrees about the X-axis so the Empty's Y-axis is pointing upward (this can be done quickly with the hotkey sequence, *R* ▶ *X* ▶ *90*).

IMPORTANT

The reason you need to make this rotation is to help the GIANTS Engine define joint limits correctly. This is the reason why I recommend using the Arrows display type for Empties. That display type makes it easier to understand which direction your axes are pointing. Things can get a little confusing because there's a difference between the global coordinate systems in Blender and GIANTS Engine. In Blender, the Z-axis is the height axis, or simply put, Z is "up". In contrast, GIANTS Engine works with the Y-axis as up. Fortunately, when you export to I3D, the exporter handles converting the rotations for you.

After you position and orient your `attacherJoint` correctly, you need to do the same for the `topReferenceNode` Empty. That Empty should still be centered on your linkage mechanism, but it should be located at the place where you want the top link to be. (Technically, if we hadn't already created the `topReferenceNode` Empty, you could select faces on the linkage in Edit mode and use the Create Empty convenience operator from the GIANTS I3D Exporter add-on.)

NOTE

If you're working on our example cultivator and you're wondering where to put the topReferenceNode Empty, don't be surprised. This model actually doesn't require that node for its connection. I've included it here as a reference in case your vehicle does need it.

Once you've positioned your attachment points, there's one final step you need to do to make sure that they're correctly identified in your vehicle mod. Like your collision components, you need to ensure that each of these Empty objects has a node ID so it can be identified as an I3D mapping in your vehicle-XML file (see Chapter 6 for more details on I3D mapping and the vehicle-XML file). The process for adding a node ID is the same as with your collision component:

1. Select your object. In this case, that object would be one of your attachment point Empties: `attacherJoint` or `topReferenceNode`.

2. In the GIANTS I3D Exporter tab of your 3D Viewport's Sidebar, enable the **Node Id** check box at the top and click the **Use Node Name** button to ensure that the functional node is using the same name as your object in your Blender file.

3. Perform Steps 1 and 2 on your other two attachment point Empties. In the provided example, there are only two nodes that require a node ID.

Now, when you export your vehicle to I3D and have it associated with a vehicle-XML file (see the next chapter), these nodes are included as I3D mappings that can be referenced elsewhere in the file.

Handling Connection Hoses

When a tool is attached to a tractor, there's more attachment points than just the towing linkage. The implement usually has hydraulics for movement, electric power, and sometimes air (for air brakes), transferred with hoses and cables. Your vehicle mod should have these hoses and cables as well. To simplify matters, I refer to both cables and hoses collectively as just "hoses" throughout the rest of this section.

Of course, hoses tend to lay differently when they're used to connect to the tractor compared to how they are when the implement is stored. Trying to animate or otherwise deform your hose meshes to lay correctly in both states can be tedious.

To make it easier to handle hoses, you can actually have two different mesh objects for each hose, one for when connected and one for when disconnected. If you let the game engine know which one is which (using your vehicle XML file), it can automatically swap meshes for you in-game. In fact, the attached hose mesh is dynamically created by the game engine, so for that you only need an Empty to indicate the connection point. That means you only need to model the hose in its disconnected state. In addition, since connections for hydraulics and power tend to be standardized, you can use the connector meshes that come with Farming Simulator rather than needing to model them yourself.

In order to facilitate all of this functionality, you need to make some more attachment points so the game engine is aware of where they are, both in the connected and disconnected states. Use the following steps:

1. **Define some reference Empties where the hoses are to be attached to the tow vehicle.** As an example, let's assume your vehicle has three hoses: one that has hydraulic fluid move into your vehicle, one for outbound hydraulics, and a third for electric power. So you need a reference Empty for each attachment point where it connects to your vehicle. Use the Create Empty operator that comes with the GIANTS I3D Exporter add-on to add your attachment reference Empties using the following naming convention:

   - `hydraulicIn01`

   - `hydraulicOut01`

   - `electric01`

- **To help with organization, add an Empty at the global origin named `connectionHoses`.** Make all three of your hose reference Empties children of your new `connectionHoses` Empty so they're part of that transform group in the game.

- **Model your hoses in the detached state.** Each hose mesh starts at the location of the reference Empties created in step 1. Be sure that each modeled hose is its own object and a child of its corresponding reference Empty. Ultimately, you should end up with three hose objects:

   - `hydraulicIn01_detached`

   - `hydraulicOut01_detached`

   - `electric01_detached`

- **Select each hose object and be sure to give it a node ID.** Use the Node Id check box in the GIANTS I3D Exporter tab of the 3D Viewport's Sidebar. Now you can deal with the connectors (also called adapters) for each disconnected hose.

- **Create an Empty for each hose and place it at the end of each one.** These are your connector Empties. Each one should be a child of its corresponding hose object. Use the following naming scheme (extending the names you already used for the hoses themselves):

   - `hydraulicIn01_connector`

   - `hydraulicOut01_connector`

   - `electric01_connector`

With your adapter Empties created, named, and correctly inserted in your vehicle hierarchy, you can begin positioning them. To get these Empties placed, it's a little more challenging than with the attachment point Empties because the way that disconnected hoses lay is rarely along the global axes. Fortunately, you can take advantage of the 3D cursor to assist with the process. Use these steps:

1. Select the hose you want to work with. In this example, let's assume you're working on the hose object named `hydraulicIn01 _ detached`.

2. Tab into Edit mode on that hose object and deselect all geometry (**Select ▶ None** or *Alt+A*).

3. While in Edge Select selection mode (*2*), select the edges that make up the open end of your hose mesh. You can quickly select all of those edges as a loop by *Alt*+left-clicking one of them.

4. Align the 3D Viewport to your selected edges by choosing **View ▶ Align View ▶ Align View to Active ▶ Front**. This should result in the 3D Viewport looking at your selected edges along an orthogonal angle. Those edges should be entirely vertical or horizontal. If **Front** doesn't work, try **Top** or **Right**. It's important to get this step correct because when you snap your 3D cursor in the next step, it's aligned to the viewport orientation.

5. Choose **Snap ▶ Cursor to Selection** and your 3D cursor is positioned at the center of your selection of edges. And because you aligned your view to match your selected edges, the 3D cursor should also match the angle of that selection.

6. Tab back into Object mode.

7. Select the Empty that's associated with the adapter that belongs to your hose. In this case, that would be the Empty named `hydraulicIn01 _ connector`.

8. Choose **Snap ▶ Object to 3D Cursor** to move your Empty to the location of the 3D cursor. Now you just need to make it have the same rotation.

9. Choose **Object ▶ Transform ▶ Align to Transform Orientation**. The base result of this isn't likely to get you what you want. However, if you expand the Last Operator panel (or call the floating version by pressing *F9*), you can change the **Orientation** drop-down menu to *Cursor*. And like magic, your Empty should match the rotation of the 3D cursor (and, by extension, the end of your hose).

Perform these steps on each of your adapter Empties and make sure that each one has a node ID using the steps covered in the preceding section. Once you complete that process, you've got all of your reference objects where they need to be in 3D space and in your vehicle hierarchy. The next step, covered in Chapter 6, is making the game engine aware of these reference nodes.

SUMMARY

In this chapter, you worked your way through the process of making your vehicle mod "physics-ready" so players can properly interact with it in Farming Simulator. You started by establishing most of your model as being a non-physics component so those pieces aren't accidentally used as part of physics calculations. From there, you went through the basic process for building and naming collision components. Then you set up your main collision component. After that, you used compound children to make sure the physics system correctly accounts for the moving parts in your model. And finally, you went through the process of adding reference nodes to your model to assist with attachment points and connection hoses.

In the next chapter, we start pulling all the pieces together in your mod by directly making adjustments to the XML files that define your vehicle.

CHAPTER 6

Setting up ModDesc-XML and Vehicle-XML

Up to this point in the book, we've been focusing on the I3D format that you export from Blender. As powerful as that format is, it's not a one-stop-shop for controlling the behavior of your mesh. In addition to your exported vehicle model in the I3D format, you also need some additional text files to bundle with your vehicle. Both files are in XML format, a versatile text-based file format that gets used in all sorts of games and applications. Specific to your mod in Farming Simulator, you need at least two files, a **mod description** file (moddesc.xml) and a vehicle file, frequently known as the **vehicle-XML** file.

This chapter starts by walking you through the basics of setting up the overall structure for your mod. Once you have the structure established, we go through the basic details in the moddesc.xml file to ensure that your mod is recognized in Farming Simulator. Then, we spend the last part of the chapter working through the fundamentals of the vehicle-XML file so Farming Simulator knows what to do with your mod. Finally, we'll see how to make the GIANTS I3D Exporter in Blender see your XML files and even update them for you as you work.

In this chapter:

- Giving your mod a home

- Building your moddesc.xml file

- Setting up your vehicle-XML file

- Getting Blender to see your XML files

TECHNICAL REQUIREMENTS

The majority of the work done in this chapter is done by editing text files. Just about any modern text editor will work (as described in Chapter 1), but the best recommendation for these files is GIANTS Studio. In addition to being a solid text editor, GIANTS

DOI: 10.1201/9781032659497-6

Studio has debugging capabilities that can help you build and troubleshoot your mod's files as you create them.

You'll also benefit by having the GIANTS Editor installed on your computer as well. With GIANTS Editor, there are a few shortcuts you can use to quickly get some templates for your mod files.

And the examples in this chapter are all based on the Kverneland Qualidisc Pro cultivator that's available on the downloads page for this book. You can reach that page at https://gdn.giants-software.com/blenderBook or by scanning the QR code at the end of this section. Of course, you're encouraged to use your own model for your mod, but this model is available if you want to follow along.

https://gdn.giants-software.com/blenderBook

GIVING YOUR MOD A HOME

So thus far in your mod-making journey, you've been working right in Blender on a file that can basically live anywhere on your hard drive. Of course, from an organizational standpoint, you should probably have a specific folder (or several) for saving your work. However, the details of where you store your .blend file haven't been overly important up to now.

But you're building a mod. Farming Simulator has some expectations with respect to where your mods live and how they're organized. Fortunately, it's not that complicated. You just need a single folder to hold all the files for your mod. Eventually, when your mod is ready, you can move your folder into the Farming Simulator mods folder. But while you're building your mod, the folder can live just about anywhere. The most common practice is to have a sub-folder in your Documents folder. For example, you might make a folder named My FS Mods. Then, within that folder, your actual mod folder can live. Using the example cultivator that we've been working with throughout this book, your folder path might look like Documents/My FS Mods/QualidiscPro.

That `QualidiscPro` folder is the destination where you want to export your I3D file from Blender. It's also the place where you're going to put the XML files covered in the rest of this chapter.

To give yourself an idea of the kind of structure that a mod should have, you can actually cheat a bit using GIANTS Editor. Go to **File ▶ New Mod from Game** and GIANTS Editor will present you with a dialog that you can use to pick any vehicle from your Farming Simulator installation and build a starter mod with that as your base, then it asks you where to build the mod's folder. If you open that folder using Windows Explorer, you can see the structure of a mod. Figure 6.1 shows the folder that GIANTS Editor creates if you use this feature to build a mod based on the Pickup 1986 vehicle.

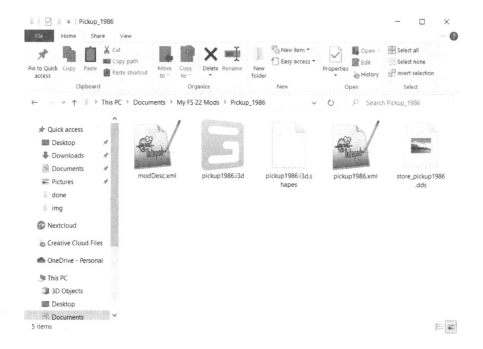

FIGURE 6.1   The resulting folder when you use **File ▶ New Mod from Game** to build a starter mod.

At its core, a mod consists of three files: the I3D file that holds your model, a modDesc. xml file, and a vehicle-XML file. All the other files are supporting files, like textures in DDS format or scripts written in Lua. As it pertains to the core XML files, though, there's an added benefit of using GIANTS Editor to create this structure. When you do this, you get those XML files already populated with some boilerplate content.

BUILDING YOUR `MODDESC.XML` FILE

The starting point for any mod is the `modDesc.xml` file. As the name implies, this file is a *mod desc*ription that Farming Simulator and ModHub reads to recognize your mod. If you used the technique described at the end of the preceding section to have GIANTS Editor build a boilerplate mod folder for you, you can open the modDesc.xml file in that folder and you should see something like this:

```
<?xml version="1.0" encoding="utf-8" standalone="no" ?>
<modDesc descVersion="60">
    <author>Me</author>
    <version>1.0.0.0</version>
    <title>
        <en>My Mod Name</en>
    </title>
    <description>
        <en>My Mod Description</en>
    </description>
    <iconFilename>icon.png</iconFilename>
    <storeItems>
        <storeItem xmlFilename="pickUp300.xml"/>
    </storeItems>
</modDesc>
```

The first line of the file (the part starting with <?xml) is known as an XML declaration. All it's doing is letting anyone (or any program) reading the file know that it's an XML file. You never need to change this line for your mods.

NOTE

XML files are organized as a series of **tags**, indicated by angled brackets around some text. Those tags have **attributes** within them with values assigned. They also have **content** within them. If a tag has content, it has an opening tag and a closing tag. The closing tag is exactly like the opening tag, it just starts with a slash (/) after the opening bracket. If the tag has no content, the slash is placed before the closing bracket. Also, because of this structure, you can nest tags within each other; this arrangement makes XML really nice for storing hierarchical data.

The Basics: Understanding the Essential Parts of the modDesc.xml File

The root tag in your modDesc.xml file is <modDesc> and it includes an attribute, descVersion. This attribute lets Farming Simulator and ModHub know what minimum version is supported. The descVersion value controls whether your mod is displayed on ModHub for particular build versions of Farming Simulator. You can check the supported descVersion for your install of Farming Simulator by checking your local game folder. Use Windows Explorer to go to C:/Users/[username]/Documents/My Games/Farming Simulator (where [username] is your username) and in that folder open log.txt in a text editor. Search that file and you should be able to see the ModDesc version for your installation of Farming Simulator. It should read something like this: ModDesc Version: 77

The next tag in your `modDesc.xml` is the `<author>` tag. That's you!   This is where you put your name, your avatar name, or your mod team's name, if you're part of a mod team.

The next tag is the `<version>` tag. Assuming you've never uploaded your mod to ModHub, you should set the content of this tag to `1.0.0.0`. As you release updates and revisions in the future, you can increment this value.

The `<title>` tag is where you give the title for your mod. In this example, you might notice that there's another tag, `<en>`, nested within this one. The reason for this is because Farming Simulator supports a wide array of different languages. The `<en>` tag gives the title for your mod in English, which is the default. If you don't give a localized name for your mod in a specific language, English will be used. The following language tags are supported: `br, cs, ct, cz, da, de, ea, en, es, fc, fi, fr, hu, it, jp, kr, nl, no, pl, pt, ro, ru, sv, tr`.

In the `<description>` tag, you give a general description of your mod. This is where you talk about the specific vehicle you've created and provide any additional details on how to use your mod. Like the `<title>` tag, you can provide localization for your description using the same language tags. As an additional note, you can use specialized CDATA syntax. Using this syntax, you can include characters that aren't supported by strict XML, such as line breaks and characters with language-specific features like the umlaut.

To use CDATA, you're basically using a specialized tag syntax that starts with `<![CDATA[` and then continues with your text. You just need to remember to finish the tag with a `]]>`. For a `<description>` tag, you might choose to something like this:

```
<description>
    <en>
        <![CDATA[This is my special text. It has line
breaks. It's also a place where I can use special characters
like ampersands (&), letters with umlauts, like this: ä
The important thing is that I'm not indenting these
lines.]]>
    </en>
</description>
```

TIP

The use of this CDATA syntax isn't limited to your description. You can also use it in your `<title>` tag as well.

The next tag in our example is `<iconFilename>`. Within this tag, you give the path to the icon for your mod that shows in ModHub. The path that you give is relative to the location of the `modDesc.xml` file. So if your icon image is in the same folder as your `modDesc.xml`, then you just need to type the file name here. See Chapter 11 for more on generating icons for your mod.

The last main tag in the modDesc.xml file is <storeItems>. The primary purpose for this tag is to point to your vehicle-XML file using the xmlFilename attribute within at least one nested <storeItem> tag. This example only features a single store item, but a mod can feature multiple store items, so your mod could include a variety of additional vehicles. Like the icon for your mod, the path to the vehicle-XML file is relative to the location of your modDesc.xml file. In most cases, you just need to use the file name with no additional path information. We get into the details of the vehicle-XML file later in this chapter.

Understanding Additional Information Provided by modDesc.xml

The tags covered in the preceding section aren't the only possible tags available in your modDesc.xml. There're additional functionality and configuration options that you can include.

Naming Additional Contributors

For example, if you're collaborating with a team to build your mod and you're using your team name in the <author> tag, you can also include a <contributors> tag where you can include the name of each person on your team. If you have a three-person team, the syntax for this tag would look like this:

```
<contributors>
    <contributor>Team Member 1</contributor>
    <contributor>Team Member 2</contributor>
    <contributor>Team Member 3</contributor>
</contributors>
```

Multiplayer Support

You can also indicate whether your mod is multiplayer-ready using the <multiplayer> tag. This is a single tag with no nesting; just the attributes supported and only. Set the supported attribute to true if your mod is multiplayer-ready and set only to true if your mod is only intended to work in multiplayer mode. As an example, if your mod can be used in both multiplayer and single player modes, your tag may look like so:

```
<multiplayer supported="true" only="false" />
```

This example enables the mod for multiplayer (the default behavior has supported="false"), so if you leave the <multiplayer> tag out altogether, your mod will only function in single player mode.

Localization

Support for multiple languages in your mod extends beyond just the title and description. You can use your modDesc.xml file as a base for translating any named item in your mod. All of this translation activity happens within the <l10n> tag (*l10n* is the standard abbreviation for *localization*, because there are 10 letters between the l and the n in that word. Silly, yes, but you don't have to type as much). As an example if you have a steel pipe in your mod that you identify with the text `typeDesc _ steelPipe`, the content of your `<l10n>` tag may look like the following:

```
<l10n>
    <text name="typeDesc_steelPipe">
        <en>Steel Pipe</en>
        <de>Stahlrohr</de>
        <es>Tubo de Acero</es>
        <nl>Stalen Pijp</nl>
    </text>
</l10n>
```

Any other named things in your mod can be added to this by adding a new `<text>` tag with translations nested within the `<l10n>` tag. Each language tag also supports the use of CDATA syntax as described earlier in the chapter, so you can make use of special characters specific to that language.

Specializations

Additional functionality can be given to your mod using the `<specializations>` tag. Within this tag, you can reference one or more external scripts so you can add features in your mod that aren't available in the base game. As an example, imagine you have a cultivator vehicle mod and you want to add mulching functionality to it. Your `<specializations>` tag may look like this:

```
<specializations>
    <specialization name="mulcher" className="Mulcher"
filename="Mulcher.lua" />
</specializations>
```

Specialization scripts are written in the Lua language and, like other file references in `modDesc.xml`, they're relative to the location of your file, so if they're in the same folder, you just need to type their file name. For more on adding custom functionality with external scripts, have a look at the book, *Scripting Farming Simulator with LUA*.

If you have specializations, you need to have a way to associate that functionality with vehicles in Farming Simulator. You can do this using the `<vehicleTypes>` tag. Using our made-up cultivating mulcher example, the content of your `<vehicleTypes>` tag may look like the following:

```
<vehicleTypes>
    <type name="cultivatingMulcher" parent="cultivator"
filename="$dataS/scripts/vehicles/Vehicle.lua">
        <specialization name="mulcher" />
    </type>
</vehicleTypes>
```

There are a couple things to notice in this example text. For one, the `filename` attribute in the `<type>` tag points to a path that starts with `$dataS`. The dollar symbol ($) is an internal variable that Farming Simulator recognizes as being the location of its local data; in this case, it's the location of the game's `Vehicle.lua` script. Secondly, note that the `<specialization>` tags within `<type>` reference the names of the specializations defined earlier in the `modDesc.xml` file. You're not limited to just the specializations you define in your file, but if you're giving custom specializations, this is how you associate them with a specific vehicle type.

Including Additional Scripts

Perhaps you've written any additional scripts that modify the game, but aren't specifically associated with the machine in your mod. For instance, you may make changes to the game's UI or other global changes. For these kinds of scripts, you should take advantage of the `<extraSourceFiles>` tag. Within that tag, you nest a `<sourceFile>` tag that points to the location of your extra Lua-coded script file. If you put that script in a `scripts` folder within your mod folder, your `<extraSourceFiles>` tag might look like this:

```
<extraSourceFiles>
    <sourceFile filename="scripts/specialCode.lua" />
</extraSourceFiles>
```

Naming Dependencies

It's possible to take advantage of features from another mod for use in your own. Not only does this make your overall mod smaller, but it also reduces the amount of work you have to do to finish your mod. This feature is rarely used for vehicle mods, but an example use would be if you have a map that has specific building mods as a requirement so they can be placed on the map. When you use features from other mods, you're making that other mod a dependency that your mod requires. You use the `<dependencies>` tag in mod-Desc.xml to let Farming Simulator (and people who use your mod) know that they need another mod installed in order for yours to work. You just need to know the folder name of the other mod. The syntax for the `<dependencies>` tag looks like so:

```
<dependencies>
    <dependency>NameOfSomeOtherMod</dependency>
</dependencies>
```

Defining Brands and Brand Colors

If your mod features a vehicle with a new brand or manufacturer, you can specify that using the `<brands>` tag. Within this tag you can add new brands by providing a logo image. To define brand colors, you use the `<brandColors>` tag and you specify your colors using values in the sRGB spectrum. The advantage of defining brand colors is that you can re-use these colors on every vehicle in your mod, giving them all a unified color palette. Using the GIANTS Software house brand, Lizard, as an example, your branding section of your mod might look like this:

```
<brands>
    <brand name="lizardEvo" title="LIZARDEVO"
image="store/brands/brand_lizardEvo.dds" />
</brands>
<brandColors>
    <color name="LIZARD_GREEN1" value="0.0176 0.4508 0.0232 0" />
    <color name="LIZARD_RED1" value="0.4508 0.0176 0.0232 0" />
</brandColors>
```

> **NOTE**
>
> You might notice that there's a convention for making some `title` and `name` attributes in all upper case text. This is more of a convention than a requirement. You're welcome to use all lower case or mixed case text in your own names.

Adding New Attachment Types

If you have attachment points in your mod that are not defined elsewhere in the game, you should use the `<jointTypes>` tag to make the game aware of the fact that there's a new attachment point in your mod. The actual specifications for that attachment point are defined in your vehicle-XML. The entry in `modDesc.xml` is just to make sure the game engine is aware of its existence. An example `<jointTypes>` tag looks like this:

```
<jointTypes>
    <jointType name="topBall" />
</jointTypes>
```

Supporting Additional Non-Vehicle Materials

In some mods, you may have materials that you need, but they're not technically part of the materials that make up your vehicle. For instance, if you have particle effects that use a unique material, you can export that material to an I3D file and then point to that file using the `<materialHolders>` tag in your `modDesc.xml`, like so:

```
<materialHolders>
    <materialHolder filename="myExtraMaterials.i3d" />
</materialHolders>
```

> **NOTE**
>
> It's worth noting that this kind of material usage is pretty advanced and most mods won't need to make use of the `<materialHolders>` tag.

Store Packs

Sometimes your vehicle mod is part of a larger ecosystem. For instance, perhaps your vehicle is specifically useful in the harvesting of potatoes. However, without having those potatoes already, there's not much that the player can do with your mod. So you can specify starter packs in the store using the `<storePacks>` tag like this:

```
<storePacks>
    <storePack name="specialLizardPotato" title="My Special Lizard
Potato Pack" image="myPotatoPack.png" />
</storePacks>
```

Once you have your store pack defined in your `modDesc.xml`, you need to assign your vehicle to that store pack in the vehicle-XML. The reason you need to do this is because a mod can consist of multiple vehicles. For instance, if you had a sports car as a vehicle in your mod, it probably wouldn't make sense to assign it to the potato store pack.

To assign a vehicle to a store pack, you include a `<storePacks>` tag within the `<storeData>` tag in the vehicle-XML. Continuing with the potato example, your addition to your vehicle-XML might look like this:

```
<storeData>
    ...
    <storePacks>
        <storePack>specialLizardPotato</storePack>
    </storePacks>
<storeData>
```

For more on vehicle-XML, have a look at Chapters 7–9.

Connection Hoses

Your `modDesc.xml` file is also where you can define new hose connections in the game without needing to use any additional scripts. You just need to point to the XML file that specifies those hoses using the `<connectionHoses>` tag. In this example, we're pointing to the standard connectors that come with the game, but also our own custom XML file:

```
<connectionHoses>
    <connectionHose xmlFilename="myConnectionHose.xml" />
</connectionHoses>
```

Bales

And the last additional bit of functionality that you can define in your modDesc.xml is in the `<bales>` tag. With this tag, you can assign different bales to your mod without needing any additional scripts for your mod. Like connection hoses, bales are defined with a separate XML file and use the following syntax:

```
<bales>
    <bale filename="objects/squarebales/squarebales240.xml" />
    <bale filename="objects/squarebales/squarebales300.xml" />
</bales>
```

SETTING UP YOUR VEHICLE-XML FILE

Once you have your `modDesc.xml` file updated for your mod, the next big thing is specifying the functions that your mod vehicle can have in the game. The file you use to do this is commonly called the vehicle-XML file. The file itself doesn't have to be named `vehicle.xml`. Farming Simulator isn't looking for that specific name. It's looking for the file that you specified in the `<storeItems>` tag within `modDesc.xml`.

However, before getting into the innards of vehicle-XML, it's important to enable Developer Mode in Farming Simulator.

Enabling Developer Mode in Farming Simulator

You're building a mod for Farming Simulator. As such, you're extending the game's functionality beyond its original design. The process of building a mod often requires a lot of restarts and reloads. That process can be more time consuming if you have to shut down the game and restart it each time you make a small change. Fortunately, there's a Developer Mode for Farming Simulator that allows you to reload your mod while still in the game.

To activate Developer Mode, you need to edit one of the game's XML files. Using Windows Explorer, navigate to `C:/Users/[username]/Documents/My Games/Farming Simulator` and look for the file named `game.xml`. Open this file using a text editor or GIANTS Studio. Near the bottom of the file is a `<development>` tag and nested within that tag is another one called `<controls>`. By default the content of the `<controls>` tag is set to `false`. Change that content to `true` and the `<development>` tag of your `game.xml` should look like this:

```
<development>
    <controls>true</controls>
</development>
```

Once you save your `game.xml` file, you should be able to reload your vehicle from the in-game console.

NOTE

It's worth noting that since you're editing the `game.xml` file within your own user folder, you're specifically enabling Developer Mode for your user on your computer. If multiple people have users on your computer and they also play Farming Simulator, their games will not be in Developer Mode.

Understanding Vehicle-XML

As with `modDesc.xml`, the very first line in your vehicle-XML is a declaration that this is an XML file. It should never need to be changed from this:

```
<?xml version="1.0" encoding="utf-8" standalone="no" ?>
```

The real work of your vehicle-XML file starts, conveniently, with the `<vehicle>` tag. If you look at other vehicle-XML files, you might notice that there are sometimes a few different attributes included in this tag. Most of these tags are covered in more detail in Chapter 9, however, the main one that you need to be concerned at this point with is the `type` attribute. With this attribute, you tell Farming Simulator exactly what kind of vehicle your mod is, much like the `<vehicleTypes>` tag in `modDesc.xml`. The type attribute tells the game which functionality from the game is available for the vehicle you're defining. Since this book is using that Kverneland Qualidisc Pro model as its example, the `type` attribute for that mod should be `cultivator`.

The rest of the tags for your mod live nested as content within your `<vehicle>` tag. A common first tag that you may want to include is an `<annotation>` tag. The tag is optional, but its content is useful for you to say that you made the file and perhaps include a brief copyright notice.

If you're building your vehicle-XML from scratch, your file should look like this:

```
<?xml version="1.0" encoding="utf-8" standalone="no" ?>

<vehicle type="cultivator">
    <annotation>Copyright (C) Me! I made this!</annotation>
</vehicle>
```

Store Data

The next set of tags within your vehicle-XML pertains to values and information that's displayed in the in-game shop. These values don't have any effect on your vehicle during gameplay, but they are useful for properly identifying it and giving a few specifications. All of this information is nested within the `<storeData>` tag.

The first, and arguably most important, tag within `<storeData>` is the `<name>` tag. As you might guess, the content for this tag is the name of your vehicle. Typically, the name does not include the brand name. So using the example of our cultivator, the `<name>` tag would read as:

```
<name>Qualidisc Pro</name>
```

As with the `<title>` and `<description>` tags in `modDesc.xml`, the `<name>` tag in vehicle-XML can have variations for other languages.

The next tag in `<storeData>` is the `<specs>` tag. Within this tag, you provide some of the working specifications of your vehicle. Remember that these are not functional values;

they're just for display in the store. The functional values are defined later in vehicle-XML. For a cultivator mod, the standard entry for specs looks like this:

```
<specs>
    <neededPower>180</neededPower>
    <workingWidth>5.0</workingWidth>
    <combination filterCategory="weights" filterSpec="weight"
filterSpecMin="900" filterSpecMax="1000" />
</specs>
```

For our specific cultivator that we're using as an example, the working area is actually 6 meters wide, so you should change the content of the <workingWidth> tag to 6.0. After the <specs> tag, you can use the <functions> tag to describe the characteristics of your vehicle in the store. To make your life easier, you can reference the standard localized text for your vehicle type, which is available as a variable. For our cultivator, the <functions> tag may look like this:

```
<functions>
    <function>$l10n_function_cultivator</function>
</functions>
```

The remaining tags in <storeData> don't have anything nested within them or have any special attributes. They're simple tags with content that's intended to be displayed in the in-game store. Here's a quick rundown of those tags:

- <image>—Specify the image you want to display for your vehicle in the store. As with all the tags that specify some kind of file path, this one is relative to your current file.

- <price>—This is the cost of your vehicle in the game. Building mods also have this tag.

- <lifetime>—The lifetime of a vehicle is the time, in hours, that the vehicle has to be in possession until the decay has reached its maximum value.

- <rotation>—The value in this tag specifies the rotation, in degrees, of the vehicle in front of the store after it's purchased.

- <brand>—This tag specifies the brand of your vehicle. If it's not a brand already recognized by Farming Simulator, the game will automatically set the brand to the GIANTS Software house brand, Lizard. To specify a new brand, you need to define it in modDesc.xml as described earlier in the chapter. The content of this tag should match the name attribute used in the <brand> tag within modDesc.xml.

- <category>—This tag is used to help with sorting vehicles in the store. For the example we've been working with, the content of this tag would be cultivators.

- `<shopTranslationOffset>`—The content of this tag are X, Y, and Z values to shift the position of your vehicle's origin when displayed in the store. It defines the spawn position. Set this correctly so the vehicle doesn't appear 1m in the air and fall to the ground. You can set this value properly by using the command `gsVehicleDebug attributes` while in the shop and reading the values in the bottom right corner.

- `<shopRotationOffset>`—Similar to the preceding tag, the *X, Y,* and *Z* content values of this tag are used to rotate the vehicle around the origin when displayed in the store. Both of the shop offset values are also important for the display of your mod in the store icon so the vehicle isn't facing away, or hovering in the air.

- `<shopFoldingState>`—This tag declares whether your vehicle is shown folded or not when in the store. Set the content to 0 for it to be open or 1 for the vehicle to be folded.

With the `<storeData>` tag filled in, your vehicle-XML should now look something like this:

```
<?xml version="1.0" encoding="utf-8" standalone="no" ?>

<vehicle type="cultivator">
    <annotation>Copyright (C) Me! I made this!</annotation>
    <storeData>
        <name>Qualidisc Pro</name>
        <specs>
            <neededPower>180</neededPower>
            <workingWidth>5.0</workingWidth>
            <combination filterCategory="weights"
filterSpec="weight" filterSpecMin="900" filterSpecMax="1000" />
        </specs>
        <functions>
            <function>$l10n_function_cultivator</function>
        </functions>
        <image>my_store_image.png</image>
        <price>24500</price>
        <lifetime>600</lifetime>
        <rotation>0</rotation>
        <brand>Kverneland</brand>
        <category>cultivators</category>
        <shopTranslationOffset>0 0 0</shopTranslationOffset>
        <shopRotationOffset>0 0 0</shopRotationOffset>
        <shopFoldingState>1</shopFoldingState>
    </storeData>
</vehicle>
```

Base Information

The next tag you need within your vehicle-XML is the `<base>` tag. In a way, the tags nested within this one continue where the `<storeData>` content left off. This is where you point to the location of your vehicle's model file in I3D format and start specifying some functional controls. These are the tags that are important to have within `<base>`:

- `<typeDesc>`—The content of this tag is the description of the vehicle type and is displayed in the help text. Like the content of the `<function>` tag in `<storeData>` you can use a variable to specify standard text, such as `$l10n_typeDesc_cultivator`.

- `<filename>`—This is the path to the I3D file with your vehicle's 3D model that you export from Blender. As with other paths, the filename path is relative to the root of your mod folder. If the file is not in a sub-folder, you just need to have the name of the file here.

- `<size>`—The attributes in this tag (`width`, `length`, `height`, `lengthOffset`) define the physical dimensions of your vehicle in meters. The `lengthOffset` attribute should only need to be adjusted if the origin of your vehicle isn't centered as you want and you don't want to re-adjust its position in Blender (adjusting relative to the Y-axis) or GIANTS Editor (adjusting relative to the Z-axis). It's mainly for the situation when multiple vehicles are purchased in the store at once. Occasionally those vehicles may collide or intersect with each other, so the `lengthOffset` attribute can help mitigate that.

- `<speedLimit>`—This is the maximum working speed of the vehicle, measured in kilometers per hour.

- `<components>`—This tag is actually a parent tag that supports multiple `<component>` tags within it. In Chapter 5, we defined a collision component and two compound children for our cultivator. The `<component>` tag here is only necessary for the main, or root component in the vehicle since the other two are specified as children. Within this tag, you have attributes for `centerOfMass`, `mass`, and `solverIterationCount`. The first two are self-explanatory. The last, `solverIterationCount`, is used to stipulate how many times the physical connection of components in the vehicle are calculated. Higher values are more accurate, but at the expense of in-game performance.

- `<schemaOverlay>`—The attributes in this tag specify which vehicle icon is set in the Help at the top left corner within the game.

Using these tags, the `<base>` section of your vehicle-XML should look something like this for our cultivator example:

```
<base>
    <typeDesc>$l10n_typeDesc_cultivator</typeDesc>
    <filename>qualidisc_pro.i3d</filename>
    <size width="15" length="4" lengthOffset="0.1" />
    <speedLimit value="15" />
    <components>
```

```
        <component centerOfMass="0 0.5 1"
solverIterationCount="10" mass="2470" />
    </components>
    <schemaOverlay attacherJointPosition="0 0" name="IMPLEMENT" />
</base>
```

Defining Attachment Points

If your vehicle is meant to be attached to something else (for example, a cultivator needs to be attached to a tractor to be towed), you use the `<attachable>` tag to give specifications on exactly how that attachment happens. In order for these attachments to work, you need to include reference nodes for them in your vehicle model.

Effectively, this means that in Blender you need to add an Empty to your vehicle's hierarchy, as covered at the end of Chapter 5. For this example, let's assume that you've created an attachment point for our cultivator and named it attacherJoint. With that information known, you can populate your `<attachable>` tag like this:

```
<attachable>
    <inputAttacherJoints>
        <inputAttacherJoint node="attacherJoint"
jointType="implement" topReferenceNode="topReferenceNode">
            <distanceToGround lower="0.6" upper="1.1" />
        </inputAttacherJoint>
    </inputAttacherJoints>
</attachable>
```

The key tag in the above example is the `<inputAttacherJoint>` tag. Within this tag, the `jointType` attribute says that this tool can be attached to the "implement" attacher joint on the tractor. For vehicles that are more like trailers, you can specify `trailer` for this attribute. If your vehicle is a trailer, then you don't need to specify anything for the `topReferenceNode` attribute. For our cultivator example, there's actually no need for a `topReferenceNode` because of the way it connects, so you would not include it here.

Within the `<inputAttacherJoint>` tag, the `<distanceToGround>` tag specifies the distance (in meters) from the attachment point of the lower link on the implement relative to the ground. They define the lowered and lifted states of the tool. If you press V in-game, the tool is lowered to the value you have in the `lower` attribute. Press *V* again and the tool is lifted to the value in the `upper` attribute. The best way to set up these values is to test in-game and tweak with a bit of trial and error.

Connection Hoses

Like with attachment points, there's a section in the vehicle-XML that you use for referencing any connection hoses that you set up, as covered at the end of Chapter 5. The tag used for these points is, unsurprisingly, `<connectionHoses>`. It's easiest to understand this section of the vehicle-XML file by first seeing an example. So using our cultivator example, the `<connectionHoses>` tag may look like this with a single hose specified:

```
<connectionHoses>
    <hose inputAttacherJointIndices="1" type="hydraulicIn"
adapterNode="hydraulicIn01_connector" node="hydraulicIn01"
length="1.4" diameter="0.015">
        <objectChange node="hydraulicIn01_detached"
visibilityActive="false" visibilityInactive="true" />
    </hose>
</connectionHoses>
```

There are a few key things to look at here. Most importantly, in the `<hose>` tag, the `node` attribute is the node ID you specified in Blender when setting up your hoses. In this example, that node ID is `hydraulicIn01`. The `length` and `diameter` are best set by setting up your vehicle in-game and adjusting to taste.

The next most important thing to focus on is the `<objectChange>` tag that's nested within the `<hose>` tag. Recall that there are two hose objects in our cultivator example. One object is dynamically generated in the game and used when the cultivator is attached to a tractor. The other object contains the hoses we modeled, showing them when the cultivator is disconnected. The `<objectChange>` tag gives you the ability to switch the visibility of objects based on whether the vehicle is attached or not. In this example, the `hydraulicIn01` node is visible by default. However, when the cultivator is not in use, that node is hidden and the `hydraulicIn01_detatched` node is displayed instead.

Also relevant to connection hoses is the `adapaterNode` attribute. Since hose connec-

tors are fairly well standardized within the game, you can make use of these connector models from the game to display when your vehicle is disconnected. As with attachment points and hose connections, you need to have an Empty in your Blender scene (or a transform group in GIANTS Editor) that indicates the location rotation where the connector models need to be placed (this is also covered in Chapter 5). Looking at the example text, the `adapterNode` attribute for the `hydraulicIn01` hose is an Empty named `hydraulicIn01_connector`.

I3D Mappings
The last major section in your base vehicle-XML file is the `<i3dMappings>` tag. The contents of this tag lists all of the nodes (objects) that you've explicitly enabled the Node Id check box for in Blender for your model. Basically, every object that you export from your `.blend` file is referenced by an index value. To make your life easier as a modder and

make your files more human-readable, it's possible to map these index values to a specific name, the node ID. That mapping process is what happens within the content of the `<i3dMappings>` tag.

Many modders go through the unnecessary effort of manually building and populating this section of their vehicle-XML. Fortunately, this section can be automatically generated for you from the GIANTS I3D Exporter in Blender. For more on how to set that up, see the section later in this chapter titled, "Getting Blender to see your XML files."

Getting Help with Your Vehicle-XML

The vehicle-XML file can easily become an enormous file. In fact, this chapter only gives you the absolute minimum that you need to get your mod to load into Farming Simulator for testing. There are a lot more tags that you can (and likely will) add to give your vehicle more functionality. Many of those tags are covered in later chapters in this book.

In any case, there are a lot of attributes and values that you need to keep track of. It can be pretty overwhelming to keep all of that in your head. Fortunately, you don't have to. The specification and documentation for vehicle-XML ships with Farming Simulator. Use Windows Explorer to navigate to your installation folder for Farming Simulator. The path should be something like `C:/Program Files (x86)/FarmingSimulator/shared/xml/documentation`. In that folder is `vehicle.html`. If you open that file in a web browser, you can see all of the possible tags and attributes in a vehicle-XML, as well as the type of data that's supposed to populate each of them. Furthermore if you edit your vehicle-XML file in GIANTS Studio, it can give you hints about the correct kinds of values to include in your file.

Testing Vehicle-XML (and Your Mod) in Farming Simulator

To view your mod in-game, you should copy your mod folder that you create at the start of this chapter and paste it in the mods folder for your local user. The path to this folder typically lives in your Documents folder, so it should be something like `Documents/My Games/FarmingSimulator20XX/mods`. With your mod folder (and all of its contents) in there, you can start the game.

Once you start, you load the mod while creating a new saved game. Using our cultivator example, that mod would be located in the Cultivator category within the in-game shop. Typically new mods are added at the end of the list.

When you find your mod, you can buy it and then also get a tractor to make sure that your attachment points work. Of course, because you haven't yet built any animations or additional functionality (see Chapter 7), there's not much more you can do. That said, because you've activated Developer Mode and your mod folder is where Farming Simulator expects it, you can edit your vehicle-XML file in this folder and make direct edits. Then, after saving, you can reload your vehicle in the game using the console command `gsVehicleReload` as covered in Chapter 14.

GETTING BLENDER TO SEE YOUR XML FILES

As you may have noted from this chapter, there's a lot of information that goes into the `modDesc.xml` and vehicle-XML files. It would be nice if some of this information could be directly exported from Blender at the same time that you export your I3D file. In particular, the `<i3dMappings>` tag in vehicle-XML is particularly tedious to try to build by hand. Fortunately, the GIANTS I3D Exporter add-on can, in fact, automatically populate and update your vehicle-XML file, especially the contents of the `<i3dMappings>` tag. Use the following steps:

1. Open Blender with the 3D model of your vehicle.

2. In the 3D Viewport's Sidebar, go to the GIANTS I3D Exporter tab.

3. Click on **Export** to get into the Export section and scroll to the bottom. Near the bottom, there's a panel labeled XML Config Files that has a single button on the right, **Add XML Config File**.

4. Click the **Add XML Config File** button and use Blender's File Browser to navigate to the location of your mod's XML files.

5. Choose your vehicle-XML and click the **Select XML** button in the File Browser. The `modDesc.xml` file doesn't need to be added at all.

With your XML files added, your Blender session might look like what's shown in Figure 6.2.

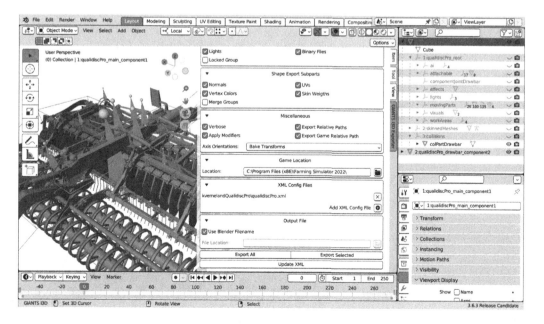

FIGURE 6.2   After you add your XML Config Files to the GIANTS I3D Exporter, you can update them right from within Blender.

And since you have made the GIANTS I3D Exporter aware of your XML files, they'll automatically be updated when you click the **Export All** button. If you just want to update the content of the XML file without re-exporting your model to I3D format, you can click the **Update XML** button all the way at the bottom of the Sidebar.

SUMMARY

In this chapter you covered the basics in setting up the primary configuration files that are necessary to have a rough-working mod for Farming Simulator. This is where your 3D model really starts to become a functional mod. You started by setting up a folder to hold the files for your mod. From there, you dug into the structure of the `modDesc.xml` file in order to describe your mod within Farming Simulator. After that, you looked at the necessary entries and structure in your vehicle-XML file so you could have a space to define the functionality of the vehicle in your mod. Finally, you connected your XML files to the working `.blend` file for the 3D model in your mod.

In the next chapter, we start adding real functionality to the mod.

CHAPTER 7

Implementing Vehicle Functions

A SSUMING THAT YOU'VE WORKED your way through the preceding chapter, you should now have a basic `modDesc.xml` and vehicle-XML file that, along with your exported I3D file, allows you to load your vehicle mod in Farming Simulator and purchase it from the in-game shop. However, even though your model is there and looks super cool, it's not really functional at this point. You haven't yet set it up to do any actual farming tasks as you play. That's what this chapter is all about.

And this chapter is a big one covering a lot of topics for functionality in your vehicle-XML file. We start by defining wheels in your vehicle. Wheels apply both to the "real" wheels like tires on a tractor, but also for wheel-like spinning components, like the discs on a cultivator. Next, we dig into defining the work areas where your vehicle affects the ground (pun intended). From there, we go into detail on how to add foliage bending nodes to your vehicle so it properly influences the crops that you drive over. And since your vehicle is affecting the ground, the next topic is using the GIANTS Engine to generate visual effects when your vehicle is working.

In this chapter:

- Defining wheels

- Setting up work areas

- Pushing away your crops with foliage bending nodes

- Creating visual effects for your vehicle

TECHNICAL REQUIREMENTS

A large component of this chapter is done by editing your vehicle-XML file in GIANTS Studio. It's possible to do this work with any text editor, but GIANTS Studio has XML features that can help you build and troubleshoot your mod's files as you create them.

DOI: 10.1201/9781032659497-7

The changes you'll make in vehicle-XML will often require you creating reference objects or modifying the existing objects in your 3D model within Blender, so it's necessary to have the recent release of Blender with the GIANTS I3D Exporter add-on installed.

GIANTS Editor is a big requirement to ensure that exported parts and functionality from Blender are going to work once they get in Farming Simulator.

And as with previous chapters, the examples in this chapter are all based on the Kverneland Qualidisc Pro cultivator that's available on the download page for this book. You can reach that page by going to https://gdn.giants-software.com/blenderBook or scanning the QR code at the end of this section. Of course, you can use your own model for your mod, but this model is available if you want to follow along.

https://gdn.giants-software.com/blenderBook

DEFINING WHEELS

Unless your vehicle mod is a custom sled or perhaps a retro manual plow, it's likely that it's going to have wheels. In fact, having a look at the cultivator example that we've been working through with this book, it technically has more wheels than you might expect. The rollers on your cultivator are meant to spin in a wheel-like fashion. Furthermore, defining your rollers as wheels also gives your cultivator something to rest on when lowered. First however, let's focus on the regular wheels at the back of the tool to illustrate the process.

Configuring Simple Wheels

To ensure that your wheels rotate correctly, you need to set up a transform group for each wheel in the vehicle. This means you need to add an Empty to your vehicle hierarchy within Blender for each wheel, and that Empty object needs to be oriented such that it can rotate cleanly around its local X-axis. In Blender, let's assume that you followed a process like what's described in Chapter 2 in the section entitled "Organizing your Blender Scene for Exporting to I3D". For the regular back wheels, they're organized in the vehicle hierarchy as being part of the back arm. So by selecting each wheel and using the Create

Empty operator that comes with the GIANTS I3D Exporter add-on you can add your wheel Empties (and name them) to match this structure:

- qualidiscPro _ root (Empty)

  - movingParts (Empty)

    – backArm (mesh)

      – wheelLeft (Empty)

      – wheelRight (Empty)

    – ...

With this basic structure in place, you can open your vehicle-XML file and add a <wheels> tag with the following content:

```
<wheels>
    <wheelConfigurations>
        <wheelConfiguration name="$l10n_configuration_valueDefault"
brand="VREDESTEIN" saveId="VREDESTEIN_DEFAULT">
            <wheels>
                <wheel filename="..." isLeft="true" hasTireTracks=
"true" hasParticles="true">
                    <physics restLoad="1.5" repr="wheelLeft"
forcePointRatio="0.3" initialCompression="35" suspTravel="0.12"
spring="31" damper="20" yOffset="0.02" />
                </wheel>
                <wheel filename="..." isLeft="false" hasTireTracks=
"true" hasParticles="true">
                    <physics restLoad="1.5" repr="wheelRight"
forcePointRatio="0.3" initialCompression="35" suspTravel="0.12"
spring="31" damper="20" yOffset="0.02" />
                </wheel>
            </wheels>
        </wheelConfiguration>
    </wheelConfigurations>
</wheels>
```

Teasing this configuration apart, the <wheelConfiguration> tag is an important one to note because it uses a default value for naming your wheel configuration. Recall from previous chapters that Farming Simulator supports localization. If you use naming that's already defined in Farming Simulator, you save time because you don't have to translate and enter those names yourself. In this example, we're using $l10n _ configuration _ valueDefault for the name attribute, which results in a string that reads, "Default" in English and other languages. Furthermore, the other two attributes, brand and saveId, are included to make use of brands and configurations that are already defined in the base game. In this case, our example is using a wheel configuration for the Vredestein brand.

Nested within each `<wheelConfiguration>` tag is another `<wheels>` tag that contains information for the actual wheels in that particular configuration. And within the `<wheels>` tag are individual `<wheel>` tags for each wheel. In our example the `<wheel>` tag has four attributes:

- `filename`—This attribute refers to an XML file that describes the wheel. In our cultivator example, we're using a definition from the base game. For the sake of space and readability, that path is abbreviated here with ellipsis, but you can see the full path in the example from GDN (or this book's Appendix)

- `isLeft`—Set this attribute to `true` to indicate that the wheel transform group is on the left side of the vehicle.

- `hasTireTracks`—If you want the wheel to generate tire tracks, set this attribute to `true`.

- `hasParticles`—If the wheel generates a dust particle system, set this attribute to `true`.

All the "work" for the wheel happens in the attributes for the `<physics>` tag that's nested within each `<wheel>` tag. In that `<physics>` tag, the most important attribute is `repr`. This attribute is the name of the Empty (your transform group) that controls that wheel. This needs to be set with the correct name or the GIANTS Engine won't know which object you're referring to. Below is a listing of each possible attribute you can include in the `<physics>` tag:

- `restLoad`—The `restLoad` attribute defines how much weight is loaded on the wheel while in resting position. You can check this value using `gsVehicleDebug physics` command in the in-game console.

- `repr`—This attribute is the transform group node of your wheel object. That same node is also used for suspension and steering.

- `driveNode`—The `driveNode` attribute is the transform group for the wheel driving rotation (about the wheel's X-axis). This attribute is optional. If you don't include it, the `repr` node is used.

- `forcePointRatio`—Use the `forcePointRatio` attribute to define where the force of the vehicle is applied on the wheel. If you set the value for this attribute to 0, that force is at the wheel's center. A value of 1 puts the force at the ground contact point.

- `radius`—Use this attribute to define the radius of your wheel object, in meters. If you are linking the wheel from an external file where the radius is already defined, you don't need this attribute. However, if you do include a radius, it overrides whatever is in the linked file. Of course, if you custom-modeled your wheels, such as with the rollers of our example cultivator, this attribute is required. Assuming you modeled it to scale in Blender, you should be able to measure this size there.

- `width`—Like the `radius` attribute, the width `attribute` defines the physical dimensions for your wheel in meters. And like `radius`, this attribute is not necessary when referencing an external file.

- `mass`—Use the `mass` attribute to let the physics system in GIANTS Engine know the weight of your wheel in metric tons. Like `radius` and `width`, this attribute isn't required if you reference an external wheel file.

- `initialCompression`—The value in this attribute shows how much the suspension system is compressed by default on a scale from 0 to 1. If the initial compression is 50%, you would use a value of 0.5 here.

- `suspTravel`—The `suspTravel` value is the maximum distance that the wheel can move vertically when it reacts to a collision.

- `spring`—The `spring` attribute defines how fast the wheel suspension will try to get the wheel back to its original position.

- `damper`—Reduce the value of this attribute and the damping of the wheel is softer.

- `isSynchronized`—Defines if the wheel rotation is synchronized in multi-player. As soon as any visual effect is linked to the wheel or a `<speedRotatingPart>` tag is referencing the wheel, this attribute should be set to `true`, which is the default setting. You should not set this attribute to `false` if the visuals are linked.

One further feature you can add to your vehicle mod is the ability to set up different configurations for different brands of wheels. Fortunately, you don't need to copy and paste all of these attributes all over again for each brand configuration. Farming Simulator defaults to inheriting the values from the configuration as defined by the `baseConfig` attribute in the `<wheels>` tag. That attribute should refer to the `saveId` value in a different configuration. For other brands, you just need to maintain the same tag structure, but point to the file name of the external wheel you're referencing. For instance, if you want to give the option to use Trelleborg wheels on your vehicle, you would add a new `<wheelConfiguration>` tag after the preceding one, like so (new tags in bold):

```
<wheels>
    <wheelConfigurations>
        <wheelConfiguration name="$l10n_configuration_
valueDefault"
brand="VREDESTEIN" saveId="VREDESTEIN_DEFAULT">
            <wheels>
                <wheel filename="..." isLeft="true"
hasTireTracks="true"
hasParticles="true">
```

```
                    <physics restLoad="1.5" repr="wheelLeft"
forcePointRatio="0.3" initialCompression="35" suspTravel="0.12"
spring="31" damper="20" yOffset="0.02" />
            </wheel>
            <wheel filename="..." isLeft="false"
hasTireTracks="true" hasParticles="true">
                    <physics restLoad="1.5" repr="wheelRight"
forcePointRatio="0.3" initialCompression="35" suspTravel="0.12"
spring="31" damper="20" yOffset="0.02" />
            </wheel>
        </wheels>
    </wheelConfiguration>
    <wheelConfiguration name="$l10n_configuration_
valueDefault" brand="TRELLEBORG" saveId="TRELLEBORG_DEFAULT">
        <wheels baseConfig="VREDESTEIN_DEFAULT">
            <wheel filename="$data/shared/wheels/tires/
trelleborg/AW309/500_50R17.xml" />
            <wheel filename="$data/shared/wheels/tires/
trelleborg/AW309/500_50R17.xml" />
        </wheels>
    </wheelConfiguration>
  </wheelConfigurations>
</wheels>
```

TIP

To get a full sense of what shared tires you can use in your vehicle from Farming Simulator, go to the install folder for the game and drill down to `data/shared/wheels/tires`. In that folder, you can find all the available tires and sizes in the game. Then you can use any one of them in your wheel configurations.

Setting Up Wheel `<speedRotatingParts>`

Ideally, your wheel Empties are located at the origin of their wheel object, but that isn't necessary for all wheel situations. As I mentioned earlier in this section, the rollers on our example cultivator behave like wheels. However, it would be pretty bothersome to add an individual Empty for every single one of them, especially since they're all rotating the same way. Furthermore, if you have fewer physical wheels listed in your vehicle-XML, you have better in-game performance.

Rather than having a bunch of physical wheels, the better approach is to use a single Empty as the transform group for all rollers and then use `<speedRotatingParts>` in your vehicle-XML to have all the roller objects rotate to match that Empty (this process is covered later in this section). The key is to place this Empty with its origin at the same height as the center of all the rollers on each side of the cultivator. You can use the following steps to add your wheel Empty for each set of rollers:

1. Select the wheel objects on one side of the cultivator. In our cultivator example, the rollers on the left are named `rollLeftBack` and `rollLeftFront`.

2. Use the Create Empty operator from the Tools section of the GIANTS I3D Exporter to add an Empty to your scene at the location of your selected objects. As with Empties that were added in Chapter 5, I recommend setting the display type for your Empty to Arrows in the Object Properties tab of the Properties editor. That display type gives a much more clear understanding of which direction your axes are rotated. Be sure that the X-axis of your Empty runs along the length of your wheel's axle so it spins without wobbling.

3. Name your new Empty something sensible (e.g. `rollLeftWheel`) and make sure it's arranged correctly in the vehicle hierarchy. In our example, the new Empty should be a sibling of the two roller objects. You can quickly adjust parent relationships from the Scenes display mode in the Outliner by clicking and dragging.

4. Select your new Empty and, from the GIANTS I3D Exporter tab in the 3D Viewport's Sidebar, enable the **Node Id** check box and ensure that it's using the same name as what's shown in Blender.

If you follow these steps for the rollers on each side of your vehicle, your updated vehicle hierarchy should look something like this (new Empties are indicated in **bold**):

- `qualidiscPro _ mainComponent1` (mesh)
  - `qualidiscPro _ root` (Empty)
    - `movingParts` (Empty)
      - `armLeft` (mesh)
  - `armLeftBackArm` (mesh)
    - `armLeftRollerArm` (mesh)
      - `rollLeftBack` (mesh)
      - `rollLeftFront` (mesh)
      - `rollLeftWheel` **(Empty)**
      - `armRight` (mesh)
  - `armRightBackArm` (mesh)
    - `armRightRollerArm` (mesh)
      - `rollRightBack` (mesh)
      - `rollRightFront` (mesh)

- **`rollRightWheel` (Empty)**

- backArm (mesh)

• wheelLeft (Empty)

• wheelRight (Empty)

  – ...

In your vehicle-XML file, the `<wheels>` tag needs to be modified to include your new roller wheels, like so (new code in **bold**):

```
<wheels>
    <wheelConfigurations>
        <wheelConfiguration name="$l10n_configuration_valueDefault"
brand="VREDESTEIN" saveId="VREDESTEIN_DEFAULT">
            <wheels>
                <wheel filename="..." isLeft="true"
hasTireTracks="true" hasParticles="true">
                    <physics restLoad="1.5" repr="wheelLeft"
forcePointRatio="0.3" initialCompression="35" suspTravel="0.12"
spring="31" damper="20" yOffset="0.02" />
                </wheel>
                <wheel filename="..." isLeft="false"
hasTireTracks="true" hasParticles="true">
                    <physics restLoad="1.5" repr="wheelRight"
forcePointRatio="0.3" initialCompression="35" suspTravel="0.12"
spring="31" damper="20" yOffset="0.02" />
                </wheel>
                <wheel>
                    <physics restLoad="1.2" repr="rollLeftWheel"
width="1" radius="0.27" useReprDirection="true"
forcePointRatio="0.1" initialCompression="40" suspTravel="0.03"
spring="90" damper="60" rotationDamping="0.006" brakeFactor="0"
supportsWheelSink="false" />
                </wheel>
                <wheel>
                    <physics restLoad="1.2" repr="rollRightWheel"
width="1" radius="0.27" useReprDirection="true"
forcePointRatio="0.1" initialCompression="40" suspTravel="0.03"
spring="90" damper="60" rotationDamping="0.006" brakeFactor="0"
supportsWheelSink="false" />
                </wheel>
            </wheels>
        </wheelConfiguration>
        <wheelConfiguration name="$l10n_configuration_
valueDefault" brand="TRELLEBORG" saveId="TRELLEBORG_DEFAULT">
```

```
            <wheels baseConfig="VREDESTEIN_DEFAULT">
                <wheel filename="$data/shared/wheels/tires/
trelleborg/AW309/500_50R17.xml" />
                <wheel filename="$data/shared/wheels/tires/
trelleborg/AW309/500_50R17.xml" />
                <wheel />
                <wheel />
            </wheels>
        </wheelConfiguration>
    </wheelConfigurations>
</wheels>
```

> **NOTE**
>
> Notice the empty <wheel> tags in the second <wheelConfiguration> tag. These empty tags indicate that the game should use the wheels in the first configuration. If you don't include these empty tags, the game won't load those wheels for that configuration.

It's important to understand that the content of the <wheels> tag relates to individual wheels. Their rotations are controlled by the movement of the vehicle. However, if you're using one wheel to dictate the rotation of two rollers, as we are in our example cultivator, you need to explicitly define the rotation in your vehicle-XML. For that, you need to make use of the <speedRotatingParts> tag. This tag is used to control the rotation of parts as the vehicle moves forward and backward.

Once you have node IDs for each of your rotating parts, you can add the following <speedRotatingParts> tag to your vehicle-XML:

Once you have node IDs for each of your rotating parts, you can add the following <speedRotatingParts> tag to your vehicle-XML:

```
<speedRotatingParts>
    <speedRotatingPart node="rollLeftFront" radius="0.27"
wheelIndex="3" />
    <speedRotatingPart node="rollLeftBack" radius="0.27"
wheelIndex="3" />
    <speedRotatingPart node="rollRightFront" radius="0.27"
wheelIndex="4" />
    <speedRotatingPart node="rollRightBack" radius="0.27"
wheelIndex="4" />
</speedRotatingParts>
```

The thing that makes these parts work is the wheelIndex attribute. Notice that both left roller parts share the same value for that parameter while the right roller parts also share a value. In this example, the reason why the left rollers are using a wheelIndex value of 3 is because the <wheel> tag containing the rollLeftWheel reference is the third one. Likewise, the fourth <wheel> tag refers to rollRightWheel, so the wheelIndex for rollRightFront and rollRightBack is 4.

> **NOTE**
>
> If you compare this example text to the actual integrated example of our cultivator that you can download from the GDN, you may notice that the wheelIndex attributes have different values. That's because the integrated example is more detailed and has the full vehicle description whereas this text is here to show basic concepts.

In addition to the node attribute for the <speedRotatingPart> tag with the correct name as you set in Blender, you need to pay close attention to the radius attribute. In particular, you need to determine whether the value for this attribute should be positive or negative. If you watch these parts rotate in-game and some of them are spinning in the wrong direction, you need to make a change. In this example, if you see that the right rollers are spinning in the wrong direction, then you'd change the radius attribute to -0.27.

Adding Wheel Chocks

You can also specify wheel chocks that get shown when your vehicle is being detached. Most of the work for that is defined in your vehicle-XML, but you do first need to add a parking node so the game knows where to place the chock. So, in Blender, you need to add an Empty (use the Create Empty feature of the GIANTS I3D Exporter add-on) at the location where the chock should be. Be sure to give that Empty a node ID. Once you have that work complete, you can proceed to refer to that node from your vehicle-XML using the <wheelChock> tag, as a child of the wheel associated with that chock. For our running example, the addition code in the <wheels> tag might look like so (new code in bold):

```
<wheels>
    <wheelConfigurations>
        <wheelConfiguration name="$l10n_configuration_
valueDefault" brand="VREDESTEIN" saveId="VREDESTEIN_DEFAULT">
            <wheels>
                <wheel filename="..." isLeft="true"
hasTireTracks="true" hasParticles="true">
                    <physics restLoad="1.5" repr="wheelLeft"
forcePointRatio="0.3" initialCompression="35" suspTravel="0.12"
spring="31" damper="20" yOffset="0.02" />
                    <wheelChock parkingNode="wheelChock01"
filename="$data/shared/assets/wheelChocks/wheelChock02.i3d" />
                    <wheelChock parkingNode="wheelChock02"
filename="$data/shared/assets/wheelChocks/wheelChock02.i3d"
isInverted="true" />
                </wheel>
```

```
                <wheel filename="..." isLeft="false"
hasTireTracks="true" hasParticles="true">
                    <physics restLoad="1.5" repr="wheelRight"
forcePointRatio="0.3" initialCompression="35" suspTravel="0.12"
spring="31" damper="20" yOffset="0.02" />
                </wheel>
                <wheel>
                    <physics restLoad="1.2" repr="rollLeftWheel"
width="1" radius="0.27" useReprDirection="true"
forcePointRatio="0.1" initialCompression="40" suspTravel="0.03"
spring="90" damper="60" rotationDamping="0.006" brakeFactor="0"
supportsWheelSink="false" />
                </wheel>
                <wheel>
                    <physics restLoad="1.2" repr="rollRightWheel"
width="1" radius="0.27" useReprDirection="true"
forcePointRatio="0.1" initialCompression="40" suspTravel="0.03"
spring="90" damper="60" rotationDamping="0.006" brakeFactor="0"
supportsWheelSink="false" />
                </wheel>
            </wheels>
        </wheelConfiguration>
        <wheelConfiguration name="$l10n_configuration_
valueDefault" brand="TRELLEBORG" saveId="TRELLEBORG_DEFAULT">
            <wheels baseConfig="VREDESTEIN_DEFAULT">
                <wheel filename="$data/shared/wheels/tires/
trelleborg/AW309/500_50R17.xml">
                    <wheelChock />
                    <wheelChock />
                </wheel>
                <wheel filename="$data/shared/wheels/tires/
trelleborg/AW309/500_50R17.xml" />
                <wheel />
                <wheel />
            </wheels>
        </wheelConfiguration>
    </wheelConfigurations>
</wheels>
```

In the <wheelChock> tag, there are three attributes to be aware of:

- parkingNode—This attribute is the node ID of the Empty you placed in Blender saying where the chock should go when the vehicle is detached. It's worth mentioning that if your wheel chock needs to fit in a smaller mount, you can scale the parking node object in Blender.

- filename—The filename attribute points to an external file from Farming Simulator where the chock's I3D file lives. These files all live in data/shared/assets/wheelChocks/ within the Farming Simulator installation directory, so check there to see what's available.

- isInverted—Set this attribute to either true or false, depending on whether the chock is placed at the front of the wheel or the back.

> **NOTE**
>
> Notice that, just like with the empty <wheel> tags in the second <wheelConfiguration> tag, you also need to include empty <wheelChock> tags on the first wheel to indicate that the same wheel chocks should be used from the first configuration.

On some vehicles, there are wheel chock mountings. It's certainly possible to model and include these mountings yourself, but since you're already using the wheel chock meshes from the base game, you can also use mountings as well. These mountings are not part of the <wheels> tag. Instead, you should use a system in the game engine known as *dynamically loaded parts*. In short, the base game has a whole variety of parts that are available for you to add to your vehicle. You can see them in the game folder at data/shared/assets. To make use of these parts, you need to add an Empty in Blender and give it a node ID that you can reference from the vehicle-XML within a <dynamicallyLoadedParts> tag.

In our example with the wheel chocks, we added two Empties, to our .blend file, wheelChockSupport01 and wheelChockSupport02. Those Empties are referenced in our vehicle-XML like so:

```
<dynamicallyLoadedParts>
    <dynamicallyLoadedPart node="0"
linkNode="wheelChockSupport01" filename="$data/shared/assets/
wheelChocks/wheelChockSupport01.i3d" />
    <dynamicallyLoadedPart node="0" linkNode="wheelChockSupport02"
filename="$data/shared/assets/wheelChocks/wheelChockSupport01.i3d"
/>
</dynamicallyLoadedParts>
```

In our example cultivator vehicle-XML (see the Appendix), this tag is added after the <wheels> tag.

Improving Performance with Merge Children

With a bunch of moving wheels, it's possible to adversely affect the performance of your vehicle in-game. However, if all of the parts are moving in the same way, you can tell the GIANTS I3D Exporter to merge them as a single object on export. In our example cultivator, you can use this feature on the array of discs at the front of the vehicle. Use the following steps to set it up on the left arm discs:

1. Select all of the discs on the left arm.

2. Move the 3D Cursor to the median of your selection (**Object ▶ Snap ▶ Cursor to Origin**).

3. Add an Empty (**Add ▶ Empty ▶ Plain Axes**) and name it `armLeftDiscs`.

4. Make your new `armLeftDiscs` Empty a child of the `armLeft` mesh object and make all of your discs on that arm a child of that Empty.

5. Note that all of the disc objects need to have their local origins oriented such that they rotate about their local X-axis.

6. Select your `armLeftDiscs` Empty and go to the Attributes section in the GIANTS I3D Exporter tab of the 3D Viewport's sidebar. You need to enable a few attributes here to ensure that merging works correctly.

7. Expand the Rendering panel and enable the **Merge Children** check box about half-way down the panel. This check box does the work of exporting all of the child discs as a single object.

8. Expand the Object Data Texture panel and enable the **Export Position** and **Export Orientation** check boxes. These parameters are what make the animation actually work. What's happening here is although the discs are being exported as a single object, they're each still assigned an index and an animated texture is generated. The game engine uses a shader and that texture to dynamically render the discs with the correct positions and orientations. When you enable these check boxes, make sure that the **File Path** field is correctly set with the name of the animated texture you want the exporter to generate.

9. Select any disc in the set of discs in the vehicle.

10. Go to the Material section in the GIANTS I3D Exporter tab and load the current material by clicking the **Load Shader** button at the bottom of the tab. Check to ensure that the disc is using the vehicle shader.

11. Still in the Material section of the GIANTS I3D Exporter tab, set the **Shader Variation** drop-down menu to either *vtxRotate* or *vtxRotate_colorMask*.

12. Still in the Material section, go to the Texture Path panel and set **mTrackArray** to point to the path of your generated texture named in step 8. Of course, if your array on the other side of your vehicle is different, you would need to have a duplicated material, but a different mTrackArray for the other side.

13. Click **Apply** to save your changes to the material.

> **NOTE**
>
> As covered in Chapter 3, in Farming Simulator 25 and beyond, *mTrackArray* has been renamed to *trackArray* and *vtxRotate* is no longer available.

After you export your I3D file of your vehicle, you have one further modification that you need to make to your vehicle-XML. Much like with the rollers described earlier in this section, you need to have an entry in your vehicle-XML to help define the rotations of your merged children. And just like with the rollers, you do this step in the `<speedRotatingParts>` tag. Taking the text from the earlier example, you would add two new `<speedRotatingPart>` tags, one for the left discs and one for the right, like so (new code in bold):

```
<speedRotatingParts>
    <speedRotatingPart node="rollLeftFront" radius="0.27"
wheelIndex="3" />
    <speedRotatingPart node="rollLeftBack" radius="0.27"
wheelIndex="3" />
    <speedRotatingPart node="rollRightFront" radius="0.27"
wheelIndex="4" />
    <speedRotatingPart node="rollRightBack" radius="0.27"
wheelIndex="4" />
    <speedRotatingPart shaderNode="armLeftDiscs"  radius="-0.30"
groundReferenceNodeIndex="1" />
    <speedRotatingPart shaderNode="armRightDiscs" radius="-0.30"
groundReferenceNodeIndex="1" />
</speedRotatingParts>
```

Note that in the newly added tags, there's not a `wheelIndex` attribute. Instead, there's a `groundReferenceNodeIndex` attribute that you use to reference the ground reference node on the vehicle.

Once you have this set up, you don't need to make any additions or changes to your vehicle-XML file. Everything else is handled by the GIANTS I3D Exporter add-on.

> **NOTE**
>
> At this point, it's a good idea to test your vehicle and this material-based rotation using the steps covered in Chapter 3 in the section titled, "Testing Your Material in the GIANTS Editor."

SETTING UP WORK AREAS

This mod that you're creating is for Farming Simulator, so as a mod vehicle, you want your implement to affect the area on the field. To make this happen, you need to define some references so the game knows when your implement is activated, what area of the ground it affects, and some "guardrails" in preparation for being used by AI workers.

Configuring Work Areas

Every working tool like a cultivator or mower (collectively referred to as *implements*) has a specific work area. That is, there's a region below and around the implement that gets affected when it's activated. In order for the game engine to understand the dimensions of this work area, you need to create some reference points in your vehicle hierarchy. As with most other reference points, the game engine expects these as transform groups, so that means you need to create some more Empties in Blender.

The first thing you need to do is add an organizational Empty that serves as the parent transform group for your work area references. Add an Empty to your scene (**Add ▶ Empty ▶ Plain Axes**) and name it workAreas. The workAreas Empty is best located at your vehicle origin (likely the world origin) and a child of your vehicle's root transform group.

Now, as children of the workAreas Empty, you need three more Empties. Here's a list of each one with its required name and position:

- workAreaStart—Place this Empty at the front left corner of your desired work area near the ground. Recall that in Chapter 6, we set the working width for our cultivator to 6 m in the <specs> tag. Since our vehicle's origin is at its center, we know that the X-axis value for this Empty needs to be at *3.0*. The Z-axis location is *0* and the Y-axis location needs to be placed visually using the Move tool.

- workAreaWidth—This Empty should share the same Y- and Z-axis values as workAreaStart, but the negative value of the X-axis number. So in this case the X-axis value should be *-3.0*.

- workAreaHeight—This Empty's naming may be a bit confusing since it defines the backmost extent of the work area, It should share the same X- and Z-axis values as workAreaStart, but with a Y-axis location that's placed visually at the back of you desired work area.

With these Empties placed, GIANTS Engine can infer a parallelogram that defines your work area, as shown in Figure 7.1.

FIGURE 7.1 The three Empties that are children of the `workAreas` Empty imply a parallelogram that defines your vehicle's working area.

IMPORTANT

Remember to give all four of your working area Empties (the three parallelogram Empties and their parent) node IDs from the GIANTS I3D Exporter tab in the 3D Viewport's Sidebar. Then when you export, your vehicle-XML is updated with the correct I3D mappings.

Back in your vehicle-XML file, you need to add a tag section so your work area is recognized. The tag you use is, logically, `<workAreas>` and you structure it like so:

```
<workAreas>
    <workArea type="cultivator" functionName="processCultivator
Area">
        <area startNode="workAreaStart" widthNode="workAreaWidth"
heightNode="workAreaHeight" />
        <groundReferenceNode index="1" />
    </workArea>
</workAreas>
```

TIP

In the `<workArea>` tag, the `type` and `functionName` attributes reference the functionality of the work area. You can look at the base game's XML for reference on different vehicle types to help you populate these attributes in your own mod.

In addition, the `<workArea>` tag supports a `disableBackwards` attribute that, if you set it to `true`, disables the working area while driving backwards. With that attribute set that way, your vehicle only does work while driving forward.

Defining Your Ground Reference Node

One of the most important things you need to establish is the location of your vehicle's ground reference node. This is a transform group that lets the game engine know that your implement is active to work. For our cultivator example, when the ground reference node transform group is lower than the ground, the cultivator starts working.

Because the ground reference node is a transform group, you need to add an Empty in your Blender scene. You want the location of this Empty to be aligned with the bottom of the cultivator's tines. Name the Empty something sensible, like `groundReferenceNode` and In terms of hierarchy, make this Empty a child of your `workAreas` Empty that you created in the previous section.

As with all other reference Empties in your Blender scene, be sure to give both Empties a node ID by enabling the **Node Id** check box in the GIANTS I3D Exporter tab of the 3D Viewport's Sidebar.

With your ground reference node added to your vehicle hierarchy, you need to make a section for it in your vehicle-XML using the `<groundReferenceNodes>` tag, like so:

```
<groundReferenceNodes>
    <groundReferenceNode node="groundReferenceNode"
threshold="0.1" />
</groundReferenceNodes>
```

In addition to using the correct name in the node attribute, you should also check the threshold attribute. By setting this attribute to 0.1, you're telling the game engine that the cultivator should be active when the ground reference node is 10cm *above* the terrain. This threshold is particularly useful when the terrain your vehicle is working is uneven, causing the ground reference node to not always be touching the ground. Also, you may recall that there is a groundReferenceNode attribute for the `<workArea>` tag and for the `<speedRotatingParts>` tag. That attribute is an index. Since this is the first (and only) `<groundReferenceNode>` tag in `<groundReferenceNodes>`, its index value is 1. If you added a second `<groundReferenceNode>` tag, that one's index would be 2, and so on.

Helping Your Vehicle Know the Distance to the Ground with Ground Adjusted Nodes

Similar to the ground reference node, your vehicle may need some additional Empties to help calculate the distance to the ground for various moving parts (see "Defining Moving Parts" in Chapter 8). You can do this for each moving part by adding two Empties, one is a ground adjusted node and the other is a raycast node. When the vehicle is active in the game, the ground adjusted node is translated to the surface of the terrain while the raycast node remains in its place within the vehicle hierarchy.

In our cultivator example, it makes sense to have two sets of these Empties, a pair for each arm of the tool. These Empties should be children of their respective arms. So your vehicle hierarchy in Blender's Outliner should look something like this:

- qualidiscPro _ mainComponent1 (mesh)
  - qualidiscPro _ root (Empty)
    - movingParts (Empty)
      - armLeft (mesh)
  - armLeftGroundAdjustNode (Empty)
  - armLeftGroundRaycastNode (Empty)
      - armRight (mesh)
  - armRightGroundAdjustNode (Empty)
  - armRightGroundRaycastNode (Empty)
  - ...

In terms of placement, both of these Empties should be in the same location and at the same height as the part of your vehicle that's meant to rest on the ground. In the case of the cultivator that we're using as an example, the adjustment plates on the outside of each arm serve as our reference height, as shown in Figure 7.2.

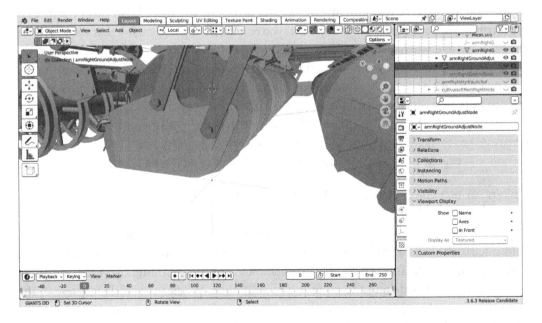

FIGURE 7.2 Use the lowest part of your tool as the reference height for your ground adjusted node and raycast node.

After you've added your Empties, you can add a `<groundAdjustedNodes>` tag to your vehicle-XML, like so:

```
<groundAdjustedNodes>
    <groundAdjustedNode node="armLeftGroundAdjustNode"
yOffset="0.3" minY="0" maxY="0.3" moveSpeed="0.5"
resetIfNotActive="true">
        <raycastNode distance="0.4" node="armLeftGroundRay
castNode" />
        <foldable minLimit="0" maxLimit="0.09" />
    </groundAdjustedNode>
    <groundAdjustedNode node="armRightGroundAdjustNode"
yOffset="0.3" minY="0" maxY="0.3" moveSpeed="0.5"
resetIfNotActive="true">
        <raycastNode distance="0.4" node="armRightGroundRaycast
Node" />
        <foldable minLimit="0" maxLimit="0.09" />
    </groundAdjustedNode>
</groundAdjustedNodes>
```

Note that the `<raycastNode>` tag is located within the content of the `<groundAdjustedNode>` tag. This arrangement helps the game engine more easily make the association between the two nodes. Also, because the arms on our cultivator are foldable, there's a `<foldable>` tag included as well.

> **NOTE**
>
> It's worth mentioning that the ground adjusted node is only updated when the current folding state for your vehicle is within the limits of 0–0.09. So in the case of our example cultivator, this would be while the tool is lowered.

With this section added, you're able to refer to the height calculation it provides elsewhere in your vehicle-XML, such as when defining your moving parts. For instance, in Blender, you could add a reference node Empty as a child of the ground adjusted node to do movements based on the current node position. You can see this kind of usage in the integrated example referenced in the "Technical requirements" section of this chapter.

Setting up AI Areas and the AI Collision Node

Now it's time to set up nodes that can be used by the game's AI workers. To start, you need a new Empty to serve as a transform group container for all your AI reference nodes. Add a new Empty to your scene (**Add ▶ Empty ▶ Plain Axes**), name it `ai`, and put it at the same level in your hierarchy as your workAreas Empty. As for physical location, it's best to keep this Empty at your vehicle's origin.

As children of the `ai` Empty, you'll need a bunch of other Empties. Fortunately, you can take advantage of the work you've already done with work areas. Use the following steps:

- Select the three Empties in your `workAreas` transform group: `workAreaStart`, `workAreaWidth`, and `workAreaHeight`.

- In the 3D Viewport, duplicate your selected Empties (**Object ▶ Duplicate**) and right-click to ensure that you don't move them from their current positions. All three of your new Empties should still be selected.

- In the Scenes view of the Outliner, click and drag your new Empties so they're children of the `ai` Empty.

- Rename your new Empties (double-click each of their names in the Outliner or use the *F2* hotkey) accordingly:
  - `workAreaStart.001` ▶ `aiMarkerLeft`
  - `workAreaWidth.001` ▶ `aiMarkerRight`
  - `workAreaHeight.001` ▶ `aiMarkerBack`

- Adjust the position of `aiMarkerBack` such that it's centered on the X-axis (so set its X-axis value to *0.0*).

At this point, you've created nodes for your AI markers, but the game engine AI also needs references for the overall size of your vehicle. If the size of your vehicle is significantly different from your working area (such as in a fertilizer spreader that spreads to a work area of 30m, despite being much smaller than that), you need three more Empties:

- Select aiMarkerLeft, aiMarkerRight, and aiMarkerBack.

- Back in the 3D Viewport, duplicate these markers just like how you created them (**Object ▶ Duplicate ▶** right-click).

- Rename your new Empties:
  - `aiMarkerLeft.001` ▶ `sizeMarkerLeft`
  - `aiMarkerRight.001` ▶ `sizeMarkerRight`
  - `aiMarkerBack.001` ▶ `sizeMarkerBack`

- Adjust the positions of your new size markers so they cover the area of your vehicle. In our example, we just need to move `sizeMarkerBack` a little farther back in the Y-axis.

One final bit of setup that you need to do is define a collision trigger. The collision trigger is a boundary that the AI worker uses to know how to stop if a person, another vehicle, or an object is in the way. The size of this boundary is defined in your vehicle-XML, but it needs an Empty as a reference. Use the Create Empty operator that comes with the GIANTS I3D Exporter add-on to add an Empty at the front center of the vehicle and give it a sensible name like `aiCollisionNode`.

Once you have your collision trigger Empty added, make it a child of your `ai` Empty. Your AI hierarchy within your vehicle should look something like this:

- `ai`
  - `aiCollisionNode`
  - `aiMarkerLeft`
  - `aiMarkerBack`
  - `aiMarkerRight`
  - `sizeMarkerLeft`
  - `sizeMarkerBack`
  - `sizeMarkerRight`

As always, once you have all of your reference nodes in place, be sure to go to the GIANTS I3D Exporter tab in the 3D Viewport's Sidebar and enable the **Node Id** check box for each.

With your references added in Blender, you can re-export your I3D file and hop back into your vehicle-XML file. Within this file, you need to add an `<ai>` tag that ultimately makes use of all the Empties you've added. For our example, the `<ai>` tag should look like this:

```
<ai>
    <needsLowering value="true" />
    <areaMarkers leftNode="aiMarkerLeft" rightNode="aiMarkerRight"
backNode="aiMarkerBack" />
    <collisionTrigger node="aiCollisionNode" width="6.6"
height="2.4" />
    <sizeMarkers leftNode="sizeMarkerLeft"
rightNode="sizeMakerRight" backNote="sizeMarkerBack" />
    <collisionTrigger node="aiCollisionTrigger" />
    <allowTurnBackward value="false" />
    <turningRadiusLimitation rotationJointNode="componentJointDraw
bar" wheelIndices="1 2" />
    <toolReverserDirectionNode node="aiMarkerBack" />
</ai>
```

Aside from pointing to all the reference objects you added in Blender, there are a few more tags and attributes that your mod can make use of. The following is a list of each of these additional tags:

- `<needsLowering>`—If your implement needs to be lowered before it can actively work, add this tag with a `value` attribute set to equal `true`.

- `<allowTurnBackward>`—By default, vehicles aren't configured to be used in reverse. If you want to allow turning in reverse with your vehicle (such as vehicles attached to the 3-point linkage without wheels), add this tag and include a `value` attribute set to `true`.

- `<turnRadiusLimitation>`—Most farm equipment isn't designed to take hard 90-degree turns. Use this tag to help the AI calculate a maximum turn radius. To use this tag, you need to indicate values for the `rotationJointNode` attribute and the index values for the regular wheels on the tool. The `rotationJointNode` attribute refers to a drawbar component (if available) or a regular attacher joint.

- `<toolReverseDirectionNode>`—for tools with wheels that can reverse, include this tag to help the AI do the reversing. You need to include a node at the back center of the vehicle. In this example, the `aiMarkerBack` Empty was re-used. It's worth noting that this tag can only be used if the `<allowTurnBackward>` tag is set to `false`. With this tag set, the vehicle can drive straight backwards to shrink the size of a turn.

If your vehicle is like our example cultivator and meant to be attached to a tow vehicle, there's an additional tag that you should include to handle when the AI worker drives the tool on the street: `<agentAttachment>`. This tag is included in the content of the `<ai>` tag and the attributes in it are used by the AI worker to properly calculate the vehicle size and rotation points. From our example cultivator, the content of the `<ai>` tag looks like this (bold for new content):

```
<ai>
    <needsLowering value="true" />
    <areaMarkers leftNode="aiMarkerLeft" rightNode="aiMarkerRight"
backNode="aiMarkerBack" />
    <collisionTrigger node="aiCollisionNode" width="6.6"
height="2.4" />
    <sizeMarkers leftNode="sizeMarkerLeft"
rightNode="sizeMakerRight" backNote="sizeMarkerBack" />
    <collisionTrigger node="aiCollisionTrigger" />
    <allowTurnBackward value="false" />
    <turningRadiusLimitation rotationJointNode="componentJointDraw
bar" wheelIndices="1 2" />
    <toolReverserDirectionNode node="aiMarkerBack" />
    <agentAttachment jointNode="attacherJoint"
rotCenterWheelIndices="1 2" width="2.9" height="3.6" length="7.5"
lengthOffset="3.25" />
</ai>
```

As you can hopefully see from the example text, the `<agentAttachment>` tag comes with a number of attributes that you can use to pass information to the AI worker. The following is a description of each attribute:

- `jointNode`: This attribute is the name of the main attacher joint while your vehicle is used on the road. If your tool doesn't drive on wheels, then you don't need to include this attribute.

- `rotCenterWheelIndices`: This attribute is a little tricky to describe. It's a list of wheel indices (separated by spaces) that represent the rotation pivot of a "trailer like" tool, such as our example cultivator. As with the `jointNode` attribute, if your tool doesn't drive on wheels, then you shouldn't include this attribute. Alternatively you could use the `rotCenterPosition` attribute to define the rotational center position independent of the wheels.

- `width`: The width of the vehicle while it's in transport mode or driving on the street.

- `height`: The height of the vehicle while being towed.

- `length`: The length of the vehicle while being towed.

- `lengthOffset`: The offset from the vehicle's main component or the rotation pivot, if defined. In our example, the rotation pivot is defined by the wheel indices, so that's our reference for the offset.

NOTE

For turn table trailers, there are agent attachment definitions required for the front and the back part. For reference, have a look at the files for trailers in the base game. In addition, you can use the `gsVehicleDebug ai` command, as covered in Chapter 14, to see the AI agent attachment and AI agent boxes.

As you might imagine, since there's an `<agentAttachment>` tag for towed, or "trailer like" vehicles that are controlled by AI workers, then there should be a tag for tractors and other vehicles that can be driven by the AI helper. That tag is the `<agent>` tag. This tag would also live in the content of the `<ai>` tag and has the following attributes:

- `frontOffset`: This attribute is distance from the `steeringCenterNode` on your vehicle, which is typically the center of the rear wheels, to the steering wheels (typically the front wheels).

- `width`: The width of the vehicle.

- `height`: The height of the vehicle.

- `length`: The length of the vehicle.

- `lengthOffset`: The offset from the vehicle's steering center node or the rotation pivot, if defined.

PUSHING AWAY YOUR CROPS WITH FOLIAGE BENDING NODES

For mods that feature vehicles that can dynamically move through the game, it's important to set up foliage bending. With foliage bending, you can define the area that the machine bends plants, bushes, and similar features on the terrain.

For foliage bending you don't have to add any additional transform groups to your model. You can typically use transform groups or objects you already have in your vehicle.

Then you specify an area around the origin of those objects. For our cultivator example, we need three foliage bending nodes: one for the main body of the vehicle and one for each of the two arms.

With that knowledge, the `<foliageBendingNodes>` tag in your vehicle-XML might look like the following:

```
<foliageBendingNodes>
    <bendingNode minX="-1.35" maxX="1.35" minZ="-3.3" maxZ="1.3"
yOffset="0.6" />
    <bendingNode minX="-0.3" maxX="0.3" minZ="1.3" maxZ="4.5"
yOffset="-0.6" />
    <bendingNode minX="-0.3" maxX="2.95" minZ="-2.35" maxZ="1.0"
yOffset="-0.5" node="armLeft" />
    <bendingNode minX="-2.85" maxX="0.3" minZ="-2.35" maxZ="1.0"
yOffset="-0.5" node="armRight" />
</foliageBendingNodes>
```

Of course, it's often difficult to visualize these minimum and maximum values. Your best option is to save your vehicle-XML file and load your mod in the game. From there you can expand the console and use the gsVehicleDebug command. With the command entered, you can use the `gsVehicleDebug attributes` command in the in-game console and Farming Simulator draws the bounding boxes for each of your reference areas, including working areas and foliage bending lines (if those lines aren't visible, try pressing *F5* to enable debug lines).

Looking at the foliage bending lines, they should appear in the colors green and red. The green area activates foliage bending whereas the red area sets the bending to 100%. Just make sure that your red box covers the vehicle boundaries.

CREATING VISUAL EFFECTS FOR YOUR VEHICLE

One of the best ways to add realism to your vehicle mod is to have it kick up dust and affect the ground while it's working. We refer to these features as visual effects.

Adding a Particle System

For instance, say you want to have dust come from the ground while your vehicle is working. This is a particle effect. Particle effects require some kind of geometry to spawn from, often referred to as an emitter. For Farming Simulator, the situation is the same. You need to create an emitter object of some sort for your vehicle.

In Blender, use the following steps:

1. Ensure that your 3D cursor is at the world origin (**Object ▶ Snap ▶ Cursor to World Origin**). This way any new objects are added at the zero point on your vehicle.

2. Add a new Empty to your scene (**Add ▶ Empty ▶ Plain Axes**), name it `effects`, and move it into your vehicle hierarchy at the same level as your `workAreas` and `ai`

Empties. The `effects` Empty serves as a transform group for holding any objects related to visual effects.

3. Add a mesh plane to your scene (**Add ▶ Mesh ▶ Plane**), name it `dustEmitter`, and make it a child of your `effects` Empty.

4. In Edit mode, adjust the geometry of your `dustEmitter` plane to roughly fit the working area of your vehicle as shown in Figure 7.3.

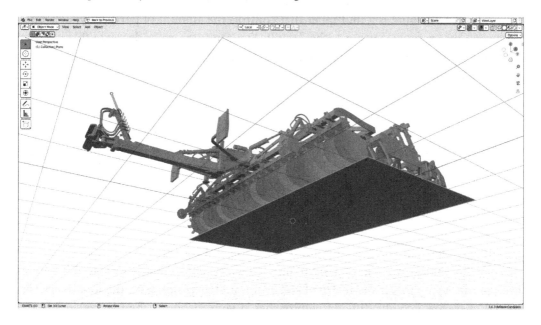

FIGURE 7.3   Add a plane to your vehicle hierarchy that will serve as your particle emitter.

5. Add an I3D mapping for your `dustEmitter` by enabling the **Node Id** check box in the GIANTS I3D Exporter tab of the 3D Viewport's Sidebar.

6. Still in the GIANTS I3D Exporter tab, switch to the Attributes section and use the **Physics** drop-down menu to choose *EmitterShape*.

7. Scroll to the bottom of the GIANTS I3D Exporter tab and click **Apply Selected** to apply the pre-defined *EmitterShape* attributes to your `dustEmitter` object.

8. Switch back to the Export section of the GIANTS I3D Exporter tab and re-export so your I3D file and vehicle-XML file are up to date.

Now that you have geometry to emit particles, you can open your vehicle-XML in GIANTS Studio and add a `<workParticles>` tag, like so:

```
<workParticles>
    <particle>
```

```
        <node node="dustEmitter" refNodeIndex="1"
particleType="SOIL_SMOKE" emitCountScale="1" />
    </particle>
</workParticles>
```

The key attributes in the <node> tag in this setup are the `particleType` and `emit-CountScale` attributes. The `particleType` attribute uses a specific text string that lets the game engine know which particle system to use for your specified emitter. The `emit-CountScale` attribute is a multiplier that controls the amount of particles your emitter produces. Our example is using 1, the default. You can increase or decrease this value for your own mod. A word of caution, though: the more you increase `emitCountScale`, the higher the impact on in-game performance.

> **TIP**
>
> Because of the way that the <workParticles> tag in vehicle-XML file is set up, you can use these same steps to add multiple particle systems to your vehicle. You just need to add another <node> tag.

Adding Soil Effects

Ground dust adds one level of realism to a vehicle, but for tools that actually affect the soil (plows, cultivators, etc.), it's good to have an effect that shows that the tool is moving through the earth. This is the realm of soil effects and, depending on the tool that you've created, there are a couple different approaches at your disposal. The two covered in this section are particle-based sweep effects and custom effect array textures.

Using Particle-Based Effects

In a vehicle like a regular cultivator there are plow-shaped parts (sweeps) that push the soil as they go through it. By spawning a particle system at the front of each of these parts, you can give the effect of dirt being thrown up as the tool moves through it. To set up this effect, you need to add a reference Empty for every sweep in the vehicle. That Empty should be added to your vehicle hierarchy as a child of the `effects` Empty and named something sensible like `sweepEffectNode01`. As for positioning, you don't need to be precise, but your `sweepEffectNode01` Empty should be located near its corresponding mesh, closer to the front of the part so the effect shows as it's tearing through the ground. Give your new Empty a node ID from the GIANTS I3D Exporter and re-export.

Now you can add this effect to your vehicle-XML by nesting an <effect> tag within the <workParticles> tag that you've already created. With your previous smoke emitter particle system, your <workParticles> tag should look like this:

```
<workParticles>
    <effect workAreaIndex="1">
        <effectNode effectClass="CultivatorMotionPathEffect"
effectType="CULTIVATOR" linkNode="sweepEffectNode01">
```

```
        <motionPathEffects textureFileName="$data/effects/
cultivator/arrays/sharedCultivatorSweepArray01.dds" numRows="20"
rowLength="18" minFade="0.07" isCultivatorSweepEffect="true" />
        </effectNode>
    </effect>
    <particle>
        <node node="dustEmitter" refNodeIndex="1"
particleType="SOIL_SMOKE" emitCountScale="2.5" />
    </particle>
</workParticles>
```

The end of the <workParticles> tag is the same as before. The main difference is the addition of the <effect> tag. That tag starts by specifying a particular work area using the workAreaIndex attribute. If your cultivator only has a single work area (similar to the one in our example), this value remains at 1. Within the <effects> tag, the <effectNode> tag, and specifically the linkNode attribute of that tag is used to reference the Empty you added in Blender. The other attributes, effectClass and effectType use keywords that the game uses to know which prebuilt effect to use.

Within the content of the <effectNode> tag is one further tag, <motionPathEffects>. For simplicity's sake, you can take advantage of a built-in texture that already comes with Farming Simulator using the $data variable to point to the Farming Simulator game folder.

> **NOTE**
>
> In the <motionPathEffects> tag, it's important to note that if you're using the default sharedCultivatorSweepArray01.dds, the numRows, rowLength, and minFade attributes should have the shown values. For custom effect array textures, the values can be different as you can see in the next section.

With that one example complete, we would need to repeat this process for each sweep in your cultivator, adding a new <effect> tag and its content tags for each one. We'd also have to place a reference Empty in our Blender file for each disc as well.

Setting up Custom Effect Array Textures
In contrast to the regular cultivator described in the previous section, our example cultivator is a disc harrow, so the standard sweep effects don't look right on that tool. Instead, you can use a different approach. Rather than using a particle system, you can use a custom array texture to produce the necessary effect. To let the game engine know where to place this effect, and generate the necessary textures, you need to add some curve objects in Blender and use a feature in the GIANTS I3D Exporter add-on to generate effect transform groups that represent the moving path for each particle. Those transform groups are then exported as a DDS texture animation file. That file is then referenced in your vehicle-XML file. While that process may seem a little complex, it really isn't. Use the following steps to do it yourself on the left arm of our example cultivator:

1. In Blender, select the `armLeft` mesh object on the cultivator file.

2. Use the Create Empty operator in the Tools section of GIANTS I3D Exporter tab of the 3D Viewport's sidebar to create a new Empty in the hierarchy, positioned at the same location as the left arm mesh's origin.

3. Name your new Empty `cultivatorEffectLeftNode`. This Empty serves as a transform group to hold your disc harrow effect objects.

4. With your `cultivatorEffectLeftNode` Empty selected, use the Create Empty operator again to create a new child Empty. Name this Empty `cultivatorEffectLeftArray _ ignore`. The _ ignore suffix ensures that this Empty and its children are skipped during export. The reason is because you're using those objects to generate textures, rather than exporting them directly.

5. Select your `cultivatorEffectLeftNode` Empty again and use the Create Empty operator to create one more Empty, named `curvesLeft _ ignore`. This Empty serves as a transform group to hold the curves that are used to generate your effect.

6. Add a new NURBS curve object (**Add ▶ Curve ▶ Nurbs Curve**) and make it a child of your `curvesLeft _ ignore` Empty. Since this curve is used to generate your effect, you can leave it with its default name.

7. In Object mode, move your new NURBS curve so its origin aligns with the outer edge of the cultivator's arm. This step doesn't have to be precise; it's a rough placement.

8. Tab into Edit mode on your curve object and edit it so it matches the angle of the closest disc, with an arc bending up to the disc, as shown in Figure 7.4. Tab back into Object mode when you're done.

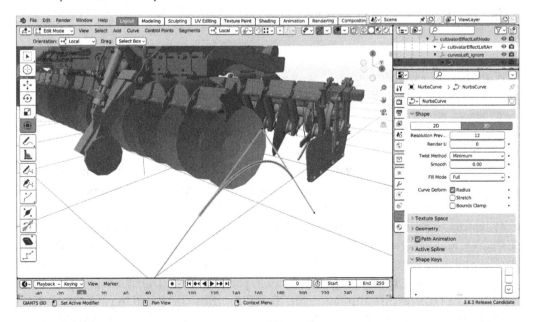

FIGURE 7.4   Edit your NURBs curve to match the angle of your outer disc, arcing up toward the disc (curve thickness was added in this image for visibility; your curve should have no thickness).

With your first curve placed, you now need to duplicate it and create an array of these curves, with at least one for every disc in the cultivator. This sounds like a tedious process, but it's quite fast if you use Blender's Repeat Last operator functionality. Use these steps:

1. Select your NURBS curve object.

2. Duplicate it with *Shift*+D. The Duplicate operator automatically puts you in a move state. Press *X* to constrain your curve object to the X-axis and move it inward toward the center of the cultivator so it lines up with the next disc.

3. Use **Edit ▶ Repeat Last** (*Shift*+R) to repeat your duplicate and move operation on your new NURBS curve. Your third NURBS curve should immediately appear aligned with the third disc on your cultivator.

4. Repeat step 3 until you have a number of curve objects matching one of the pre-defined effects in the game. For example, cultivator effects are available for 1, 3, 10, 20, 30, 40, 50, and 60 rows. So you would need to have the same number of curves as one of those values. For reference, you can check the files in your Farming Simulator installation at `data/effects/cultivator/cultivatorEffects.xml` and look for the `numRows` variable.

With all of your curves placed, your next step is to start generating your effect. The work for this step is done from the GIANTS I3D Exporter tab in the 3D Viewport's sidebar. In the Tools section, there's a button labeled **Object Data from Curve**. Click this button and a new panel named GIANTS Motion Path Tool appears at the bottom of the tab. You're going to use this panel to generate a bunch of Empties based on the geometry of the curves you just created. Use the following steps:

1. Select all of your recently created NURBS curves.

2. In the GIANTS Motion Path Tool panel, click the **Load Selected** button to populate the list in this panel with all of your selected NURBS curve objects.

3. Make a note of the value in the **Amount** field. For this example, we're leaving it at its default value, but it's necessary to know it for your vehicle-XML file. This value needs to match the number in the predefined effect. As with the number of curves in the preceding steps where you looked at the `numRows` variable in `cultiva-torEffects.xml`, there's a `rowLength` variable in that same file that should be used here.

4. In the **Group Name** text field, type `cultivatorEffectLeftArray`. This is the same name as the Empty created earlier *without* the `_ignore` suffix.

5. Click the **Create** button at the bottom of the panel. Depending on the number of curves you have, you may need to wait a minute or two for the results. When done, this operator creates a set of Empties along the path of each curve and adds them as children of the `cultivatorEffectLeftArray_ignore` Empty.

TIP

Assuming that the objects for your array are the only NURBS curve objects in your scene, you can quickly select them all by selecting one of them and then using **Select ▶ Select Grouped ▶ Type** from the 3D Viewport's header menu. You can alternatively select them all from the Outliner. Of course, if you have different sets for the left and right arms of your vehicle (for example), you'll have to deselect or hide the curves for the other side.

After the motion path tool has created all of the Empties for your effect, you can go to the Export section of the GIANTS I3D Exporter tab in the 3D Viewport's sidebar and click the **Export All** button at the bottom. You may notice that the export process takes a little longer this time. That's because the exporter is also using your array to generate a DDS texture in your mod folder. When it's done, you can check your mod folder and there should be a file named `cultivatorEffectLeftArray.dds` in there. Now you can reference this file in your vehicle-XML within the `<workParticles>` tag, like so:

```
<workParticles>
    <effect workAreaIndex="1">
        <effectNode effectClass="CultivatorMotionPathEffect" effec
tType="CULTIVATOR"                                    linkNode="cu
ltivatorEffectLeftNode">
            <motionPathEffect textureFilename="cultivatorEffectLef
tArray.dds" numRows="60" rowLength="18" minFade="0.07" />
        </effectNode>
    </effect>
</workParticles>
```

The critical tag in this example is the `<motionPathEffect>` tag, which has a `textureFileName` attribute that points to the DDS texture you just generated. The `numRows` attribute should match the number of NURBS curves you created while the `rowLength` attribute should match the value of the Amount parameter that's set in the GIANTS motion path tool. Both of these values need to match the corresponding numRows and rowLength values in the predefined effect. Custom amounts are not allowed. With this added to your vehicle-XML, you should be able to test your cultivator in-game and see the effect appear on the discs on the left arm. Once you have it working, you can use this same process for the discs on the other side, as well as the rollers on each side.

SUMMARY

And so endeth a monster chapter on adding functionality to your vehicle mod. You started by learning how to configure wheels (and wheel-like parts) in your mod. From there, you defined the working area for your vehicle so the game engine knows how it affects the terrain. Naturally this extended to the addition of foliage bending nodes to further effect vegetation as your vehicle goes over it. And finally, to give life to your vehicle while it's working, you added visual effects to the working parts of your mod. Whew. Great work.

In the next chapter, we go a bit more in-depth on adding animations to your vehicle mod.

CHAPTER 8

Animating Your Vehicle

Complex farming equipment often has moving parts that need to be animated. It could be that arms fold up on harvesting equipment, support arms or feet lower when the vehicle is stored, or the moving lattice on a scissor lift. In any case, you need to have the ability to control those animations. In contrast to the linear keyframe-style animation that's used in film and television, GIANTS Engine relies on your vehicle-XML for controlling your animations. Getting into it, this chapter starts with setting up a basic animation by first walking through setup on animating attachable parts. From there, we move forward to animating the folding process, including the movement of linked parts. As an additional bonus, we take a high-level view of animating your vehicle in Blender to get a sense of the movement and timing without needing to export all the way to Farming Simulator. Finally, the chapter ends by showing how to get sounds to play when your animations are triggered in the game.

In this chapter:

- Setting up basic animation

- Controlling the folding process

- Defining moving parts

- Including sounds with your animations

- Previsualizing animations by animating in Blender

TECHNICAL REQUIREMENTS

The majority of the work for this chapter happens on your vehicle-XML file, so you'll need GIANTS Studio or a text editor. For checking or adjusting your vehicle hierarchy, you should have Blender with the GIANTS I3D Exporter add-on installed. And if you want to test how these animations work, it's best to test your mod in-game.

In an ideal world, you can do everything in this chapter using your own vehicle file. However, all of the examples from the cultivator example that we've been working with in other chapters. If you haven't downloaded that file, you can get it here:

DOI: 10.1201/9781032659497-8

https://gdn.giants-software.com/blenderBook

SETTING UP BASIC ANIMATION

Farming equipment typically has moving parts. In addition to rotating pieces like wheels (as covered in Chapter 7), many vehicles have arms that fold for storage. Folding often involves multiple moving parts that rotate on hinges or slide along cylinders. Rather than keyframing these kinds of animations in an external tool like Blender, the animations for your vehicle mod are all defined in your vehicle-XML file. Any part of your mod can be animated, including non-visible meshes, like collision meshes.

As a simple example, using our cultivator that we've been working with, we animate the support feet that are part of the cultivator's mesh. This way, your machine has some support structure and is therefore prevented from sinking into the ground. For this specific example, you start by adding a `<support>` tag within your already existing `<attachable>` tag. Think of the `<support>` tag as a trigger function for running your animation. Using the content of the `<attachable>` tag from Chapter 6, your updated `<attachable>` tag content should look like this (new text in bold):

```
<attachable>
    <inputAttacherJoints>
        <inputAttacherJoint node="attacherJoint"
jointType="implement" topReferenceNode="topReferenceNode">
            <distanceToGround lower="0.6" upper="1.1" />
        </inputAttacherJoint>
    </inputAttacherJoints>
    <support animationName="moveSupport" />
</attachable>
```

The `<support>` tag uses an `animationName` attribute to specify an animation named `moveSupport`. Of course, that animation doesn't yet exist. You define that now by adding an <animations> tag in your vehicle-XML. For this example, the content of that tag looks like this:

```
<animations>
    <animation name="moveSupport">
        <part node="supportFeet" startTime="0" endTime="0.75"
startTrans="0 0.88746 2.095" endTrans="0 0.5 2.095" />
        <part node="supportFeetLockBolts" startTime="0.00"
endTime="0.01" startVisibility="true" endVisibility="false" />
        <part node="supportFeetLockBolts" startTime="0.74"
endTime="0.75" startVisibility="false" endVisibility="true" />
    </animation>
</animations>
```

Teasing apart the details in this bit of text, you're using the name attribute within the <animation> tag to tell the game engine that you have an animation named moveSupport. This is the same name you referenced in the <support> tag within <attachable>. Now, within the <animation> tag, you have <part> tags that define the movement you want on specifically named nodes in your exported I3D file. The breakdown of the attributes in this tag is as follows:

- node—The text you enter as the value for this node is a named node ID in your I3D file. In this case, we have our visual support feet. These meshes also include a compound child collision named supportCollisionLeft.

- startTime—This number is the time, in seconds, that you want the animation of this part to start. Typically, you want the animation to begin immediately, so you want this value to be 0. However, if you want a delay, set the value higher.

- endTime—Corresponding with the startTime attribute, the endTime attribute is when you want the animation of that part to complete, in seconds. This value should be greater than the value in the startTime attribute.

- startTrans—The startTrans attribute defines the location in X, Y, and Z coordinates that the object you're animating should be in when it starts. This location is in local coordinates, so it's important to pay attention to these values. Recall that in Blender, the Z-axis is the vertical axis, while in Farming Simulator, it's the Y-axis. To get the correct values, it's a good idea to open your I3D file in the GIANTS Editor to check translation distances and check the direction of your axes. In this example, the origin for the supportCollisionLeft object is at the local origin.

- endTrans—Similar to startTrans, the endTrans attribute dictates where the object should translate to when it's done animating. You often arrive at this value by a bit of trial and error, but you can try to do some measuring in Blender or GIANTS Editor.

In addition to the attributes used in this example, there are a handful of additional attributes at your disposal when creating your animation. Here's a list of what's available:

- startRot/endRot—Like the startTrans and endTrans attributes in the example for controlling the translation of your part, the startRot and endRot attributes control the X, Y, and Z rotation for your part in degrees.

- startScale/endScale—Rounding out the full suite of transforms, the startScale and endScale values give you animation control of the X, Y, and Z scales for your part. The values you use for this attribute are multipliers, so a value of 1 1 1 is the original scale while 0.5 0.5 0.5 is half the original size.

- startVisibility/endVisibility—Set the values for this attribute to be true or false, based on the visibility you want the object to have at the start and end of the animation.

- tangentType—The tangentType attribute gives you control over the timing of your animation. Set this attribute to spline to have a little bit of acceleration and deceleration on your movement. Use linear for more jarring and abrupt movement.

- componentJointIndex—This attribute defines the index of the joint definition in the base <components> tag of your vehicle-XML. This attribute is required to use the limit attributes covered next. The animation attributes (starting and ending rotation and scale) refer to the defined node attribute, whereas limits refer to this componentJointIndex attribute.

- startTransLimit/endTransLimit—This attribute lets you change the translation limit of the defined component joint as mentioned in the previous bullet. The limit is defined in meters and opens in positive and negative directions the same way. For example, a limit of 0 0.5 0 allows your component to move 50 cm up or down.

- startRotLimit/endRotLimit—This attribute is similar to the translation limit we covered. This limit opens the rotation of the component joint around a certain axis. The value is defined in degrees and opens in both directions by the same value. On our example cultivator we use this limit for the freely rotating drawbar.

IMPORTANT

All translations and rotations are done using the local coordinate system. What I mean is that a part's coordinate space is defined by the parent of that object. This is in contrast to Blender, which only shows global coordinate values for your selected object.

CONTROLLING THE FOLDING PROCESS

One of the most common animations for vehicles is the ability to fold parts, often for storage. Assuming that you've set up your vehicle properly in Blender so it exports with a proper vehicle hierarchy in the I3D format, there's no additional setup that you need to do in Blender. All of your configuration and animation take place in your vehicle-XML.

The process starts by adding a `<foldable>` tag in your vehicle-XML. Not only does this tag let the game engine know that your vehicle has foldable parts, but it also serves as the trigger mechanism for naming your animation. The content for our cultivator example might look something like this:

```
<foldable>
    <foldingConfigurations>
        <foldingConfiguration>
            <foldingParts startMoveDirection="1"
foldMiddleAnimTime="0.1">
                <foldingPart animationName="folding"
speedScale="1" />
            </foldingParts>
        </foldingConfiguration>
    </foldingConfigurations>
</foldable>
```

At first blush, this example may appear to have some pretty excessive nesting in order to name a single animation. However, this nesting is for good reason. Some vehicles can have multiple independent folding configurations. For instance, you may have a vehicle with optional arms that the player can choose from the shop. You would need to have multiple `<foldingConfiguration>` tags to support those animations.

As it pertains to the actual folding animation, just like the `<support>` tag in the support example at the start of this section, the `<foldingPart>` tag has an `animationName` attribute that references an animation, which ultimately is defined in the `<animations>` tag. The only difference is that the `<foldingPart>` tag in this example also incorporates a `speedScale` attribute that serves as a multiplier for the overall speed of the named animation. Of course, the default speed scale is 1, so if you want the animation to move at its originally defined speed, the `speedScale` attribute is not necessary. That said, it doesn't hurt to include it, and keeping it in your vehicle-XML gives you the ability to more easily tweak and refine the timing of your animation later.

In addition to the speedScale attribute, there are a few more attributes that you can specify in the `<foldingParts>` tag:

- `startMoveDirection`—This attribute defines the initial spawn state for the vehicle. If you set this attribute to -1, the vehicle will use the animation state at its earliest start time. If you set `startMoveDirection` to 1, then your vehicle's spawning position is what it looks like at the end of its animation.

- `startAnimTime`—With this attribute you can specify the start state even more precisely, giving you the option to define a spawning pose that's partially through the animated sequence.

- turnOnFoldDirection—The turnOnFoldDirection attribute defines in which direction the tool is unfolded and can be set to either -1 or 1. The value you choose for this attribute determines the text shown in the help menu and the vehicle schema display. By default, it's the opposite of startMoveDirection.

- foldMiddleAnimTime—By using this attribute, the folding animation is divided into folding (press *X* in-game) and lowering (press *V* in-game). The value for this attribute should be set to a number between 0 and 1 (but not equal to either). Consider it a percentage of the overall animation time defined in the <animation> tag (covered next). If this attribute is not defined, your vehicle will have just a plain folding animation when you press *X* in-game.

In our cultivator example, there are quite a few folding parts. Not only do we have left and right wheel arms, but there is also a back arm that's used to actually lower the vehicle. Then there are the main arms on the left and right. Furthermore, the rollers on each arm have their own secondary arms that also get folded. Fortunately, all of this folding is pretty easy to coordinate in the <animations> tag. With modifications to account for this movement, the content of our updated <animations> tag looks like this (new parts in bold):

```
<animations>
    <animation name="moveSupport">
        <part node="supportFeet" startTime="0" endTime="0.75"
startTrans="0 0.88746 2.095" endTrans="0 0.5 2.095" />
        <part node="supportFeetLockBolts" startTime="0.00"
endTime="0.01" startVisibility="true" endVisibility="false" />
        <part node="supportFeetLockBolts" startTime="0.74"
endTime="0.75" startVisibility="false" endVisibility="true" />
    </animation>
    <animation name="folding">
        <part node="backArm" startTime="0.0" endTime="1.0"
startRot="0 0 0" endRot="-25 0 0" />
        <part node="wheelArmLeft" startTime="1.0" endTime="1.5"
startRot="-16 0 0"  endRot="0 0 0" />
        <part node="wheelArmRight" startTime="1.0" endTime="1.5"
startRot="-16 0 0"  endRot="0 0 0" />
        <part node="armLeftBackArm" startTime="1.0" endTime="1.5"
startRot="4.7 0 0"  endRot="0 0 0" />
        <part node="armLeftRollerArm" startTime="1.0"
endTime="1.5" startRot="-4.7 0 0" endRot="0 0 0" />
        <part node="armRightBackArm" startTime="1.0" endTime="1.5"
startRot="4.7 0 0"  endRot="0 0 0" />
        <part node="armRightRollerArm" startTime="1.0"
endTime="1.5" startRot="-4.7 0 0" endRot="0 0 0" />
```

```
        <part node="armLeft" startTime="2.0" endTime="9"
startRot="0 0 0" endRot="0 0 90" />
        <part node="armRight" startTime="1.5" endTime="8.5"
startRot="0 0 0" endRot="0 0 -90" />
    </animation>
</animations>
```

In this updated section, you have a new `<animation>` tag with a `name` attribute set to `folding`, the same name referenced in the `<foldable>` tag. Within this tag, as with the earlier `moveSupport` example, there are individual `<part>` tags for each part that's supposed to move in this animation. You're animating the rotation on the `armLeft` and `armRight` parts with this bit of XML.

DEFINING MOVING PARTS

In meatspace farming equipment, there are typically smaller parts (arms and hydraulics, for example) that do the actual work of lifting, rotating, or otherwise moving the larger parts of the vehicle. In the virtual space of a game, rotating large parts is as easy as adjusting a few parameters, as shown in the previous section. However, for realism, you still want those smaller parts to move. So, in effect, we have a situation where the game behavior is the inverse of what happens in reality. In the game, we animate the large part and treat the movement of smaller parts as dependencies of that large animation.

Specific to Farming Simulator, there's a pretty specific definition of "moving parts" as it pertains to animations. In general moving tools are manually controlled by player input or they're triggered by another animation, such as folding. Those moving tools then, in turn, trigger an update of a moving part, such as a hydraulic cylinder. With moving parts, you can update a variety of other parts, including wheels, component joints, attacher joints, and even other moving parts. Also, you can use moving parts to align specific nodes to others. This feature is particularly useful in the case where you have expanding and compressing hydraulic cylinders. And rounding out the full capabilities of moving parts, they can also have chains of dependent parts that allow them to update one another.

Setting Up Hydraulics

A commonly occurring moving part in farming equipment is hydraulic pistons, used in meatspace machines as actuators to do the "heavy lifting" of moving large parts. In Farming Simulator, the hydraulics on your vehicle are moving parts that are dependent on the movement of the large pieces that they're attached to. To get your hydraulic pistons to work, there is a little bit of setup you need to do to your model in Blender. Specifically, the parts of your hydraulic system need to be separated into two base objects: the hydraulic cylinder and the hydraulic piston. Of course if you have multiple sets of hydraulic actuators, each of them needs to be separated into these two base objects.

In addition, you need to create one reference transform group per piston that you can refer to from your vehicle-XML to control the movement and animation of your hydraulic parts. As with previous examples, the transform groups are defined in Blender as named Empties in your vehicle hierarchy. Most critically, these Empties need to be correctly aligned with the orientation of your hydraulics so the movement looks correct and you don't end up with a piston that intersects with its cylinder at an odd angle.

Getting these orientations correct in Blender can be a tedious process using just Blender's built-in tools. Fortunately, the GIANTS I3D Exporter add-on has some convenience operators that help with this process. Let's assume that you have a single hydraulic assembly that's already been separated into two objects, `armLeftHydraulic` and `armLeftHydraulicPunch`. Use the following process to correctly align the orientations of your parts and then position and orient your reference Empties:

1. Select your cylinder object and switch into Edit mode.

2. Select the geometry that the cylinder is supposed to rotate about. Typically this is some kind of cylinder mesh that's meant to be a pin.

3. From the GIANTS I3D Exporter tab in the Sidebar, go to the Tools section and click the **SelectionToOrigin** button to set your object origin for your cylinder at the center of your current selection.

4. Return back to Object mode.

5. Select your piston object and perform steps 2–4 on it.

6. In Object mode, select your piston object and *Shift*+`select` your cylinder object. This order of selection makes your cylinder object the current active object.

7. Make your piston object a child of the cylinder object (**Object ▶ Parent ▶ Object**). Alternatively, you can drag and drop from the Scene display type in the Outliner.

8. *Shift*+`select` your piston object to keep it in your selection set while also making it the active object.

9. From the Tools section of the GIANTS I3D Exporter tab, click the **AlignYAxis** button. This button is a shortcut to quickly have the local Y-axis of any selected object aligned to the active object. In this case, you're aligning the origin of the cylinder to point toward the piston. And since the piston is a child of the cylinder, the operator also aligns the piston's origin to match.

10. With your piston object selected, go back to the Tools section of the GIANTS I3D Exporter tab and click the **Create Empty** button to create an Empty that's a child of your piston. This new Empty also shares the exact same orientation as your piston.

11. Name your new Empty something reasonable, like `armLeftHydraulicRef`.

12. Be sure that you have added node IDs for all the parts of your hydraulic assembly, including the mesh objects and the Empties.

With the parts of your hydraulics assembly correctly set up, you can move forward to controlling the animation of that assembly in your vehicle-XML. The process starts by adding a new tag, `<cylindered>`. Within this tag, the controls for your hydraulic assembly are nestled in a `<movingTools>` tag and a `<movingParts>` tag. The content of the `<movingTools>` tag defines which nodes have their movement dependent on the movement of the animated parts. In this example, that would be the hydraulic cylinder. The `<movingParts>` tag gets more specific about the actual referenced movement. The contents of these tags look like this:

```
<cylindered>
    <movingTools>
        <movingTool node="armLeft">
            <dependentPart node="armLeftHydraulic" />
        </movingTool>
    </movingTools>
    <movingParts>
        <movingPart node="armLeftHydraulic" referencePoint="armLef
tHydraulicRef" referenceFrame="armLeftHydraulicRef">
            <translatingPart node="armLeftHydraulicPunch" />
        </movingPart>
    </movingParts>
</cylindered>
```

Breaking down the text, the animation for our hydraulics assembly is triggered by the movement of the armLeft node, as indicated by the node attribute of the `<moving-Tool>` tag. This is the node that's folded in the preceding section. Our hydraulic cylinder is listed with that tag as a dependent part using the `<dependentPart>` tag. With that dependency chain defined, you can move down to the `<movingParts>` tag and note that within that tag, there's a `<movingPart>` tag that also references the cylinder object. And just as important, that tag has the following two attributes:

- referencePoint—This attribute refers to a node in your vehicle that defines the X and Z rotation of your moving part.

- referenceFrame—This attribute refers to a node in the vehicle that defines the Y rotation of your part.

NOTE

The axes listed in the preceding bullets refer to the axes as they are in Blender, not in the game.

Because in our case the hydraulics assembly is always pointing along the same angle to the object named in the `referencePoint` attribute, we can specify the same node in the `referenceFrame` attribute as well. That said, depending on the movement of the `referencePoint` node in relation to your moving part, you may still need a custom `referenceFrame` attribute. Basically, you have to ensure that the moving part is never pointing outside of the range of a hemisphere defined by the `referenceFrame` node. If it does, then the part will flip. So if you find your moving part flipping in-game, chances are good that you need to add a custom `referenceFrame` to fix that. Have a look at Figure 8.1 to get an understanding of how the reference frame helps define the valid rotation range.

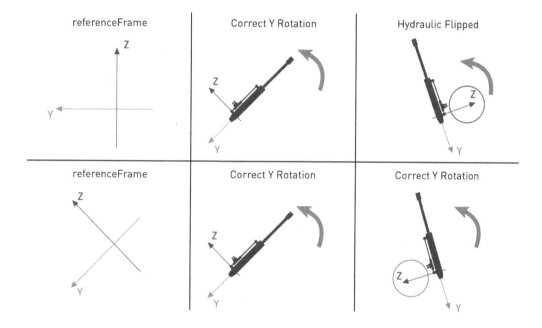

FIGURE 8.1   Use a `referenceFrame` node to specify the valid rotation range for your hydraulics.

The last key piece in this code is the `<translatingPart>` tag. This tag indicates that the specified node (in this example, the hydraulic piston) is translated along its local Y-axis when the moving part is updated. With this configuration, your hydraulic piston should move into and out of the hydraulic cylinder as the left arm of the cultivator is folded and unfolded.

Setting Up Moving Arms

Hydraulics aren't the only moving parts to take into consideration. Often there are also lever arms and other assemblies that move along as dependent animations relative to the large movement of the main animation. These additional moving parts and linkages need to be accounted for as well. Fortunately, the process for moving arms is nearly identical to that of hydraulics. The only difference is the type of dependent movement you're describing. All of this work still happens within the `<cylindered>` tag in your vehicle-XML.

Our example cultivator doesn't have these kinds of moving linkages, but other vehicles do. For this scenario, let's assume that you have a vehicle with some moving arms that are also triggered by the folding action of the left arm. We'll also assume that you've already separated the parts of the linkage into parts and added the necessary reference Empties to your vehicle hierarchy. Your <cylindered> tag content may include the following bold tags:

```
<cylindered>
    <movingTools>
        <movingTool node="armLeft">
            <dependentPart node="armLeftPart01" />
        </movingTool>
    </movingTools>
    <movingParts>
        <movingPart node="armLeftPart01" localReferencePoint="armL
eftPart02" referencePoint="armLeftPart02Ref" referenceFrame="armLe
ftPart01RefFrame">
            <dependentPart node="armLeftPart02" />
        </movingPart>
        <movingPart node="armLeftPart02" referencePoint="armLeftPa
rt02Ref" referenceFrame="armLeftPart02RefFrame" />
    </movingParts>
</cylindered>
```

In the <movingTools> tag, you added another dependent part named armLeft-Part01. Then, in the <movingParts> tag, a new <movingPart> tag is added for that armLeftPart01 object. This is where the dependency chain gets a little complex. Notice that there's an additional localReferencePoint attribute that points to another object named armLeftPart02. That's a second-arm linkage in this chain of dependencies. By setting it as a local reference, the movement of the two objects is bound together. Also take note that although this moving part is pointing to the arm-LeftPart02Ref transform group as the referencePoint attribute, it uses its own armLeftPart01RefFrame transform group for the referenceFrame attribute. And to complete the chain, the content of this tag lists armLeftPart02 in a <dependentPart> tag which, in turn, requires that you add a specific <movingPart> tag for armLeftPart02 with its own transform groups for referencePoint and referenceFrame.

TIP

Reading all of this as plain text or even seeing it in images can be a bit confusing. In fact, the only way to check if it's working is by testing the animation from within Farming Simulator. Technically, you can previsualize the movement a bit by setting up an Armature object in Blender with an IK constraint, but that's a bit out of scope for this book.

When you have a properly-configured set of moving arms, they should move in coordination with the part that drives all of the movement. In this example, when the `armLeft` object is rotated, the reference nodes move with it, and those nodes drive the rotation on `armLeftPart1` and `armLeftPart2`. Figure 8.2 shows a visualization of how this configuration behaves.

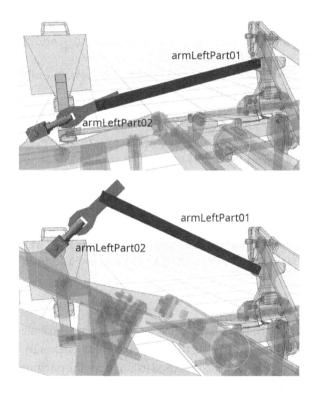

FIGURE 8.2 At the top, our example moving arms before the `armLeft` object is rotated, and at the bottom, those same arms after rotation.

INCLUDING SOUNDS WITH YOUR ANIMATIONS

For a fully interactive mod, it's useful to include sounds with the animations of your vehicle. Fortunately, you don't have to go out and record your own farming equipment sounds unless you really want to. You can take advantage of the sound templates that ship with Farming Simulator. You can find the template's XML file at `C:/Program Files (x86)/Farming Simulator/data/sounds/soundTemplates.xml`. Use the named items within the `<template>` tags in that file as references in your vehicle-XML.

To use a sound with an animation, you include it within the corresponding `<animation>` tag within the overall `<animations>` tag. As an example, say you want to use the `defaultHydraulicSmall` sound template and have it play during the folding animation in our existing example. Your added tags may look like this:

```
<animations>
    <animation name="moveSupport">
        <part node="supportLeft" startTime="0" endTime="0.5"
startTrans="0 0 0" endTrans="0 -0.385 0" />
        <part node="supportRight" startTime="0" endTime="0.5"
startTrans="0 0 0" endTrans="0 -0.385 0" />
    </animation>
    <animation name="folding">
        <part node="armLeft" startTime="0.2" endTime="3"
startRot="0 -90 0" endRot="0 -90 90" tangentType="spline" />
        <part node="armRight" startTime="0.4" endTime="3.2"
startRot="0 -90 0" endRot="-90 -90 0" tangentType="spline" />
        <part node="groundReferenceNode" startTime="0" endTime="1"
startTrans="0 0 1" endTrans="0 1.5 1" />
        <sound template="defaultHydraulicSmall" startTime="0.2"
endTime="3.2" volumeScale="0.1" pitchScale="1.3" />
    </animation>
</animations>
```

Just like with animated parts, the `startTime` and `endTime` attributes are specified in seconds. In addition, you also have two further attributes, `pitchScale` and `volumeScale`. As their names imply, these attributes can be used to attenuate the pitch and volume of the sound from the template. Optionally, you can also add a `direction` attribute. Set the `direction` equal to `1`, and the sound plays when the animation is run in the positive direction. If you set the `direction` equal to `-1`, the sound plays when the animation is run in reverse.

You also have the ability to play a "one-shot" sound. For example, when you reach the end of an animation sequence, you need some kind of metallic impact sound to play. For that kind of scenario, you use the same `<sound>` tag with a `template` attribute, but the only other attribute you need is `startTime`. If you don't specify an `endTime` attribute, the sound will play once at that time and then stop.

PREVISUALIZING ANIMATIONS BY ANIMATING IN BLENDER

When you're trying to create the animations for your mod, it's critical to get a good sense of what the timing looks like on those animations. However, all of your timing is managed from your vehicle-XML file. The work of building animations is an iterative process where you make little tweaks and then watch the animation to check the movement and timing. That means the general workflow looks something like this:

1. Add `<animations>` and `<movingParts>` tags in your vehicle-XML with your best guess for timing.

2. Launch Farming Simulator.

3. Load your mod and the vehicle in that mod.

4. Play your animation to check movement and timing.

5. Go back to Step 1 and make adjustments.

IMPORTANT

Unfortunately, animations from Blender do not export when you use the GIANTS I3D Exporter add-on. Blender animations are not currently supported by the exporter. So when you're animating in Blender, you're doing it entirely as a means of previsualization. However, there's a lot of value (and time savings) in being able to get your timing right first. Then all you have to do is put the right numbers in on your vehicle-XML file. Furthermore, previsualizing in Blender is really helpful when setting up skinning, like for hydraulic hoses. See Chapter 12 for more on this topic.

That's a lot of steps to go through with every adjustment to timing. Of course, this list of steps isn't entirely fair. Once you have your mod and vehicle loaded in Farming Simulator, you can make changes to your vehicle-XML and reload from the in-game console using `gsVehicleReload` (see Chapter 14). However, what if you wanted to check your animation before you even export to the I3D format? What if you wanted to know which Empties (transform groups) or parent objects to move to make a particular animation work? All of these things can be done from within Blender while you're still building your vehicle.

This way, you can know what to put in your vehicle-XML well in advance. You can spend a lot less time tweaking your timing with numbers in your vehicle-XML and instead tweak the timing with more visual animation tools.

So this section is dedicated to understanding how to animate in Blender through the lens of a Farming Simulator modder. We'll start by talking about getting your Blender session set up for animation. Then we will cover the actual work of animating in Blender.

Setting up for Animating

The first thing to do when you're setting up to animate within Blender is choose the right workspace. Now, you can certainly animate from any workspace within Blender's interface, but there is one workspace that's specifically dedicated to that task: the Animation workspace.

Choose the Animation workspace by clicking on its tab among the others at the top of the Blender window. When you choose the Animation workspace, you should see something like what's shown in Figure 8.3.

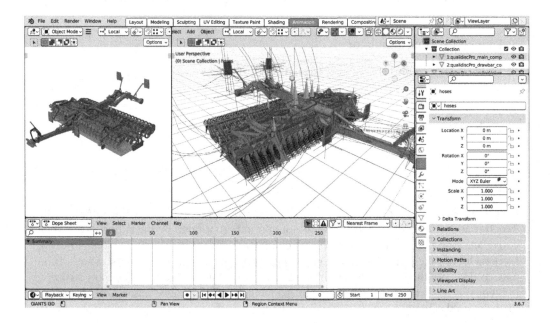

FIGURE 8.3   Blender's Animation workspace is the best place to create animations in Blender.

Visually, the Animation workspace is not all that different from the Layout workspace that you typically use by default. In addition to a 3D Viewport dedicated to the camera view, the main difference is at the bottom of the workspace. The Timeline editor is compressed to just show its header, and above it, there's a Dope Sheet editor. The Dope Sheet editor is one of the primary editors used for animating within Blender. This editor allows you to easily see all of the keyframes in your animation and also use those keyframes to tweak your timing.

NOTE

A *keyframe* is kind of like a save state for properties in time. When animating, the process consists of moving parts to define a *pose* and storing the properties that define that pose as a keyframe. By storing a series of poses at different points along the timeline, you can create an animation. Blender handles the transition, or *interpolation*, from one keyframe to the next.

Adjusting Settings to Best Visualize Animation

Remember that you're animating in Blender to previsualize the movement. This means that it's critical to make sure that Blender uses units that make sense to you as a game modder and that it plays your animation at the right speed.

The first of these tasks is handled by correctly setting up your units of time in Blender. Most people who animate in Blender do so for television and film, and those animators tend to think of time in terms of *framerate*, frames per second, or fps. In those media, the fps is constant, typically at 24 or 30 fps. This is how Blender is set to work by default, with a playback speed of 24 fps and time shown in the interface as frames.

For games, however, the fps can vary depending on how powerful the computer is and how complex the graphics are. So instead of frame rate, it's better to measure time in seconds. Fortunately, you can adjust Blender's interface to better reflect this need. Use the following steps:

1. In the Dope Sheet, navigate to **View ▶ Show Seconds** to have the time show up in seconds plus frames. Of course, the default frame rate is somewhat difficult to convert to fractions of a second. To fix that, go to the next step.

2. In the Output tab of the Properties editor, go to the Format panel and change the **Frame Rate** drop-down to *Custom*. This setting allows you to choose any arbitrary frame rate that you want. When you choose this option from the menu, Blender reveals two more properties: **FPS** and **Base**.

3. Adjust the **FPS** property to *100*. Now you have 100 frames per second, which easily translates to fractions of a second.

Now you have timing that more easily translates to what you enter in your vehicle-XML.

The next thing you want to set up is Blender's playback environment. If Blender can't play your animation in real time, then you're not getting a good sense of its timing. That would negate the benefit of trying to previsualize your animation in Blender, so it's important to get this next part right. The default setting for Blender is to play every frame of your animation. Now, not all computers can keep up with a frame rate of 100 fps, so you need to change this behavior using the following steps:

1. In the Timeline editor at the bottom of the workspace, click on the **Playback** roll-out.

2. At the top of the Playback roll-out, change the **Sync** drop-down to *Frame Dropping*. Figure 8.4 shows where to find this setting in Blender's interface.

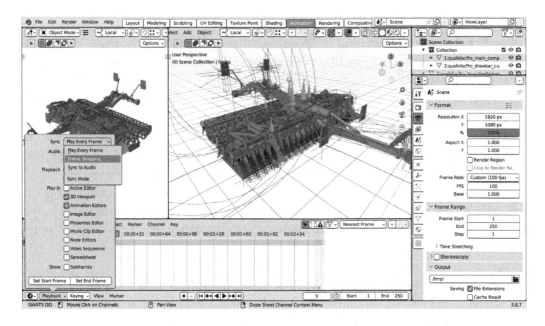

FIGURE 8.4   Change the Sync setting in the Playback roll-out to Frame Dropping so your animations playback in real time.

With this change in settings, Blender skips frames in order to make sure your playback speed matches real time. There's a chance that if you have a low-performance computer, you might see some stuttering or stopping in the video when it plays back, but the benefit is that you're going to actually see things happening at an accurate speed. From there, you can ensure that your movement looks and feels right.

Creating a Keying Set

Now, it's entirely possible for you to go ahead right away and start animating. Just move part of your vehicle around and set keyframes. However, remember that your purpose here is to animate the same properties that you're planning on animating in your vehicle-XML file. Sometimes you animate components; sometimes it's Empties that are transform groups; and other times you're animating objects directly. However, you're not animating everything. You're animating controllers and using parent relationships to dictate the rest of the movement in your vehicle.

So, from an animation standpoint, your best course of action is to only focus on the parts of your vehicle that are actually being animated. There are two tools you can use to facilitate this workflow, keying sets and disabled selection.

Starting with the former of those two things, let's set up a keying set. Simply put, a *keying set* is a collection of properties that can be keyframed together in one shot. Keying sets are created from the Scene tab on the Properties editor. In that tab is a panel labeled Keying Sets. Expand that panel by clicking on it, and you're greeted with an interface for creating your own keying set.

By default this panel is pretty empty. Blender ships with a handful of default "convenience" keying sets, but this panel is for building your own custom or *absolute keying sets*. Use the following steps:

1. Click the Plus (+) button to the right of the list box at the top of the Keying Set panel. Upon clicking this button, Blender adds a blank keying set to the list box, unimaginatively named *Keying Set*.

2. Double-click your new keying set to rename it to something more useful. In this example, maybe you name it *Folding Arms* to reflect that this keying set contains properties for the folding arms on our example cultivator. You can create as many keying sets as you would like, but for this example, I'm just walking you through one.

Congratulations! You've made your first keying set. Of course, it's not doing anything for you right now because it's empty. Now you need to add keyable properties to your new keying set. Use the following steps:

1. Click your keying set's name in the list box at the top of the Keying Set panel in Scene Properties. By selecting your keying set here, you're making it your active keying set.

2. In the 3D Viewport or the Outliner, select the object that holds the properties that you want to animate. Using our example of the folding arms on our sample cultivator, you might select the *armLeft* object.

3. In the Object tab of the Properties editor or the Item tab of the 3D Viewport's Sidebar, right-click any of the rotation values and choose **Add All to Keying Set** from the menu that appears. Since folding is only done with rotation, there's no need to include location or scale in the keying set. Back in the Keying Sets panel of Scene Properties, you should see *rotation_euler* added to the list box in the Paths sub-panel.

4. Repeat these steps for every property you want to include in your keying set. In our example, that would be just the two arms.

When you finish building out your keying set, you might have a Keying Set panel that looks like what's shown in Figure 8.5.

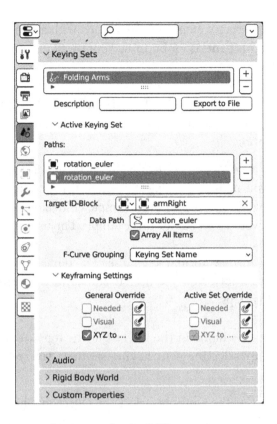

FIGURE 8.5   Building a custom keying set for the folding arms on our example cultivator.

Animating in Blender

Since you have your keying set all configured and set up, the workflow for animating in Blender is incredibly fast. To start, you need to insert keyframes for your first pose, or rest position. In the Dope Sheet, use the following steps:

1. Move the timeline cursor to the beginning of your timeline. The label on the timeline cursor should read *00:00+00,* meaning zero minutes, zero seconds, and zero frames.

2. Ensure that you're using the desired keying set. You can do this from the Scene tab of the Properties editor or from the Keying roll-out in the Timeline editor.

3. In the 3D Viewport's menu choose **Object ▶ Animation ▶ Insert Keyframe**. For faster access, you can press the *I* hotkey. All of the properties in your keying set have their values stored in a keyframe now.

Fantastic! You have your first pose set. All you have to do now is keyframe your next pose using the following steps:

1. In the Dope Sheet, move the timeline cursor forward in time. This is your best guess for how long the movement should take. At this point, you don't need to be overly precise. You just need somewhere to set the pose.

2. Back in the 3D Viewport, select your objects and adjust them to suit your second pose. In our folding arms example, you'd select each arm object and rotate it.

3. Insert your second keyframe (**Object ▶ Animation ▶ Insert Keyframe**, or press *I*).

IMPORTANT

When animating, it's important that you only select and modify the objects in your keying set. There's no risk of accidentally keying the wrong object, but there is the risk that you might move an object away from its natural rest position, giving you an inaccurate previsualization of your animation. To get around this, some people choose to set a "rest pose" keyframe for every object in their model on the first frame. That way, if you accidentally move something out of place, it'll snap back to its rest position the moment you scrub forward or backward in time.

Now you have two keyframes. And with two keyframes, you have an animation; you can play the animation by clicking the Play button in the Timeline editor at the bottom of the workspace. Because you set Blender to play using frame dropping, your animation should play close to real time and you can decide whether the timing matches what you want. Pause the animation by clicking the Pause button in the Timeline editor.

Now, let's assume that you didn't guess the correct timing right off the bat. You're going to need to adjust your timing. Use the following steps:

1. In the 3D Viewport, select the objects in your keying set (**Select ▶ Select Grouped ▶ Keying Set**). If you have selectability disabled for every object outside of your keying set, you can select all (**Select ▶ All**) and only your keying set objects are selected. The reason for making this selection is because the default behavior in the Dope Sheet is to only show keyframes for selected objects.

2. In the Dope Sheet deselect all keyframes (**Select ▶ None**).

3. Still in the Dope Sheet select all the keyframes in your second pose. The fastest way to do this step is by clicking the keyframe indicator in the Summary channel. Doing so selects all of the other keyframes at that same time in the Dope Sheet.

4. Adjust the position of the keyframes in your second pose by pressing and releasing the *G* hotkey, then move your mouse cursor left and right. To make the animation play faster, move the pose left. To make it play slower, move the pose right.

5. When you have the pose at a time that works, *left-click* to confirm moving those keyframes.

After you find a timing that works for you, you can look at the position of the keyframes in your second pose. This is the duration of the animation that you enter in your vehicle-XML file. Have fun!

SUMMARY

What a moving chapter! (Sorry… animation pun. I couldn't help myself.) Having reached this point, you started by seeing how to set up a basic animation. From there, you built on that knowledge to understand how to control the folding process on your vehicle mod. Then you saw how to define and animate other moving parts—including dependent parts—on your vehicle. After that, you took a look at animating your vehicle in Blender to get a preview of the movement without needing to export and test in Farming Simulator. Finally, you closed the chapter by adding sound to play when your animation is triggered.

In the next chapter, we'll get into adding those extra bits of polish on your mod that help make the experience truly immersive.

CHAPTER 9

Adding Extra Vehicle Features

A T THIS POINT, YOUR vehicle mod should be functional to the point that you can probably use it as part of a real game. However, this game is Farming Simulator, emphasis on *simulator*. The idea is to make the in-game experience feel genuine and immersive. That means adding features to your mod that re-enforce that immersive experience. This chapter is about adding some of those features. We start by seeing to it that your vehicle works at different parts of the day by adding light sources on it. After that, we cover the process of adding a license plate to your vehicle mod. All of your vehicle work is contained in a vehicle-XML file, so it's worthwhile to ensure that what you put in yours actually fits the structure expected by the game, so we end the chapter by covering how to validate your vehicle-XML file.

In this chapter:

- Implementing light sources
- Adding a license plate
- Validating your vehicle-XML

TECHNICAL REQUIREMENTS

As with the previous chapter, the majority of the work in this chapter is done from your vehicle-XML file. This means you'll need to be sure that you have GIANTS Studio or a suitable text editor installed. Also, to reference locations and add Empties on your vehicle mod, you'll need Blender and the GIANTS I3D Exporter add-on.

The examples provided in this chapter should work on any vehicle mod, but you may find it useful to reference our example cultivator that we've been working with throughout the book. That file can be downloaded at the following URL:

DOI: 10.1201/9781032659497-9

https://gdn.giants-software.com/blenderBook

There's also the vehicle-XML file for that cultivator included in this book's appendix.

IMPLEMENTING LIGHT SOURCES

For a dose of realism, you can add lights to your vehicle mod. You have the option of using light objects that come with Farming Simulator or building your own general light sources. This section walks you through the process of setting up both.

Referencing Shared Lights from Farming Simulator

It's worthwhile to have a look at where the shared lights are within the Farming Simulator game files. Use Windows Explorer to navigate to `C:/User Programs (x86)/Farming Simulator/data/shared/assets/lights` and in that folder you'll find a set of subfolders with all the lights that ship with Farming Simulator. These lights can be re-used in your mod.

To make use of these shared lights, you need to add an Empty to your vehicle hierarchy in Blender and make sure that Empty has an associated Node ID for export. Then, within the `<lights>` tag in your vehicle-XML, you can reference the game lights using the `<sharedLight>` tag, like so:

```
<lights>
    <sharedLight linkNode="rearLight05_01" filename="$data/shared/
assets/lights/lizard/rearLight05_left.xml" />
</lights>
```

This bit of mark-up tells the game engine to use the light defined in the shared assets folder of Farming Simulator and place it at the location of an Empty in the vehicle named `rearLight05 _ 01`.

Working with Real Light Sources

General light setup starts with adding light objects in Blender. These lights are responsible for shining colored light on the environment around your vehicle. Use the following steps:

1. Position your 3D cursor near the center of your light. If your light is a separate object, you can probably speed this process up by using **Object ▶ Snap ▶ Cursor to Selected** in the 3D Viewport's header menu. Otherwise you may need to do the same process, but first select the specific geometry of your light in Edit mode.

2. Add a new Spot light (**Add ▶ Light ▶ Spot**) and rotate it so the cone of the light faces the direction that you want the light to point.

3. Name the light something reasonable (e.g. `backLightLeft`). If you have multiple light sources for the same function, such as headlights or brake lights, a good practice is to make one light object a parent of the other. Then, when you refer to the parent object in the vehicle-XML, the child automatically shares the same behavior. In this example, you might name your left light `backLightsHigh` and then make the right light `backLightRight`, a child of `backLightsHigh`.

4. Add your light to your vehicle hierarchy. It may be tempting to nestle all of your lights under an Empty as a transform group like you've done for effects and working area, but since the lights need to move with the parts of your vehicle that may also move, it's probably better to make your light a child of the object that's holding your light geometry. In our example, that would be the back arm of the cultivator.

With your light positioned, go to the Object Data tab of the Properties editor so you can configure the actual properties of your new light objects. There are some standardized light settings that are used for lights in Farming Simulator, based on whether the light is red (such as brake lights in the rear), orange (for turning signals), or white (for head lights). The following are the standardized settings for each of those light types. Use these values when configuring your lights in Blender in the Object Data tab of the Properties editor:

- **Back lights** (red)
    - **Color:** rgb(0.5, 0.0, 0.0)
    - **Specular:** 1.00
    - **Radius:** 0.25 m
    - **Custom distance:** 2.5 m
    - **Size:** 130°
    - **Blend:** 0

- **Turn lights** (orange)
  - **Color:** rgb(0.31, 0.14, 0.0)
  - **Specular:** 1.00
  - **Radius:** 0.25 m
  - **Custom distance:** 4 m
  - **Size:** 120°
  - **Blend:** 0
- **Position lights** (white)
  - **Color:** rgb(1.0, 1.0, 1.0)
  - **Specular:** 1.00
  - **Radius:** 0.25 m
  - **Custom distance:** 4 m
  - **Size:** 120°
  - **Blend:** 0

Once you have your light placed and its properties correctly adjusted, you can prepare it for export. Use these steps in the GIANTS I3D Exporter tab of the 3D Viewport's SIdebar:

- Enable the **Node Id** check box. At this point, this step should be nearly automatic for you.
- In the Attributes section of the GIANTS I3D Exporter tab, go to the Predefined panel and choose the correct *Lights—Real* template from the **Non-Physics** drop-down menu.
- Scroll to the bottom of the tab and click the **Apply Selected** button.

> **NOTE**
>
> You need to perform this process (add the light object, configure its settings, and prep for I3D) for each light source on your vehicle. Then you can export to I3D and update your vehicle-XML

In your vehicle-XML, you add your lights by using the `<lights>` tag. Having lights shine on your game environment can have a dramatic effect on game performance, so you can take advantage of the `<high>` tag within the contents of your `<lights>` tag. By using this tag, you let the game engine know that it should only use the enclosed features if the game is set to use high-performance settings. As an example, tools only use real lights within the `<high>` tag.

The lights you've added in this section are referred to as *real lights* because of their behavior, so the `<realLights>` tag is where they ultimately live. Assuming you've created lights in your vehicle hierarchy for brake lights and turn signals, your `<lights>` tag may look like this (new tags in bold):

```
<lights>
    <sharedLight linkNode="rearLight05_01" filename="$data/shared/
assets/lights/lizard/rearLight05_left.xml" />
    <realLights>
        <high>
            <light node="backLightsHigh" lightType="0" />
            <turnLightLeft node="turnLightLeft" />
            <turnLightRight node="turnLightRight" />
            <brakeLight node="backLightsHigh" />
        </high>
    </realLights>
</lights>
```

Looking at the XML text, you might notice that the `backLightsHigh` node is named twice. The reason is because this light has two functions. The first function is refined by the `lightType` attribute in the `<light>` tag while the other function is that of a brake light, which is not controlled by the `lightType` attribute at all. Lights can have different types. Having the `lightType` attribute set to 0 defines it as a default light. Below is a list of the different light types and their values (in-game, you can cycle through light levels by pressing *F*; the order of those levels in the game is defined by the tractor XML files and doesn't necessarily follow this order):

- **0**: Default light
- **1**: Rear work light
- **2**: Front work light
- **3**: High beam
- **4**: Pipe light

You may also notice that there's a `<high>` tag that contains all of the lights in this example. The existence of such a tag may make you wonder if there's a `<low>` tag and what it does. The high and low designations are related to game performance. If the player has the game set to use low resources, then the lights in the `<low>` tag are used. Typically, they're the same lights, but fewer of them and with slightly different cone angles and ranges. You can refer to the lights in base game vehicles for reference. It's important to note that the `<low>` tag only works for tractors. For tool-type vehicles, the `<low>` tag should only be used for front lights and work lights. You can check out the base game files for reference.

ADDING A LICENSE PLATE

You can also add custom license plates to your vehicle mod that's automatically generated, much like shared lights and hose connectors. Likewise, the process for adding a license plate follows the same steps. You need to add an Empty in your vehicle hierarchy (name it something that makes sense, like `licensePlateBack`) and assign it a Node ID for export. From there, it's a matter of referring to that node from your vehicle-XML, like this:

```
<licensePlates>
    <licensePlate node="licensePlateBack" position="BACK"
preferedType="SQUARISH" placementArea="0.3 0.15 0.3 0.3" />
</licensePlates>
```

Your vehicle can have multiple license plates to account for being on the front and back of it, though this example only has the back plate. The following is a quick explanation of each attribute in the `<licensePlate>` tag:

- node—As with other references, this attribute is the name of the Empty in your Blender file.

- position—The value for this attribute should either be FRONT or BACK, in all caps. In the game shop, players can configure the vehicle to have plates on the front, back, both, or neither. So setting this value lets the game engine know which plate this one is.

- preferredType—Like the position attribute, this one requires an all-caps string that is either ELONGATED or SQUARISH. This option does depend a bit on the license plates that are available on the map that the player is using. For instance, U.S. vehicle plates are always of the SQUARISH type. If the vehicle is loaded in a U.S. map, the game engine places squarish plates, even if you've defined ELONGATED.

- placementArea—The last attribute, placementArea, defines the maximum dimensions of the plate in meters. The value of this attribute consists of four numbers, each corresponding to one side of the plate relative to the origin of your placement node. The order of the sides goes clockwise, starting at the top, so top, right, bottom, left. If the plate of the map is bigger than the defined placement area, the plate is shrunken to fit.

> **NOTE**
>
> The `<licensePlates>` tag also has a single attribute that you can optionally set, called `defaultPlacement`. This attribute is a string value, either set to NONE or BOTH. It defines the default placement index, independent of the map setting in the game. For example, the U.S. map has no plates by default, but for cars and trucks, you can have plates enabled by setting this option to BOTH.

VALIDATING YOUR VEHICLE-XML

As indicated by the name we've been using, vehicle-XML is a file in XML, or eXtensible Markup Language. On the surface, it doesn't seem like there's a whole lot that's special about XML. It's basically a text file with some very specific rules about how you format the text within that file. Those rules cover things like defining tags with the angled brackets (< and >), and that attributes are specified with an equals sign (=). Outside of those rules, though, XML is designed to be really flexible about what kind of data is being stored and how it's represented.

So what defines which tags and attributes are valid for use in a Farming Simulator mod? Those things aren't part of XML as a language and need to be defined somewhere. These definitions are the job of an *XML schema*, which, interestingly enough, is defined in an XML-formatted text file called an XML Schema Definition, or XSD. For editors that support them (like GIANTS Studio and Visual Studio Code), you can load an XSD and use it to help confirm that what you're writing in your XML file is valid data.

NOTE

"Valid" in the context of this section means that the data is something that GIANTS Engine (the game engine behind Farming Simulator) expects and knows what to do with. If the data causes an error in the game, it's not valid. Using an XML schema can help you catch and fix these kinds of issues before they become real errors in testing.

You can get the XSD for vehicle-XML from the GDN at the following URL: https://validation.gdn.giants-software.com/xml/vehicle.xsd. However, you don't have to manually download the XSD to use it. By including this URL in your <vehicle> tag, a modern editor like GIANTS Studio will be able to automatically get the XSD (assuming you have an active internet connection). In our example cultivator, it's the second line of the vehicle-XML, reading like so:

```
<vehicle type="cultivator" xmlns:xsi="http://www.w3.org/2001/
XMLSchema-instance" xsi:noNamespaceSchemaLocation="https://
validation.gdn.giants-software.com/xml/vehicle.xsd">
```

NOTE

You may notice that the URL in this example has fs22 in it, indicating that this is the XSD for Farming Simulator 22. If you're building your mod for a different version of Farming Simulator, the fs22 text should be changed to match the version you're using.

I mentioned earlier that in many modern text editors and development environments, you can load the XSD to help you validate your vehicle-XML as you write it. You'll need to refer to the documentation of those tools to see how to do it for the specific one you're using. However, if you're working with GIANTS Studio, there's nothing special that you need to do.

Because the primary use of GIANTS Studio is to help you develop mods, it's already configured to make use of the XSDs in Farming Simulator.

To get an understanding of how the XSD can help you in GIANTS Studio, let's load up the quick example vehicle-XML from the beginning of Chapter 6, but with two minor changes (in bold):

```
<?xml version="1.0" encoding="utf-8" standalone="no" ?>

<vehicle thing="cultivator" xmlns:xsi="http://www.w3.org/2001/
XMLSchema-instance" xsi:noNamespaceSchemaLocation="https://
validation.gdn.giants-software.com/xml/vehicle.xsd">
    <annotation>Copyright (C) Me! I made this!</annotation>
</vehicle>
```

The biggest change is including the XSD reference in the <vehicle> tag. The other change is a modification of the type attribute to instead be thing, which is invalid for the vehicle XML schema. Now, if you start a new mod in GIANTS Studio with this as your vehicle-XML, GIANTS Studio gives you a warning, indicating that the thing attribute is not a valid part of the XML schema for a vehicle-XML, as shown in Figure 9.1.

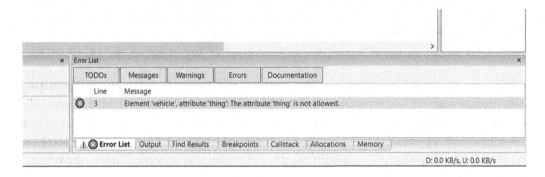

FIGURE 9.1 GIANTS Studio gives you a warning when you're using invalid tags in your vehicle-XML.

In addition to reporting mistakes in your vehicle-XML, having the XSD in GIANTS Studio is also great for giving you meaningful suggestions and recommendations for attributes in your tags. In addition to that, it shows a description of each attribute, so you know the correct kind of data to put into it. Figure 9.2 shows an example of one of these recommendations.

```
1  <?xml version="1.0" encoding="utf-8" standalone="no" ?>
2
3  <vehicle type="cultivator" xmlns:xsi="http://www.w3.org/200:
4      <annotat type            Description: Vehicle type is!</annotation>
5  </vehicle>                   Type: String
6                               Required: no
```

FIGURE 9.2 GIANTS Studio gives recommendations for attributes which include descriptions of each one, as defined in the XSD for vehicle-XML.

> **TIP**
>
> Of course, it can be a little bit tedious to rely on recommendations for every single tag and attribute in your vehicle-XML. A better approach is to make use of the example vehicle-XML documentation file available on the GDN here: https://validation.gdn.giants-software.com/vehicle.html.

SUMMARY

Although this chapter went by quickly, the tools and features in it give you that little bit of additional polish to help your mod feel real. You started by adding lights to your vehicle so it can illuminate the environment in-game. Then you completed the chapter by adding a license plate as a nice finishing touch. And finally, you got a bit technical and did an exploration of XML schemas and ways to validate that your vehicle-XML is written properly.

In the next chapter, we start getting into ways to optimize your mod for in-game performance by taking advantage of merge groups.

CHAPTER 10

Creating Merge Groups

M ODELS FOR FARMING EQUIPMENT tend to have a lot of parts. With enough of those parts in the same environment at the same time, any game engine is going to eventually struggle to maintain playable performance while managing those parts. This is where you start making optimizations. GIANTS Engine, the game engine behind Farming Simulator, supports a really handy optimization called *merge groups*. This chapter is all about setting them up. We'll start with covering what they are and how they're useful. Then we'll dive right in and start building a merge group on our example cultivator by first walking through the process of adding parts of the vehicle to the merge group. And finally, we create a bounding volume for the merge group.

In this chapter:

- Understanding merge groups

- Assigning objects to your merge group

- Creating a custom bounding volume

TECHNICAL REQUIREMENTS

All of the work in this chapter happens in Blender with the GIANTS I3D Exporter add-on. You should also have a vehicle model that you want to create as your mod. If you don't have your own vehicle, you can use the example cultivator that we've been working on in the rest of the book, available here:

DOI: 10.1201/9781032659497-10

https://gdn.giants-software.com/blenderBook

UNDERSTANDING MERGE GROUPS

It may surprise you, but if you've worked through Chapter 7, you've already had a little bit of exposure to the concept of merging. In the Defining Wheels section of Chapter 7, the concept of merge children is introduced. The core principle is the same for merge groups: you're telling the game engine to consider a group of objects as a single object, while still retaining the ability to rotate the parts around their individual origins. This merging structure is an optimization that can help maintain good in-game performance even with a complex vehicle model.

Of course, because it's an optimization, not all objects in your model can be part of a merge group. There's a specific set of conditions that need to be met in order to add parts as a member of a merge group. Here's a quick rundown of those conditions:

- **All members of the merge group need to have the same material.** If you have parts with different materials, you can still take advantage of merge groups; you'll just need to have more than one. When you're using a multi-material setup in mods for Farming Simulator 25 and newer, the basic material settings (diffuse, normal, specular, and shader variation) need to be the same for all members of the merge group.

- **There need to be multiple members of a merge group.** Simply put, you can't have a merge group that only has a single member.

- **Members of a merge group can't change scale or visibility during the course of gameplay.** For example, it's a common practice to hide bolt objects on a vehicle when it's in its folded state. Those bolts can't be part of any merge group.

- **Skinned meshes (see Chapter 10) can't be part of a merge group.** So, as an example, hoses don't qualify to be part of a merge group. Fortunately, hoses don't often have the same material as other parts of the model, so they wouldn't be a part of a larger merge group anyway.

- **All members of the merge group must fit within the space of a bounding volume that you've defined (see the next section).** If your vehicle folds, the size of the bounding volume needs to also account for the folded state of the vehicle as well.

ASSIGNING OBJECTS TO YOUR MERGE GROUP

You start by adding objects to your merge group. Like transform groups in the rest of your vehicle, merge groups have their own internal hierarchy. However, that hierarchy isn't easily visualized or managed from Blender's Outliner. Instead you need to use the Rendering panel in the Attributes section of the GIANTS I3D Exporter tab in the 3D Viewport's Sidebar.

Defining a Merge Group Root

As with any hierarchy, the merge group hierarchy needs to start with a source, a *root*. Technically speaking, this can be any member of the merge group, but for the sake of organization (and your own sanity), it's a good idea to go with a hierarchical tree that's similar to the organization you've already set up. In our cultivator example, the central beam in our model, `qualidiscPro _ vis` works as a good merge group root.

Use the following steps to define the root node for your merge group:

- Select the object that you intend to be your root node. In this example, that would be `qualidiscPro _ vis`.

- Go to the Attributes section in the GIANTS I3D Exporter tab and click the **Load Current** button at the bottom to ensure you're not using older data.

- Expand the Rendering panel and make the following adjustments:

  - Change the **Merge Group** value to *1*.

  - Enable the **Merge Group Root** check box.

- At the bottom of the tab, click the **Apply Selected** button to apply your changes to your selected object.

Figure 10.1 shows a close-up of the GIANTS I3D Exporter tab with these specific settings correctly set.

| Decal Layer | 0 |
| Merge Group | 1 |

☑ Merge Group Root

Bounding Volume _____ | Merge Group 1 ⌄ |

☐ CPU Mesh

FIGURE 10.1 Use the Merge Group value to define the merge group for your selected object and enable the Merge Group Root check box to define it as the root node.

IMPORTANT

It's important that your merge group root is a static, non-animated part of your vehicle. The bounding radius is linked to the root, so if you rotate the root, you'd also be rotating the bounding radius, which complicates matters. If you don't have static parts in your intended merge group, you can add an Empty to your scene at your vehicle's origin and set that Empty as your merge group root.

Adding other Objects to Your Merge Group

Once you have your merge group root defined, you can start adding more parts to your merge group. The process of adding an object to a merge group is nearly identical to the steps defined in the preceding section. The only difference is that you need to make sure that the Merge Group Root check box is disabled. Otherwise, you'll end up with multiple objects competing to be the root node.

NOTE

Remember that objects in a merge group must all have the same material, can't be skinned, and can't have their visibility or scale animated during gameplay. Furthermore, GIANTS Engine is limited to 60 objects per merge group.

As you work, it's a good idea to periodically do an export from Blender and test your vehicle in the GIANTS Editor. When you test, individual objects in your model should now appear as transform groups, but you should still be able to rotate them on their local pivots, as shown in Figure 10.2.

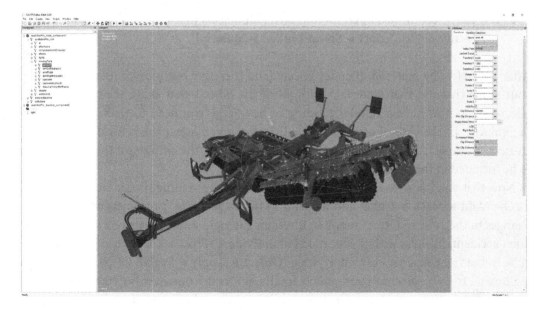

FIGURE 10.2 With merge groups, your parts of the merge group are a single transform group in GIANTS Editor, but individual parts of the group can still be rotated on their local axes.

> **IMPORTANT**
>
> If you're using merge groups, be sure that in Blender, you go to the GIANTS I3D Exporter tab in the 3D Viewport and, in the Export section. Within the Shape Export Subparts panel, enable the **Merge Groups** check box.

CREATING A CUSTOM BOUNDING VOLUME

To build a merge group, everything starts with a custom *bounding volume*. Simply put, a bounding volume is a box that takes up the same amount of space as the member parts in your merge group.

> **IMPORTANT**
>
> It's critical that you account for all states of the parts in your merge group. So if your vehicle has a folding animation (like our example cultivator), you need to make sure that your bounding volume is as tall as your vehicle in its folded state while also being wide enough to accommodate your vehicle in its open state.

Because you know that all of the objects in a merge group need to have the same material, there's a trick you can do to understand how big your bounding volume needs to be. You can select all of the objects in your scene that share the same material datablock. Use the following steps:

1. Select one of the parts in your model that you know should be part of the merge group.

2. Use the Select Linked operator and select all objects that share the same material as your active object (**Select ▶ Select Linked ▶ Material**).

After you select by material, Blender selects (and therefore outlines) all of the objects in your scene that use that material. With all of the objects that share the same material selected, you now have an understanding of how large you need to make your bounding volume. In the case of our example cultivator, if you select the central `qualidis-cPro _ vis` part, and use this trick, you should see that the entirety of the model needs to be included in the bounding volume.

Now that you know roughly how large your bounding volume should be, you can add a cube (**Add ▶ Mesh ▶ Cube**) and adjust it to the correct size. I recommend making the changes to the cube in Object mode so it retains the right angles in its box shape and you don't accidentally mess with the locations of individual vertices. Then, after you have your cube to the right size, you can apply scale (**Object ▶ Apply ▶ Scale**). Of course, adding a big box all the way around your vehicle totally blocks it from view, so, like with physics components in Chapter 5, you can go to the Object tab in the Properties editor and, in the Viewport Display panel, change the **Display As** drop-down menu to *Wire*.

With your cube added, you need to make it part of your vehicle hierarchy and let the GIANTS I3D Exporter know that you intend to use it as the bounding volume for your merge group. As far as adding the volume to your vehicle hierarchy, it doesn't actually need to be a child of anything. You can just use naming to place it at the bottom of the stack.

In our cultivator example, there are two base Empties in the scene, 1:qualidiscPro _ main _ component1 and 2:qualidiscPro _ drawbar _ component1. Recall from Chapter 2 that the 1: and 2: prefixes on object names are used for ordering your scene and are recognized by the GIANTS I3D Exporter add-on. So for this example, name your cube 3:qualidiscPro _ boundingVolume _ mergeGroup1 and its name will drop to the bottom of the list in the Outliner.

All that's left now is making the exporter aware that the cube is meant to be a bounding volume for a merge group. The work for this phase is all done from the GIANTS I3D Exporter tab in the 3D Viewport's Sidebar. Select your bounding volume object and use the following steps:

1. In the Attributes section, click the **Load Current** button at the bottom of the tab to ensure that you're not using any leftover data.

2. Expand the Rendering panel and next to the Bounding Volume label, ensure that *Merge Group 1* is selected from the drop-down menu.

3. At the bottom of the tab, click the Apply Selected button to make sure that the merge group assignment is made.

And that's it! You now have a bounding volume set for Merge Group 1. Using our example cultivator as an example, your Blender session may look like what's shown in Figure 10.3.

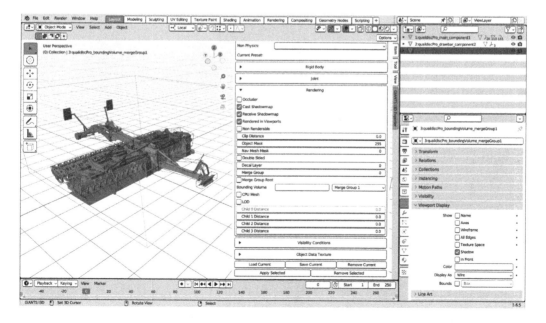

FIGURE 10.3 Create a bounding volume to contain the objects of your merge group.

SUMMARY

In this chapter, you saw how to optimize your mod's in-game performance by using merge groups. You started by discovering what merge groups are and how they can help manage a bunch of parts in your mod. Then you added individual parts of your mod to that merge group using the GIANTS I3D Exporter. Finally, you added a bounding volume for your merge group.

In the next chapter we cover another helpful optimization tactic, level of detail meshes.

CHAPTER 11

Building Level of Detail (LOD) Meshes

CONTINUING THE TOPIC OF optimization that was started in Chapter 10, there's something else that you can do to increase in-game performance when your vehicle mod is used. In short, the game engine for Farming Simulator supports the ability to switch meshes for your vehicle based on the distance from the viewing camera. To manage this feature, the engine relies on *level of detail*, or LOD, meshes. This chapter is all about LOD. We start by understanding what exactly LOD is. From there, we get into some of the tools available in Blender to help you model your LOD meshes. After that, we close the chapter by showing how to use merge groups to manage your LODs without changing anything outside of your .blend file. And finally, we start the process of setting up your model in Blender so it exports to I3D with support for LOD meshes.

In this chapter:

- Understanding LOD

- Modeling your LOD meshes

- Setting up a merge group to manage your LOD

- Adjusting your vehicle hierarchy and setting attributes to control LOD meshes

TECHNICAL REQUIREMENTS

The work of setting up LOD meshes is all done in Blender with the GIANTS I3D Exporter add-on. Because LOD control is managed with merge groups, it would be beneficial to use whatever example file you set up from Chapter 10 for the work in this chapter. You can use our example cultivator that's available at https://gdn.giants-software.com/blenderBook (or you can scan the QR code below), but you'll need to add a base merge group, as described in Chapter 10. At the end of the chapter, you can test your results using the GIANTS Editor.

DOI: 10.1201/9781032659497-11

https://gdn.giants-software.com/blenderBook

UNDERSTANDING LOD

At its very core, the *level of detail* (LOD) feature in a game engine does the work of swapping meshes for an object based on that object's distance from the camera. At this point, you should be well aware of how many different objects go into a vehicle mod. And you should know that each of those 3D objects can have fairly high geometry counts, depending on how detailed you make them. Well, that high-resolution geometry looks great when you're close-up to the vehicle, but all of that detail gets lost when the vehicle is tooling around in the background. However, even though you can't see the detail, every bit of it is still being processed by the game engine. As you might imagine, this scenario can have a negative impact on in-game performance.

To keep high playability, it's possible to tell the game engine to use a lower-resolution model when it's a specific distance from the player camera. By having multiple versions of your model to display based on that distance, you're creating levels of detail (hence the name).

Of course, for the performance increase that you get with creating and using LOD meshes, there are some trade-offs. The biggest trade-off is for you, the mod creator. You basically have to model your vehicle all over again. Of course, since you already have the high-resolution version of your vehicle, creating versions in lower resolutions is typically faster and easier, especially with some of the tools covered in the next section.

The second trade-off comes in the form of hard drive space. Because there's, in total, more geometry data stored in your mod, it takes up more space on hard drives and takes longer to download from the ModHub. That said, if you can make optimizations to ensure that the game maintains a good framerate, it's probably worth sacrificing a little bit of hard drive space and a few more seconds of download time.

MODELING YOUR LOD MESHES

The process of creating an LOD mesh can vary a bit depending on the topology of your starting mesh, but it generally takes much less time to create than your original high-resolution model. In fact, it's often a good idea to duplicate **Object ▶ Duplicate Objects** in your high-resolution mesh and use that as your starting point. The added benefit of using this approach is that your LOD mesh ends up at the same place in your vehicle hierarchy as the original. When you create your duplicate mesh, be sure to give it a sensible suffix to clearly indicate that it's a LOD mesh. For example, in our cultivator, if you duplicate the left arm, `armLeft`, the name of the LOD mesh for that part should be something like `armLeft _ lod`.

Another helpful feature in Blender for building LOD meshes is Blender's scene statistics. In the header of the 3D Viewport, expand the Overlays roll-out and enable the Statistics check box. When you enable this feature, the upper left of the 3D Viewport shows statistics on the number of objects, vertices, faces, and so on in your scene, as shown in Figure 11.1. As an additional bonus, when you're in Edit mode, the Statistics overlay only shows the values relevant to your active object.

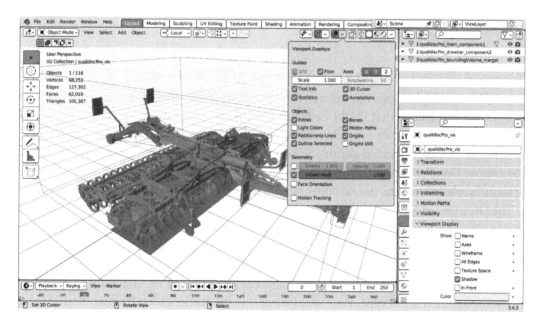

FIGURE 11.1   Enable the statistics overlay to see the number of vertices in your model.

Once you've duplicated and properly named your LOD mesh, you can start the work of creating the lower-resolution version. The work at this stage is not technically difficult, though I will admit that it can be a little hard, emotionally speaking. You're going to spend this stage removing all of the hand-crafted details that you added to your original high-resolution model. If you spent a lot of time getting your model as visually accurate as possible, it can be difficult to get rid of those small parts that took the most amount of time to get right. But that's the job. Here are some tips that can help you along the way:

- Be absolutely brutal with what you remove. Anything that doesn't contribute to the overall silhouette of the part should be either removed or replaced with more simplified geometry.

- Look to remove small detailed pieces. Bolts, straps, brackets… all of these things are great candidates for removal. Because these small parts often have a lot of geometry to look correct, you can often drop your 3D model's vertex count by half with this tip alone.

- You may also consider updating the textures on your material to "paint in" those small parts to give the illusion that they're still there in the low-resolution version.

- Anything at the bottom of the vehicle is a great candidate for removal. Most of the time, when you're looking at the vehicle from a distance in-game, you're not going to see the bottom of it.

- Don't worry about floating parts. If you delete a bracket and the thing it was holding up is just floating in space, that might be perfectly fine and not noticeable at all from a distance.

Sometimes, even after going through this process, the geometry from your original object may still be too high. However, before you start re-modeling those pieces, there's one further feature in Blender that might be helpful in this situation. Blender's Decimate modifier can be really great for procedurally reducing the geometry of a model. You add the modifier from the Properties editor in the Modifiers tab. Click the **Add Modifier** button and choose *Decimate* from the drop-down menu that appears (Decimate is in the second column, labeled Generate, because this modifier generates new, albeit reduced, geometry).

The Decimate modifier gives you the ability to somewhat intelligently reduce the geometry in your model with some handy sliders. For most game-ready vehicle models, the default **Decimation Type** of *Collapse* tends to give the best results. If your model has a topology that has a lot of face loops and grid-like topology, you may want to try the *Un-Subdivide* type, but that tends to be more commonly used on character models. For the Collapse decimation type, your main control is the **Ratio** slider. By default, this value is set to 1.000, indicating that you're still at the original geometry. Lower this value, and you should interactively see your model update in the 3D Viewport. Furthermore, at the bottom of the Decimate modifier, there's a *Face Count* value that lets you know how many faces are remaining in your model after the modifier has done its work.

Between reducing those detail pieces and using the Decimate modifier, you can often quickly drop the face count on your model to a fifth of what it was in your original. As an example, Figure 11.2 shows the armLeft object in our example cultivator in the original high-resolution version and a lower-resolution LOD mesh. The high-resolution version of that part has over 8700 faces, while the LOD version clocks in at around 2300 faces.

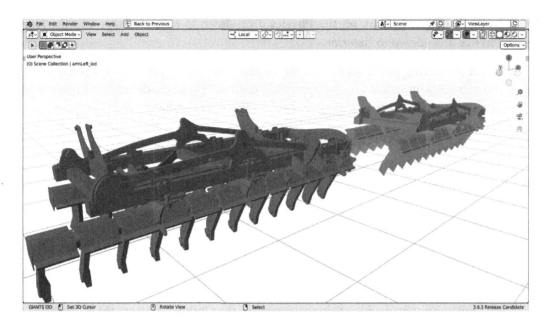

FIGURE 11.2   By reducing the number of small, detailed parts and using Blender's Decimate modifier, this part has a LOD mesh with 70% less geometry.

IMPORTANT

You don't need to explicitly apply the Decimate modifier on your LOD mesh. When you export to the I3D format using the GIANTS I3D Exporter, that add-on automatically applies all modifiers on the exported objects. This way, you can maintain some flexibility, and if you need to adjust the Decimate modifier in the future, you have that option available to you.

SETTING UP A MERGE GROUP TO MANAGE YOUR LOD

Although you can manage LODs directly, we can use merge groups to more easily manage the display of LOD meshes without changing the vehicle hierarchy. If you went through the steps in Chapter 10, you should already have one merge group for your high-resolution model. Now you need to create another merge group that the game engine can use to control which mesh is displayed on-screen.

What's next is assigning your LOD meshes to that merge group. For each LOD mesh in your mod, you need to set a few attributes in the GIANTS I3D Exporter to ensure that the game engine knows what to do with them. Use the following steps for each of your LOD meshes:

1. Go to the Attributes section in the GIANTS I3D Exporter tab.

2. At the bottom of the tab, click **Load Current** to ensure that no left-over data is applied to your selected object.

3. In the Predefined panel, set the **Physics** drop-down to *ExteriorShape* and the **Non Physics** drop-down to *Exterior*.

4. In the Rendering panel set the **Merge Group** value to *2*. This assumes you're using the merge group defined in the preceding section. If your model has multiple merge groups, this value should correspond to the one you're using for your LOD meshes.

5. At the bottom of the tab, click **Apply Selected**.

And, like with the process covered in Chapter 10, you need a bounding volume for your LOD's merge group. Use these steps:

1. Select the bounding volume you created for your original merge group.

2. Duplicate that bounding volume (**Object ▶ Duplicate Objects**) and press *Esc* to ensure that it's in the same location as the original.

3. Rename your new bounding volume to `4:qualidiscPro _ boundingVolume _ mergeGroup2` by double-clicking its name in the Outliner or using the *F2* hotkey.

4. Back in the 3D Viewport, go to the GIANTS I3D Exporter tab in the Sidebar and switch to the Attributes section.

5. Click the **Load Current** button at the bottom of the tab to ensure that you're not using any leftover data.

6. Expand the Rendering panel and next to the **Bounding Volume** label, ensure that *Merge Group 2* is selected from the drop-down menu. This example assumes that your only other merge group is the one with the high-resolution model. If you have multiple merge groups, set this drop-down to one that you haven't used yet.

7. At the bottom of the tab, click the **Apply Selected** button to make sure that the merge group assignment is made.

ADJUSTING YOUR VEHICLE HIERARCHY AND SETTING ATTRIBUTES TO CONTROL LOD MESHES

Since your LODs are managed by a merge group, there's actually not very much extra work that needs to be done with respect to your vehicle hierarchy. In fact, it's best if your LOD meshes are each children of their corresponding high-resolution mesh in the vehicle hierarchy. This is why in the "Modeling Your LOD Meshes" section, I suggested duplicating your high-resolution object as a starting point, then making your duplicated mesh a child of the original high-resolution one. Taking that approach helps ensure that your LOD mesh is in the correct location in the hierarchy and therefore transformed the same as the high-resolution object without requiring any changes to your vehicle-XML.

That said, there is one additional tweak you need to make. So far, all you have are a bunch of objects (hopefully with _ lod at the end of their names) that are members of a merge group. Currently, there's nothing to tell the game engine that you're actually using LODs or when those LOD meshes should be activated. Fortunately, this step is easily managed from the merge group root. Recall from Chapter 10 that you had to designate one object in a merge group as being the root of that group. In that example, we used one of the mesh objects, but it could just as easily be an Empty that you're using as a transform group.

In fact, the way we organized our LODs in our example cultivator is by making an Empty to serve as the transform group that holds each of the merge group root objects. Then you can put your LOD settings on that Empty. The layout could look something like what's shown in the Outliner in Figure 11.3.

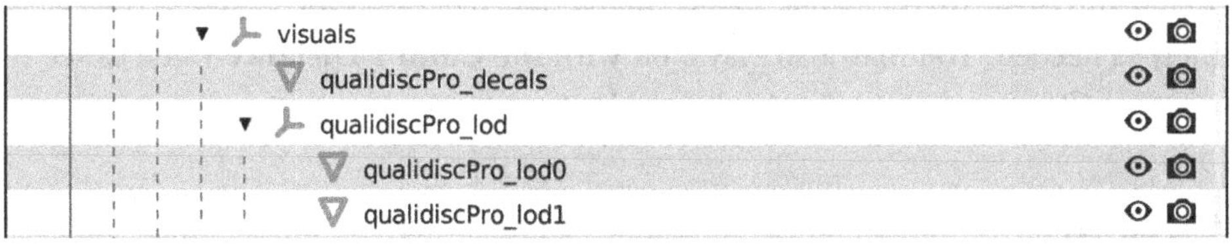

FIGURE 11.3   A hierarchy for holding merge group roots for your LODs.

In Figure 11.3, there's an overall parent Empty called `visuals` that contains multiple visual elements, including the decal mesh and the transform group for your LOD merge group roots. That Empty, `qualidiscPro _ lod` is where you put your LOD settings. Select that Empty and use the following steps:

- In the Attributes section of the GIANTS I3D Exporter tab, expand the Predefined panel.

- In the **Physics** drop-down menu, choose *Default* to set all attributes on your Empty to their default settings.

- Still in the Attributes section, expand the Rendering panel.

- In the Rendering panel, make sure you have the following settings:

  - **LOD**: *enabled*

  - **Child 1 Distance**: *40* (this value is in meters)

- Click **Apply Selected** at the bottom of the tab.

When you enable the **LOD** check box on your parent Empty as described in these steps, the exporter understands that all children of that Empty are switched based on the distances defined. This way, you can give yourself multiple LODs, not just two. The way that works is that each child of your Empty is the mesh root for each LOD merge group, in order. So using our cultivator example, your structure might look like this:

- `qualidiscPro _ lod`

  - `qualidiscPro _ lod0` (high-resolution LOD)

  - `qualidiscPro _ lod1` (middle-distance LOD)

  - `qualidiscPro _ lod2` (long distance LOD)

The distance for triggering the merge group associated with `qualidiscPro_lod2` is defined with the **Child 2 Distance** property.

Once you have those steps completed, you should be able to export your vehicle from the Export section of the GIANTS I3D Exporter tab and then test your mod in GIANTS Editor by moving the scene camera away from your vehicle. At a distance of 40 meters, the high-resolution meshes should swap out for your low-resolution LOD versions.

From here, you can test in-game to decide if your LOD meshes have too much or too little detail and make further adjustments in Blender (like tweaking values in the Decimate modifier) as needed. You may also play a bit with the **Child 1 Distance** value to see if you get better results nearer or farther from the player camera.

IMPORTANT

When testing your LODs, make sure you go into the Graphics Settings menu in Farming Simulator and ensure that it's set to 100% LOD distance. If you configure it with *Very High*, the switch between meshes could be way too early if the player is using *Medium* or *Low* graphics settings.

It's worth mentioning that although using merge groups makes the process of defining and switching LOD meshes pretty easy, they're not strictly required. You can put LOD settings on a regular object and have its LOD mesh as a child of that object. This approach is really useful when, for example, you're building configurations.

SUMMARY

In this chapter, you learned about using level of detail meshes as an optimization technique for your mod. You started by discovering what LODs are and how they benefit in-game performance. Then you were exposed to some techniques that you can use in Blender to more quickly build your LOD meshes. From there, you set up a merge group to help GIANTS Engine manage your LODs. And finally, you made a small tweak to your vehicle hierarchy and set some configuration options to let the game engine know that you're using LODs and which merge group to associate with them.

In the next chapter, we step a little bit away from optimization and start talking about details. Specifically, we're covering the process of skinning meshes to assist with deforming animations, like for hoses.

CHAPTER 12

Constructing Hydraulic Hoses

A T THIS POINT IN your mod build, your vehicle is almost fully functional in-game. However, you may have found it tricky to handle these hoses in your game model, particularly when animating parts as described in Chapter 8. The challenge is that unlike most other parts of farming equipment, which are made of steel and other hard materials, hoses tend to be made of more flexible materials. They bend and deform relative to whatever they're attached to. The standard tools you use for animating other parts of your vehicle at the object level simply don't have the control you need for hoses. This is where armatures and the process of *skinning* come into play and that's the core topic of this chapter.

The chapter starts by explaining what an armature is in Blender and how Blender's rigging system gives you control over deforming geometry like hoses. From there, we get right into the process of adding bones to your armature so they move with the parts of your vehicle that you've already animated. And finally, we can start assigning weights on our meshes that correspond to the bones in your armature, giving you the ability to control how your hoses bend.

In this chapter:

- Understanding armature objects in Blender

- Adding armature bones that move with your vehicle

- Assigning vertex weights to control deformations

TECHNICAL REQUIREMENTS

All of the work for this chapter is done within Blender using its native tools. Of course, you still need the GIANTS I3D Exporter add-on to get your mod exported into Farming Simulator, but there's no need to touch your vehicle-XML.

If you don't already have your own vehicle that you're working with to create a mod, you're welcome to take advantage of our cultivator example, available here:

DOI: 10.1201/9781032659497-12

https://gdn.giants-software.com/blenderBook

UNDERSTANDING ARMATURE OBJECTS IN BLENDER

A *deforming* object is one that changes shape in the course of an animation. Unlike the metal beams and bolts that make up most of a vehicle, deforming objects like hoses can bend, twist, and stretch. In 3D software, artists typically use some kind of intermediary skeleton object to control those deformations. In Blender, that object is called an *armature*. Blender's armature objects consist of one or more bones. The geometry of your hose meshes is associated with specific bones by using vertex groups that share the same name as the bones. Furthermore, you can control the influence that a bone has by assigning a weight to a vertex for each vertex group that it's a member of. All of this may sound rather complex, but the concepts start to make more sense once you start working through a real example.

> **NOTE**
>
> If you've worked with skeleton objects in other software, please note that Blender's armatures are subtly different. In other applications, like Autodesk Maya, the core unit of a skeleton is a joint, and bones are merely the parent-child relationship between joints. In Blender, it's different. The core unit of an armature in Blender is a bone, which has a head and a tail. The head of the bone typically corresponds with what other applications call a joint. So if you look at other vehicle mods and see bones with the word "joint" in their name, just know that for all intents and purposes, those are still just bones.

To keep things simple, it's best to have the origin of your armature object live at the same origin as your root object in your vehicle (which, incidentally, should also be the same location as the world origin). Ensure your 3D Cursor is located at the world origin by navigating to **Object ▶ Snap ▶ Cursor to World Origin** in the 3D Viewport's header. Once you've done that step, you can add an armature object to your scene by choosing **Add ▶ Armature**.

Blender's base Armature object consists of just one bone, named Bone. From the Outliner (or using the *F2* hotkey), rename your armature to hoseRig and that initial bone to rootBone. While you're at it, you should also create a transform group to contain all of your deforming parts and your rig. Add an Empty (**Add ▶ Empty ▶ Plain Axes**) and name it something sensible. In our cultivator example, the name for our Empty is skinnedMeshes. Using either the Outliner or Blender's parenting operator, make your hoseRig armature a child of the skinnedMeshes Empty. Likewise, to keep things fully organized, all of your deformable objects (in this case, your hoses) should, in turn, be children of your hoseRig armature object. At this point, your Blender session might look something like what's shown in Figure 12.1.

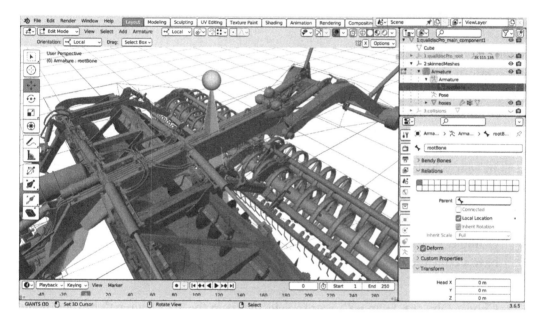

FIGURE 12.1   Add an Empty to serve as the transform group for your skinned meshes and include both your armature object and the meshes that it's meant to deform as children of that Empty.

ADDING ARMATURE BONES THAT MOVE WITH YOUR VEHICLE

Now that you have a strong foundation for your rig, you can start adding bones to your armature. The work of adding bones to your armature is similar to the process of adding Empties to your scene for things like the location of hose connectors or a license plate. The difference is that you need to add bones within the context of your armature object rather than just in Object mode within Blender. So there are a few extra steps.

Also, there are some important distinctions to make when setting up bones for your vehicle mod when compared to the rigging process described for Blender that you may find in tutorials online. Most importantly, you should actively avoid building a chain of bones that aligns with your hoses. Not only is that kind of approach overkill for most situations, each bone represents another vertex group in your mesh object with corresponding weight assignments (see the next section). All of that adds up to being more data that the game engine has to process, which can result in slower in-game performance.

Secondly, you may be tempted to simply create a new armature object for each bone that you need. After all, it's just like working with Empties, right? Well, not really. Armatures and their member bones are a lot like being their own self-contained transform groups. There's a large organizational advantage to keeping your bones in a single armature unless you absolutely need to break out into multiple objects.

Finally, don't think of your armature as being a traditional armature-based character rig where the whole character is controlled by bones in the armature. In fact, for your vehicle mod, the reverse is actually the case. The bones in your armature are actually controlled by the objects that you've already animated. They, in turn, only control the animation of your hose meshes.

Adding Bones to Your Armature

Now, with all of that preamble out of the way, you can start adding bones to your armature. Like mesh objects in Blender, armature objects have an Edit mode that you can toggle with the Tab hotkey. You add bones in Edit mode. However, don't jump right into Edit mode on your `hoseRig` armature just yet. Like objects in Blender, new bones are placed at the location of the 3D cursor. Typically, you want to place bones at the origins of the main moving parts in your vehicle. So the best workflow is to place the 3D cursor right at one of those origins. Use the following steps:

1. **Select the object whose origin you want your new bone to share.** In our cultivator example, we have a folding animation on the `armLeft` object, so it makes sense to have a bone there as well. Therefore, for this step, the `armLeft` object is what we've selected.

2. **Choose Object ▶ Snap ▶ Cursor to Selected from the 3D Viewport's header menu.**

3. **Select your armature object.** In this case, that would be the `hoseRig` object.

4. **Tab into Edit mode on your armature object.**

5. **Add a new bone at the location of the 3D Cursor with Add ▶ Single Bone.**

6. **Name your new bone something sensible using the Outliner or the *F2* hotkey.** In this example, our new bone is named `armLeftBone`.

7. **Tab back into Object mode.**

With one bone added, you repeat this process for each bone you intend on having in your model. Don't worry about creating parent-child relationships between bones. Remember, the bones are ultimately going to be controlled by the objects in your vehicle mod, not the other way around. Using this process on our example cultivator, your result may look like what's shown in Figure 12.2.

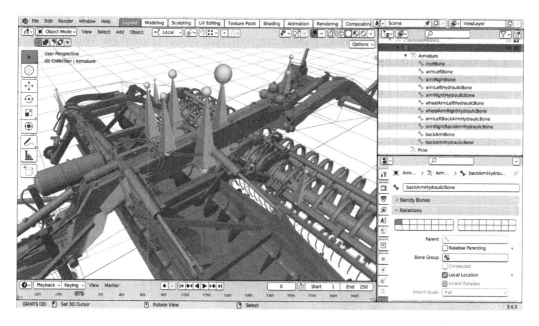

FIGURE 12.2   Add bones for each animated part of your vehicle.

Setting Constraints on Your Armature Bones

After you have all of your bones in place, you need to ensure that they move when their corresponding part of your vehicle moves. Normally, you'd control this behavior in a parent-child relationship. However, since all of your bones are encapsulated within the armature object, those kinds of relationships are difficult to create in the Outliner as you've done before.

Instead, you need to take advantage of another one of Blender's rigging features, *constraints*. Simply put, a constraint is a rule that you put on an object (or, in this case, a bone) that dictates how it moves or relates to other objects in the scene. For armature objects in Blender, you need to put constraints on individual bones. This process is done in a special mode that's exclusive to armatures called Pose mode. With your armature object selected, you can access Pose mode from the pie menu that appears when you press *Ctrl*+Tab or by using the Mode drop-down menu in the 3D Viewport's header.

Once you're in Pose mode, you should see that a new tab appears in the Properties editor, called Bone Constraints. What you want to do here is add a Child Of constraint to your selected bone and then configure that constraint to point to the object that you want to behave as its parent. Using the example of the `armLeftBone` in your `hoseRig` armature, use the following steps:

1. **In Pose mode, select the bone you want to work on.** In this example, that would be `armLeftBone`.

2. **From the Bone Constraints tab of the Properties editor, click the Add Bone Constraint button and choose Child Of from the menu that appears.** The Child Of constraint is in the fourth column, labeled Relationship. When your constraint is added, the bone should have a green color overlay.

3. **From the Child Of constraint panel, use the Target field to choose the object you want to be your bone's parent.** In this example, that object is armLeft. You can either choose it from the list or click the eyedropper icon and pick the object you want from the 3D Viewport.

4. **Tab back into Object mode and test your constraint by selecting the parent object and moving it around.** The bone you set the constraint on should move with it. In this case, you'd select `armLeft`, and you should see `armLeftBone` move with it.

Figure 12.3 shows the Child Of constraint added to the armLeftBone bone.

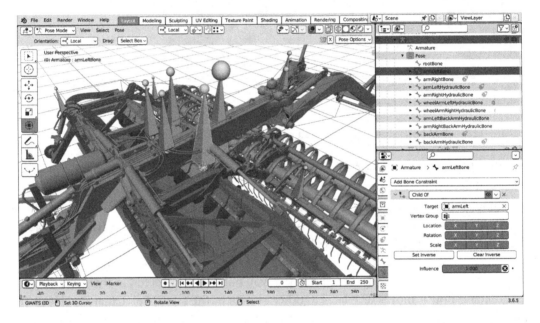

FIGURE 12.3   Use the Child Of bone constraint to bind the movement of your bones to the animated parts of your vehicle.

ASSIGNING VERTEX WEIGHTS TO CONTROL DEFORMATIONS

At this point, your bones are all in place, and they move in accordance with the animated objects in your vehicle, but they're still not influencing the behavior of your hoses. In order to have your deformations, you need to now make an association between your hoses object and your armature bones. That association is defined by vertex groups on your hoses object.

> **IMPORTANT**
>
> The key here is that vertex groups in your hoses object must have the exact same name as the bones in your armature.

Fortunately, there's an incredibly handy shortcut in Blender to help you automatically create the necessary vertex groups. This function is built into Blender's parenting operation. In most of the examples throughout this book, I've been recommending that you set up your parent-child relationships by using the drag-and-drop capabilities built into the Scene view of the Outliner. Unfortunately, by taking this approach, you do miss out on some automation that Blender has built-in.

The upside is that it doesn't matter if you've already made your hoses object a child of your `hoseRig` armature. You can still take advantage of this feature. From the 3D Viewport, use the following steps:

1. **Select your hoses object.** In this example, that would be `hoses`.

2. *Shift*+**select your armature object to add it to the selection and make it the active object.** The armature object in this example is `hosesRig`.

3. **Run the parenting operator and specifically choose With Empty Groups as the one to use (Object ▶ Parent ▶ With Empty Groups).** When you run this operation, Blender automatically creates vertex groups on your mesh object to correspond with the names of bones in your armature.

Now you can start assigning vertices to these groups. I should also note that you may be tempted to try the **With Automatic Weights** menu option in the Parenting menu, but in this case, I would discourage that. The option to use automatic weights is based on the bone's physical distance from the mesh. While that works great in traditional character rigging scenarios, it doesn't typically produce great results for the kind of rig in our models.

Assigning Weights to Your Root Bone

To more easily visualize bone weights, it's best to do this step in Weight Paint mode. As an example, let's assign all of the vertices in your hoses mesh to the root bone's vertex group. Use the following steps:

1. **Select your hoses object.** In our example, that object is named `hoses`.

2. **Switch to Weight Paint mode by using the mode drop-down menu in the header of the 3D Viewport or by using the *Ctrl*+Tab hotkey combination.** By default, you should see all of your hoses turn blue. By default, Blender visualizes weight assignments as a heat map, with blue indicating that the vertices aren't assigned to the active vertex group.

3. **Select all vertices (Select ▶ All).** You can also use the *A* hotkey.

4. **In the Object Data tab of the Properties editor, expand the Vertex Groups panel and select your root bone's vertex group from the list box.** In this example, the vertex group is named `rootBone`. When choosing this vertex group, the colors on your hoses mesh shouldn't change; it should still be blue.

5. **At the bottom of the Vertex Groups panel, ensure that the Weight property is set to 1.0.** Vertex weights are on a scale from 0 to 1, with zero meaning no influence and one meaningful influence.

6. **Click the Assign button in the Vertex Groups panel to assign the set Weight value to all selected vertices for the active vertex group.** Congratulations, you've just assigned all vertices in your hoses mesh to be fully influenced by your root bone. Your hoses mesh should now appear red to indicate that the vertices are fully influenced by the active vertex group.

IMPORTANT

Before you move forward with assigning vertices to other vertex groups, I'm going to strongly encourage you to undo what you did in the preceding example. You can either use the Undo feature or you can simply click the Remove button in the Vertex Groups panel of Object Data Properties to remove the selected vertices from the root bone's vertex group. Undoing everything may seem a little weird, but there's a good reason for this, covered in the next section.

Defining Weights for Other Vertex Groups

You can use the same basic process described in the preceding section to set weight values for your vertices and assign them to other vertex groups. However, if you try to click on vertices to select them in Weight Paint mode, you may find that something else happens. That's because the default behavior in Weight Paint mode is the ability to literally paint the weight values on your vertices by clicking and dragging your mouse cursor over them. If you want more precise selection control, you can *Shift*+click to select individual vertices or use the *B* hotkey to box select a group of them. Alternatively, you could also quickly Tab over to Edit mode and make your selection there. The selection persists across modes.

In practice, it's a good idea to start by only assigning full weight (1.0) or no weight (0.0) to vertices for a given vertex group. Then, after all of your base weights are set, work on smoothing the transition of influence between groups. There are two main approaches to smoothing your weight-group transitions. For the most artistic control when smoothing, you can take advantage of the Blur and Smear tools in Blender's Weight Paint mode. These tools are accessible from the Toolbar on the left side of the 3D Viewport when you're in Weight Paint mode, and they work similarly to their corresponding tools in image editing tools like Photoshop. Alternatively, you could do smoothing a bit more directly by selecting (*Ctrl*+left-click) the vertices at your transition point and choosing **Weights ▶ Smooth** from the header menu in the 3D Viewport.

TIP

Weight Paint mode works in Blender even when the character (your vehicle mesh in this case) is posed. In fact, one approach that can yield nice results is to rotate a moving part (like a folding arm) and then paint the weights on your hoses so the bend correctly matches the look you want. Then revert the rotation to make sure that the hose still looks good in the rest position.

As you start assigning weights to the vertices in your hose mesh, it's important to recognize that there's a key difference between how Blender handles vertex weights compared to how they're handled in GIANTS Engine. The difference is born from the fact that vertices can be members of multiple vertex groups with varying weight values.

Simply put, the game engine requires that all the vertex weights on a single vertex must add up to equal 1. In contrast, Blender doesn't have this requirement.

Ultimately, this difference means that you need to make some adjustments to your vertex weight assignments prior to exporting from Blender. Otherwise, you may run into an error or unexpected results when testing in-game. The work you have to do can be boiled down to two requirements:

- If a vertex isn't a member of any group, it should be a member of the root bone's group.

- The sum of the weight assignments for a vertex must equal 1.0

Fortunately, it's pretty easy to address both of these requirements. Each is covered in the next two sections.

Handling Ungrouped Vertices

In order to ensure that all vertices have a group, you first need to find those vertices. Blender has a built-in operator in Weight Paint mode that can help with that process. Use the following steps:

1. In the 3D Viewport, deselect all vertices (**Select ▶ None**).

2. Choose **Select ▶ Ungrouped Vertices** from the 3D Viewport's header menu to select all vertices in your mesh that are not part of a vertex group.

3. In the Object Data tab of the Properties editor, select your root bone's group in the Vertex Groups panel.

4. Still in the Vertex Groups panel, ensure that the **Weight** property is all the way up to 1.0.

5. Click the **Assign** button to assign your formerly ungrouped vertices at full influence to your root bone.

Now that all of your vertices are a member of at least one group, you can address the second requirement.

Normalizing Vertex Weights

It's important to GIANTS Engine that all the vertex group weights for each vertex add up to 1.0. When values fit within a scale from zero to one, they're known as being *normalized*. For example, let's say you have a vertex that belongs to two vertex groups, and its weight for each group is set to *1.0*. Well, $1+1=2$, so the weights on this vertex are not normalized.

TABLE 12.1   Examples of Normalized and Non-Normalized Vertex Weights

Vertex Group	Example Weight 1	Example Weight 2	Example Weight 3	Example Weight 4
body	1.0	0.5	0.5	0.25
arm1	1.0	0.0	0.5	0.25
arm2	0.0	0.0	0.0	0.5
SUM	2.0	0.5	1.0	1.0
	Not normalized	Not normalized	Normalized	Normalized

However, if you set the weight for each group to a value of *0.5*, then the sum of those weights is 1 and therefore normalized. Please note that the sum of all the weights must equal 1; any other value greater or less than 1, and those weights aren't normalized. Table 12.1 shows some examples of normalized and non-normalized weights on a single vertex.

This emphasis on normalization is important because, by default, Blender's Weight Paint mode doesn't enforce any kind of normalization between vertex groups. However, the GIANTS Engine expects normalized weights. Fortunately, there's a useful operator that can handle this process for you in one shot. Use the following steps:

1. In Weight Paint mode, select all vertices in your mesh (**Select ▶ All**).

2. From the 3D Viewport's header menu, choose **Weight ▶ Normalize All**.

And just like that, all of the vertices in your hoses object should be normalized such that the sum of their vertex group weights equals one. And with that, you can export your vehicle and test it in-game.

SUMMARY

This chapter was focused on the process of *skinning* your mesh, or more plainly put, controlling the deformable parts of your vehicle (hoses) with armatures and vertex groups. You started by getting an understanding of Blender's armature objects and how they can be used to control the behavior of other meshes. Then you got right to work by adding an armature object and bones inside it, aligned with parts of your vehicle. And finally, you assigned the vertices in your hoses mesh to vertex groups that correspond with bones in your armature. When you were finished, your hoses were able to bend with your vehicle as it animated.

In the next chapter, we focus on how your mod, and more specifically, your mod's icon, appears in the in-game shop.

CHAPTER 13

Generating Icons

YOU'VE GONE THROUGH ALL this effort to create your mod; you may as well make it look nice and presentable in the in-game store. The biggest part of that puzzle is having some really nice icons for your vehicles and for your mod. Fortunately, there's a tool that helps you simplify the process of creating these icons, and that's what this chapter is all about. The chapter starts by introducing you to the Farming Simulator Icon Generator and its basic setup. Then we'll cover the task of using the Icon Generator to produce store icons for each vehicle in your mod. And finally, we'll use the same tool to create an icon for your whole mod.

In this chapter:

- Getting the Farming Simulator Icon Generator

- Building a store icon for individual vehicles

- Creating an icon for your overall mod

TECHNICAL REQUIREMENTS

In order to go through the steps in this chapter, you're going to need a complete (or nearly complete) mod. At minimum, you need a mod folder populated with your `modDesc.xml` file and your vehicle-XML, as well as any I3D files that go with it. If you don't have a completed mod yet, you can use the example files from our cultivator example (see the URL and QR code after this paragraph). Alternatively, you can use the New Mod from Game feature of GIANTS Editor, as described in Chapter 6. You'll also need a working copy of Farming Simulator and GIANTS Editor installed on your computer.

DOI: 10.1201/9781032659497-13

https://gdn.giants-software.com/blenderBook

The final requirement for this chapter is the Farming Simulator Icon Generator program, but the details on that are covered in the next section.

GETTING THE FARMING SIMULATOR ICON GENERATOR

The easiest way to generate store icons for your mod is with a free tool from GIANTS Software that's available on the GDN. Log in to your account on the GDN and go to the Downloads page (https://gdn.giants-software.com/downloads.php). At the bottom of this page, in the section titled Modding, there's a link for the Farming Simulator Icon Generator. Click the link to download the program to your hard drive. The Icon Generator tool doesn't actually need to be installed; it's bundled in a compressed folder. So you can right-click it in Windows Explorer and choose **Extract All** from the context menu. You can choose to extract the folder to anywhere on your hard drive; just remember where you do it.

NOTE

It's worth mentioning that bundled in the ZIP file with the Farming Simulator Icon Generator executable is a PDF file with a handy description of how to use the tool, along with a change log that describes changes from one version to the next.

Once the program is extracted, you should be able to launch the Farming Simulator Icon Generator. It should look similar to what's shown in Figure 13.1.

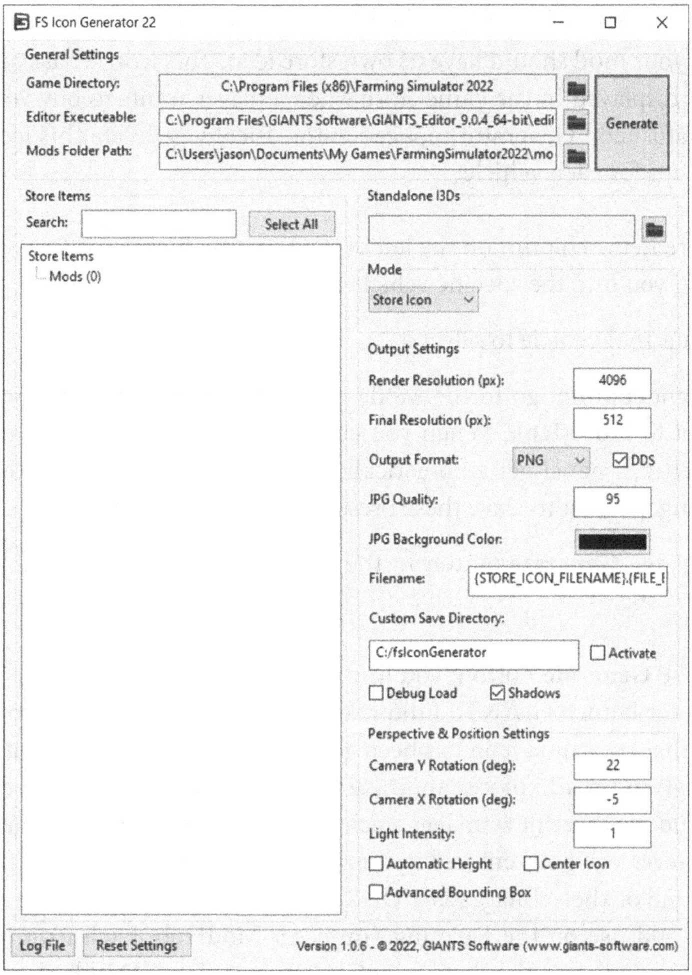

FIGURE 13.1   The Farming Simulator Icon Generator is a pretty simple program when you first launch it.

With the Farming Simulator Icon Generator installed and running on your computer, there are a few setup steps you need to go through. Most importantly, you need to point the program at the correct paths on your hard drive for Farming Simulator, GIANTS Editor, and the folder where your mod lives. The Icon Generator typically does a pretty good job of finding Farming Simulator and GIANTS Editor, though if you have your mods folder in a non-standard location, it may have some difficulty. For instance, if you followed the example in Chapter 6, you may have your mods folder located at Documents/My FS Mods/.

Once you have all those settings correctly entered at the top of the window, you should see the Store Items column on the left populated with each of the mods in that folder. Now you can start making your icons.

BUILDING A STORE ICON FOR INDIVIDUAL VEHICLES

Each vehicle in your mod should have its own store icon. This icon is basically a thumbnail image that gets displayed in the game store when a player wants to buy your vehicle. The Farming Simulator Icon Generator tool can automatically generate this icon for you. Use the following steps for each vehicle:

1. In the Store Items column on the left of the Farming Simulator Icon Generator, drill down until you find the specific vehicle that needs an icon.

2. Click the desired vehicle to select it.

3. On the right column, go to the Mode panel and ensure that the drop-down menu there is set to **Store Icon**. When you choose this drop-down, a lot of values in the Output Settings panel get automatically populated. Unless you know exactly what you're doing, it's best to leave these presets in place.

4. Click the large **Generate** button in the upper right of the Farming Simulator Icon Generator.

After clicking the **Generate** button, you just need to wait a minute or so. You should see the Icon Generator launch GIANTS Editor, and then, shortly after that, you have a dialog informing you that your mod icon has been generated. When it's done, you can open your mod's folder in Windows Explorer and take a peek at what was generated. In your mod folder, you should see three new images, each with the same name. That name should correspond to whatever you have entered in the `<image>` tag within `<storeData>` in your vehicle-XML. One of these images is a DDS image for use in-game. The other is a PNG for general use and use on the Farming Simulator ModHub. Each icon file is an image 512×512 pixels in size. And the third is in GIM format. The GIM file stores metadata for converting images to DDS. If you want to manually convert files to DDS, you can use the GIANTS Texture Tool, also available on the GDN.

If you like the icon, then you're good to go. However, for some vehicles, the default camera values don't always give the most flattering view. If that's the case for your icon, there are some controls that you can use to tweak and then re-generate your icon. In the bottom right corner of the Farming Simulator Icon Generator, there's a panel labeled Perspective & Position Settings. Most of the time, you shouldn't adjust the values in this panel. All of the base game icons are rendered with these default settings. However, you have the option of "sweetening" the framing on your icon with these values. Generally, you don't have to do more than adjust the **Camera Y Rotation (deg)** value a bit. For instance, you can set this value to 45 to get a view of your vehicle from its front left corner. That value can work particularly nicely for tools that are wider than they are long.

After you set a value that you think may work, click the **Generate** button at the top of the window again. Your old icon is overwritten with the new one. If you're satisfied with those results, you can move on to performing the same process on your other vehicles. If it's still not to your liking, you can tweak further and keep regenerating until you get icons that you like.

As you build your icons, it's possible that your vehicle may appear to be "floating" in the generated icon. This can happen for a number of reasons, including having your vehicle's root placed somewhere different in your .blend file. Whatever the reason, there's a relatively simple fix. In your vehicle-XML file, you can add a couple tags within the content of the <storeData> tag. In particular, you may want to include the offset tags, <shopTranslationOffset> and <shopRotationOffset>. The content of each of these tags gives X, Y, and Z axis offsets for translation and rotation, respectively. For our example cultivator, the tags in our <storeData> tag look like this:

```
<storeData>
...
    <shopTranslationOffset>0 -0.185 0</shopTranslationOffset>
    <shopRotationOffset>-0.817 0 0</shopRotationOffset>
...
</storeData>
```

To help you pick these values more easily, you can use the gsVehicleDebug attributes command from the in-game console (more on this in the next chapter) while in the shop screen and check the values in the bottom right of the screen. That's the position and orientation when the vehicle is sitting flat on the ground. Copy these values into the <shopTranslationOffset> and <shopRotationOffset> tags to get a good icon where your vehicle looks like it's on the ground.

> **TIP**
>
> You can create icons for multiple vehicles in one batch by *Shift*+clicking each vehicle in the Store Items column on the left of the Farming Simulator Icon Generator.

CREATING AN ICON FOR YOUR MOD

In addition to the icons for each of your vehicles, you need to have a store icon for your overall mod. Not only is this icon used in-game, but it's also used on the Farming Simulator ModHub when you publish your mod to share with others (see Chapter 15). The process is similar to what's described in the preceding section for generating vehicle icons, with some subtle differences:

1. In the Store Items column on the left, select your vehicle mod. If your mod has multiple vehicles, use this opportunity to select the ones you want to show up in your icon. You can select multiple vehicles by *Shift*+clicking them.

2. On the right column in the Mode panel, set the drop-down to **Mod Icon**. As with the vehicle icon, many of the values in Output Settings automatically change once you make this selection. Leave them at the default values for now.

3. Click the **Generate** button in the upper right of the window.

Just like with the process of generating your vehicle icons, the Farming Simulator Icon Generator goes through a process of launching GIANTS Editor to generate your icon directly from your I3D file. In fact, if you only have one vehicle in your mod, the process should look identical.

If you look in your mod folder at the results, you have three new images in DDS, PNG, and GIM formats, each with `icon _` as their prefix. These images should be 256×256 pixels in size. And, like with your vehicle icon, if you're not satisfied with the camera angle or lighting in your icon, you can tweak the settings in the Perspective & Position Settings panel and then regenerate.

IMPORTANT

Unlike the store icon, the mod icon does not actually use the content of the `<icon>` tag in your `modDesc.xml` file to generate the name of your icon images. This means that if those names are different, you need to fix that. Either rename all three images that the Icon Generator created or just change the one line in your `modDesc.xml`.

SUMMARY

This chapter was short and sweet. You saw how to use the Farming Simulator Icon Generator to create icons for your mod. At the start of the chapter, you downloaded and installed the Farming Simulator Icon Generator from the GDN. Then you used that tool to create store icons for individual vehicles in your mod. And finally, you used this same tool to create an icon for your mod as a whole.

In the next chapter, we'll get into some specific commands that you can use from within Farming Simulator to test your mod and tweak it to perfection.

CHAPTER 14

Tips and Tricks for Testing Your Vehicle In-Game

Y OU'RE NEARLY DONE! IF you've worked your way through the rest of the book, it's likely that you have a functional mod for Farming Simulator. But how do you know for sure? Moreover, how can you be sure that your mod has the best in-game performance and behavior possible? The short answer: you need to test it in-game. However, although you can probably get a decent enough feel for how your mod is working in the game, it's much better if you can have some more clear numbers for your tests. Fortunately, there's a host of tools available in the game that can give you exactly that kind of information.

Those tools are what this chapter is all about. We start the chapter by going through the steps necessary to make sure you have access to in-game tools, most of which live in the in-game console. Next, we cover some cheats to quickly populate the ground so you can test vehicle behavior (for instance, harvesters need ripe crops to do their work). We also work our way through a few cheats that help you quickly modify your vehicle in-game to visualize filling, wear, and fuel. From there, we show a way to reload your vehicle-XML file without restarting the game, so you can quickly make changes and see them immediately. And finally, we dig into a command that shows detailed debugging information about your vehicle mod.

In this chapter:

- Setting up Farming Simulator for testing

- Reloading your vehicle without restarting the game

- Populating fields quickly

- Modifying your vehicle from the in-game console

- Debugging your vehicle mod

DOI: 10.1201/9781032659497-14

TECHNICAL REQUIREMENTS

The only real requirement for this chapter is Farming Simulator. You could also benefit from having GIANTS Studio or a text editor, but really, the commands and procedures covered in this chapter work whether you have a mod loaded or not. However, for some things, like gsVehicleReload (covered later in the chapter), it's useful to have a vehicle-XML file that you can actually edit. Otherwise, that command won't appear to do very much for you.

SETTING UP FARMING SIMULATOR FOR TESTING

Farming Simulator is, first and foremost, a game. So, as you might imagine, its default starting behavior is configured with that use in mind. In order to have access to the special tools and commands that are useful to you as a modder, you need to make some changes so the game starts ready for your tests.

In fact, it's likely that you've already made one critical change. In Chapter 6, within the section titled "Enabling Developer Mode in Farming Simulator", you modified the game's game.xml file to enable Developer Mode. Developer Mode gives you the ability to see the in-game console by pressing the *Tilde (~)* key twice on your keyboard. Figure 14.1 shows an example of what the in-game console looks like when you first show it.

FIGURE 14.1 The in-game console is enabled by Developer Mode and is the place where you enter most of your testing commands.

You can actually cycle through the commands that are available to you from the in-game console by repeatedly pressing *Tab*. There's a lot in there, though, and it's always better to know what a command does before running it, so it's in your best interest to hold off on actually running any of these commands.

What's even more impressive is that those commands aren't the totality of what's available to you. You can make more console commands available by launching Farming Simulator with some additional flags set. While it's possible to launch Farming Simulator from the command line with these flags, they can be easy to forget. A better approach is to make a custom shortcut for the Farming Simulator executable with these flags already set. Use the following steps:

1. **From Windows Explorer, navigate to the game folder for Farming Simulator.** It should be somewhere like `C:/Program Files (x86)/Farming Simulator/`.

2. **In that folder, right-click the Farming Simulator executable (usually named something like `FarmingSimulator.exe`) and choose *Create shortcut* from the context menu that appears.** Windows will probably warn you that you can't make a shortcut in the game folder and suggest to add it to your desktop. You should agree to that.

3. **Rename your new shortcut to `Farming Simulator Debug` by right-clicking it and choosing *Rename* from the context menu.** Of course, just naming it Debug doesn't actually set any flags for you. That's in the next step.

4. **Right-click your Farming Simulator Debug shortcut and choose *Properties* from the context menu.** A window should appear with the properties for your shortcut.

5. **Edit the *Target* field to add `-cheats` after the execution path.** Your result should look something like what's shown in Figure 14.2.

6. **Save your changes and close the window.** Now, when you double-click the `Farming Simulator Debug` shortcut, Farming Simulator will launch with those flags, providing you with even more debug commands from the in-game console.

FIGURE 14.2   Add the -cheats flag to your execution path to get more debug commands when you launch Farming Simulator.

IMPORTANT

It's important that you only use these debug flags when developing or building mods and *not* for regular gameplay. While these flags expose some useful commands and features, they do have an impact on in-game performance.

POPULATING FIELDS QUICKLY

When your vehicle mod is a tool like a harvester or cultivator, you need to have a field to do that work on and test it. While you can certainly do the work of building a field like you would in a real game, it's faster for testing purposes if you can have one already set up for you. In this section, we cover three commands you can use from the in-game console: getFieldSetFruit, getFieldSetGround, and gsTipAnywhereAdd.

gsFieldSetGround

Both the command in this section, gsFieldSetGround, and the one in the next are used to quickly cheat a field to the desired state for testing purposes. Specifically, the gsFieldSet-Ground is what you use to set the visualization and the state of a given field. However, you don't just type the command in the in-game console. You also need to include some parameters. This command has two required parameters and a variety of additional parameters. The following is a list of each parameter for the gsFieldSetGround command:

- fieldIndex: (required) This parameter is a numbered value that corresponds to the index of the field you want to modify. The index for each field is visible in the map.

- groundTypeName: (required) This parameter is a string (text) value that describes the in-game visualization for the field. The list of valid ground types includes the following choices:

  - cultivated

  - direct_sown

  - grass

  - grass_cut

  - harvest_ready

  - harvest_ready_other

  - planted

  - plowed

  - ridge

  - roller_lines

- rolled_seedbed

- seedbed

- sown

- stubble

- tillage

- none

- `angle`: This parameter is an angle that the field should be set to. The angle doesn't refer to the slope of the ground but to the general working direction. On Farming Simulator's default maps, the possible values are integers from 0 to 8, mapped from 0 to 180 degrees. In mod maps with custom ground angles, these values can be different. If in doubt, set this parameter to 0.

- `sprayTypeState`: This parameter is an integer value between 0 and 4, representing the following states:

  - 0: Nothing

  - 1: Fertilizer

  - 2: Lime

  - 3: Manure

  - 4: Liquid Manure

- `fertilizerState`: The `fertilizerState` parameter is a number that you set to 0, 1, or 2, with 0 being unfertilized and 2 being 100% fertilized.

- `plowingState`: Set this parameter to 0 to tell the game engine that the field requires plowing or set it to 1 to say the field doesn't need plowing. This value only influences the yield and not the visuals of the field.

- `weedState`: This parameter is an integer value between 0 and 9, where each value can be mapped to these states:

  - 0: No weeds

  - 1: Invisible sparse

  - 2: Invisible dense

  - 3: Weed small

  - 4: Weed medium

  - 5: Weed large

  - 6: Weed small (same as 3)

- 7: Dead small

- 8: Dead medium

- 9: Dead large

- `limeState`: If you want to set the field such that it needs lime, set this parameter to 0. If you want the field to be limed, set it to 1. This value only has an influence on the yield and not the visuals.

- `stubbleState`: The `stubbleState` indicates whether your field has been mulched, where 0 means unmulched and 1 means mulched.

- `buyField`: Set this parameter to `true` to tell the game engine that the player has bought the field if it hasn't already been bought. Set it to `false` to indicate otherwise.

- `removeFoliage`: If you'd like foliage to be removed when you set the ground state, set this value to `true` (this is the default). To keep foliage, set it to `false`.

The way these parameters work, you enter them in order with spaces between each. This setup means that the later parameters can't be set unless you also set the earlier ones. For instance, you can't set the `plowingState` parameter unless you've also set the parameters for `fertilizerState`, `groundLayer`, `angle`, `groundTypeName`, and `fieldIndex`.

As an example, enter this command in the in-game console (Figure 14.3):

```
gsFieldSetGround 45 plowed
```

FIGURE 14.3   A plowed field, created with `gsFieldSetGround`.

However, the state of the field itself is unchanged from whatever it was before you entered that command. To make that field look plowed *and* have the proper plowed state, you would enter this command instead:

```
gsFieldSetGround 45 plowed 0 0 0 1
```

The beginning of the command is the same, but you've also set the `angle` and `spray-TypeState` attributes to 0, set the field as being unfertilized, and then finally set the field itself to a `plowingState` of 1, or plowed.

gsFieldSetFruit

Much like its cousin command in the preceding section, `gsFieldSetFruit` is a command you use to change the state of a given field. And just like gsFieldSetGround, this command has an assortment of parameters that you can use with it; the first of the two being required:

- `fieldId`: (required) Like the `fieldIndex` value for gsFieldSetGround, this parameter is a number that corresponds with a specific field. In fact, this parameter is exactly like `fieldIndex`; it's just named differently.

- `fruitName`: (required) This parameter is a string value that corresponds with one of the kinds of crops you can grow in Farming Simulator. Valid `fruitName` values include (this is an example; a more comprehensive list can be found in the game data at `data/maps/maps _ fruitTypes.xml`):

  - `barley`

  - `canola`

  - `maize`

  - `wheat`

- `growthState`: The `growthState` parameter is an integer value from 0 to 15, and the meanings of those values differ depending on the type of crop. Using wheat as an example, values 1–7 relate to stages of growth. A value of 8 means that the wheat is harvestable. Setting a growthState of 9 means withered. And a value of 10 indicates that the wheat has been cut. Many crops follow this same model, but it's different for others. It's best to use a little trial and error to understand these values for a specific crop type.

- `groundTypeName`: This parameter corresponds with the same parameter in `gsSetFieldGround` and allows for all the same string values listed in the preceding section.

- `sprayTypeState`: This parameter is an integer value between 0 and 4, representing the following states:

- 0: Nothing

- 1: Fertilizer

- 2: Lime

- 3: Manure

- 4: Liquid Manure

- `fertilizerState`: The `fertilizerState` parameter is a number that you set to 0, 1, or 2, with 0 being unfertilized and 2 being 100% fertilized.

- `plowingState`: Set this parameter to 0 to tell the game engine that the field requires plowing or set it to 1 to say the field doesn't need plowing. This value only influences the yield and not the visuals of the field.

- `weedState`: This parameter is an integer value between 0 and 9, where each value can be mapped to these states:

  - 0: No weeds

  - 1: Invisible sparse

  - 2: Invisible dense

  - 3: Weed small

  - 4: Weed medium

  - 5: Weed large

  - 6: Weed small (same as 3)

  - 7: Dead small

  - 8: Dead medium

  - 9: Dead large

- `limeState`: If you want to set the field such that it needs lime, set this parameter to 0. If you want the field to be limed, set it to 1. This value only has influence on the yield and not the visuals.

- `stubbleState`: The `stubbleState` indicates whether your field has been mulched, where 0 means unmulched and 1 means mulched.

- `setSpray`: Set this parameter to `true` to have the visual texture for fertilizer and lime set when using the `limeState` and `fertilizerState` parameters.

- `buyField`: Set this parameter to `true` to tell the game engine that the player has bought the field if it hasn't already been bought. Set it to `false` to indicate otherwise.

As an example, enter the following command in the in-game console:

```
gsFieldSetFruit 45 wheat 8 harvest_ready 0 1 4
```

With this command, you are telling the game engine that field 23 should have harvestable wheat on harvest-ready ground with no set spray, partial fertilization, and more weeds than you would want as a player. In-game, your field may look like what's shown in Figure 14.4.

FIGURE 14.4   Use gsFieldSetFruit to populate a field with a crop and set the state of that crop.

gsTipAnywhereAdd

Another incredibly handy command is `gsTipAnywhereAdd`. Unlike the other commands in this section, this one isn't specific to fields, but it does pertain to the game environment for testing. Use this command to place heaps of any type of fill directly in front of your game character. And like the other commands, this one includes a number of parameters. In fact, using this command and its parameters, you can spawn windrows, which can be helpful if your mod is a baler and you need to set up a testing scenario for it.

The parameters for gsTipAnywhereAdd are as follows:

- `fillTypeName`: (required) This parameter is a string (text) value that corresponds to one of many types of fill that are available in Farming Simulator with everything from chaff to woodchips. For a comprehensive list, you can look in the game data at `data/maps/maps _ fillTypes.xml`.

- `amount`: (required) This parameter is an integer value, measured in liters, of how much of whatever heap you want to add per row. The volume is a bit difficult to imagine, so you may need to play with this value to arrive at your desired amount.

- `length:` This parameter specifies, in meters, how long your desired heap should be.

- `rows:` If you want to create rows of heaps, set this value with an integer number that corresponds to the number of rows you want.

- `spacing:` If you have multiple rows, you can use the `spacing` parameter to set the distance between each row in meters.

As an example of this command, enter this in the in-game console:

```
gsTipAnywhereAdd straw 10000 20 5 3
```

With this command, you're telling the game engine to create 5 rows of 10,000-L straw heaps 20 meters long, spaced 3 meters apart. In-game, your results should look something like what's shown in Figure 14.5.

FIGURE 14.5   Adding rows of wheat heaps with `gsTipAnywhereAdd`.

gsPalletAdd and gsBaleAdd

There are times when you just need a pallet or a bale in the game. Maybe you need to lift the pallet or move the bale around. Or, more realistically, you need to test your production placeable mod, and you need to have the goods required for the production. Whatever the reason, rather than hunting around a game map to find a pallet or bale, you can just add one quickly using the in-game console.

If you want to add a pallet, use the command `gsPalletAdd`. This command has a few parameters that you need to include when using it:

- `fillType:` (required) This parameter corresponds with the `fillTypeName` parameter used by `gsTipAnywhereAdd`. It's a string value with the name of whatever fill type you want loaded on the pallet.

- `amount:` This parameter is an integer value for the amount of your chosen fill on the pallet, measured in liters. If you don't include this parameter, the pallet spawns full.

- `worldX:` The `worldX` parameter is the location you want to place the pallet on the world map, along the East-West axis.

- `worldZ:` Like `worldX`, the `worldZ` parameter is the North-South coordinate for your pallet's location.

NOTE

If you don't include the `worldX` and `worldZ` parameters, the pallet is spawned in front of your player character.

So if you wanted to add a pallet with 1000 liters of flour in front of your player, you might use this command:

```
gsPalletAdd flour 1000
```

Likewise, you may also want to add a bale somewhere on the game map. For that, you need to use the `gsBaleAdd` command. Like `gsPalletAdd`, the `gsBaleAdd` command has a number of required parameters that you must include:

- **fillType:** As with gsPalletAdd, this parameter represents the type of material that your bale is composed of. For example, you might use `straw` as your `fillType` parameter.

- **isRoundable:** Bales can be round or they can be square. If you want the bale to be round, set this parameter to `true`.

- **width:** This parameter is the width of your bale, measured in meters.

- **height:** The height of your bale in meters.

- **length:** Your bale's length, also in meters.

- **wrapState:** This parameter is a value that represents how tightly wrapped your bale is. It's a floating point value between `0.0` and `1.0`, where `1.0` means that the bale is fully wrapped with foil. This parameter only works for grass bales.

- **modName:** If you want to test a bale that's been added through your modDesc.xml, but has the same size as the bale in the base game, you can use this parameter to force the game to load your mod bale. The string you would use for this parameter is the name of your mod's ZIP file.

Like the `gsPalletAdd` command, the `gsBaleAdd` command doesn't require you to include any coordinates for placing the bale. You use this command and the bale appears right in front of your player character.

As an example, if you want to add a square straw bale that's 1.2 m×0.9 m×2.2 m, you would use the following command in the in-game console:

```
gsBaleAdd straw false 1.2 0.9 2.2
```

Likewise, if you wanted to add a small round grass bale, you could use this command:

```
gsBaleAdd grass_windrow true 1.2 1.25 1.25
```

gsTreeAdd

Some of the work that the player does in game involves dealing with trees in and around their property. Either they're growing and harvesting from them, or they're clearing them out to make a field to grow other stuff. And of course, there are tools and vehicles that exist to help with that process. If you want to test harvesting trees, you still need to purchase them and place them via the shop. However, if you want to test clearing out cut trees of a particular type or in a particular state, it can be tricky to find exactly what you need. Fortunately, you can use the `gsTreeAdd` command to specify and place a cut tree in front of your character.

As with many other commands that you enter in the in-game console, the gsTreeAdd command has a number of required parameters you must include:

- `length`: This parameter is the length of your tree as it's lying on the ground, in meters.

- `type`: This parameter is a string value that you use to specify the type of tree that you want. A full listing of possible types can be found in the game data for your Farming Simulator install.

- `growthState`: The `growthState` parameter for trees is much like the same parameter for the `gsFieldSetFruit` command. This is an integer value from 1 to 6, defining the maturity of the tree. And like with `gsFieldSetFruit`, the meaning of each `growthState` value can differ a bit from one tree type to the next. For reference, you can look at the game data for Farming Simulator at `data/maps/maps_treeTypes.xml` and look for trees like spruce or pine in that file to understand their possible growth states.

- `delimb`: Set this parameter to `true` if you want to give your tree the appearance of being pruned.

gsMoneyAdd

Stuff in Farming Simulator costs in-game money for the player to purchase and use. Sometimes, your mod might be for a very expensive piece of equipment that a player doesn't have enough cash for when they first start playing. That means you'd need to play through the game to amass enough money to purchase your own mod, just so you could test it. While that might be fun, it's not exactly the most efficient way to test out your mod. To get there faster, you can use the gsMoneyAdd command. This command has a single parameter, amount, where you specifically say the amount of money you want to give the player. So if you need the player character to have an additional $50,000, you would type the following in the in-game console:

```
gsMoneyAdd 50000
```

MODIFYING YOUR VEHICLE FROM THE IN-GAME CONSOLE

In order to properly test out your vehicle, you need to test it in a whole bunch of different states and situations. Now, you could just use your vehicle in the game and see how it performs, but that's not the quickest way to do testing. If you want to test the tool under load or see how it looks with wear or damage, that can take a lot of time if you have to wait until game time. There're a lot of commands you can use from the console to "skip to the end" in these situations, so you can quickly see whether your mod behaves as you expect. This section includes a bunch of these commands.

gsFillUnitAdd

Let's say your mod is a tool that gets filled with corn or wheat or something and you want to test how that tool performs and looks with various amounts of fill. You could play it in the game and fill it with whatever you can find or grow, but it's faster to just use the gsFillUnitAdd command from the console. As with many commands that you run from this console, this one includes a number of parameters:

- fillUnitIndex: (required) Trailers can sometimes have multiple fill units, so you need to define an index value. If your mod only has a single unit, then set this value to 1.

- fillTypeName: (required) This is a string (text) that is the name of whatever kind of fill you want, such as wheat, straw, or maize. That's not a comprehensive list, of course, because there are a lot of types of fills. You can check the game data at data/maps/maps _ fillTypes.xml for a full list of options.

- amount: This optional parameter is the amount of fill, in liters. If you don't include a value, then the gsFillUnitAdd command fills as much volume as the vehicle can take. The amount attribute also accepts negative numbers, so you can test emptying a vehicle.

To use this command, select the vehicle that you want to fill in-game, and then run this command from the console. For instance, if you have a trailer that you want to fill with wheat, you might type the following:

```
gsFillUnitAdd 1 wheat
```

Testing the Dirtiness and Wear on Your Vehicle

Farming equipment has a rough life. It can get beat up quite a bit, and the game has visualizations to help show that wear over time. Of course, if you're short on time, you can see the results and test much quicker with console commands. In fact, there are three commands that are really helpful. The following are three commands you can use to rough-up your vehicle:

- `gsVehicleAddDirt`: As your vehicle mod is put to work, it collects dirt. Use this command to add that dirt.

- `gsVehicleAddWear`: A working vehicle takes scratches, paint fading, and staining over time. This command makes textures visible for those effects.

- `gsVehicleAddDamage`: Vehicles do occasionally get beat up. The visual part of that can be depicted using the `gsVehicleAddWear` command just described. However, a damaged vehicle also performs its tasks less efficiently. For example, a tractor has less horsepower, or a cultivator has to be pulled slower. This non-visual damage is what the `gsVehicleAddDamage` command provides.

> **NOTE**
>
> Recall from Chapter 3 that you set up a vmask for defining wear and dirt on your model. The `gsVehicleAddDirt` and `gsVehicleAddWear` commands are how you can test whether your texture placement was correct.

In all three cases, these commands take an `amount` parameter with a value between `0.0` and `1.0`. You type them in, and Farming Simulator adds a texture to reflect that level of dirtiness, wear, or damage. For example, if you wanted to set a vehicle as being halfway dirty, you'd use the following command:

```
gsVehicleAddDirt 1
```

However, if you want your vehicle halfway dirty, you would use this:

```
gsVehicleAddDirt 0.5
```

These commands also accept negative values, so if you want to make your vehicle clean again, you can use this command:

```
gsVehicleAddDirt -1
```

Adjusting Fuel and Temperature Levels

When you're driving a vehicle from your character's POV, you can see the vehicle's dashboard instruments, including fuel levels and the vehicle's engine temperature. If you want to test the dashboard displays for these levels, it's easiest if you can see them change directly. There are two commands that can help you do these tests:

- `gsVehicleFuelSet`: Type this command in the in-game console with a parameter for the value you want, measured in liters, and your vehicle will have that fuel level.

- `gsVehicleTemperatureSet`: Similar to the preceding command, use this one with a parameter for the temperature, in degrees (Celsius), and your vehicle's motor temperature will change to reflect that value.

gsCameraFovSet

Sometimes, it's not about the vehicle itself, but how a particular part of the vehicle looks. The default field of view for the in-game camera doesn't always show you all the details you need to see when checking your model. To help with this situation, you can use the `gsCameraFovSet` command to directly modify the field of view (FOV) for the current game camera. The `gsCameraFovSet` command takes a single parameter value for the field of view, measured in degrees. So if you want to zoom in on a part of your mod to check it without the distortion that sometimes comes from being close, you might enter a command like this:

```
gsCameraFovSet 15
```

Figure 14.6 shows this command in action. On the left, you see the interior of a tractor using the standing in-game field of view, and on the right, you see that same view, but with a much tighter FOV, for checking the dash instruments.

FIGURE 14.6   On the left, dash instruments in standard FOV. On the right, that same view with a tighter FOV.

RELOADING YOUR VEHICLE WITHOUT RESTARTING THE GAME

When you make tweaks to your vehicle mod, you're going to want to test those tweaks quickly. This is especially true when doing quick adjustments to values in your vehicle-XML file. It can be bothersome to have to restart Farming Simulator, rebuy your vehicle, and then look for differences. In fact, if you're looking for differences, it can be difficult to notice them at all if you have to go through that process every time.

Fortunately, you don't have to. The `gsVehicleReload` command is in the in-game console. When you run this command, Farming Simulator re-parses your vehicle-XML file and reloads your I3D file. This means that it doesn't matter if you make a change in Blender or in GIANTS Studio. The `gsVehicleReload` command updates everything.

Generally speaking, most of the time, you're going to just use this command directly, with no parameters. However, the command does have some useful parameters:

- `reset`: By default, this parameter is set to false. Set it to true (e.g. `gsVehicleReload true`), and when your vehicle is reloaded, it's completely reset to its initial spawn state.

- `radius`: This parameter is a distance in meters. Any vehicles within that radius will be reloaded all at once. This parameter is especially handy for pallets, which can't be entered or attached. With the `radius` parameter, you can just walk by the pallets and reload them.

So, for example, if you want to reload all vehicles within 25 meters to their initial spawn state, you would enter the following command:

```
gsVehicleReload true 25
```

DEBUGGING YOUR VEHICLE MOD

The majority of the commands given in this chapter so far are commands that perform some action in-game, be it setting up a field or reloading your vehicle. However, most of the time when you're testing your mod, the most useful thing you can get is information. How big is your work area? What's the weight of your vehicle? How hard is the tractor's engine working when it tows your vehicle? With this kind of information, you can adjust the values in your vehicle-XML file to yield better results. When it comes to providing you with this kind of information, two incredibly useful commands are `gsVehicleDebug` and `gsVehicleDebugLOD`.

gsVehicleDebug

The best way to understand the `gsVehicleDebug` command is to actually use it. Launch Farming Simulator with the shortcut you created earlier in this chapter and load your vehicle mod. You'll need to enter the vehicle for the debug overlays to display properly. From the in-game console, type `gsVehicleDebug` and press *Enter*. If you hide the in-game console, you should see that the HUD has been updated with some additional options, along with some vehicle-specific information hovering over your vehicle, as shown in Figure 14.7.

FIGURE 14.7 The `gsVehicleDebug` command gives you a ton of information via the in-game HUD.

In truth, the `gsVehicleDebug` command toggles a whole debugging mode within Farming Simulator, with its own set of interactive options that you can display. By default, you're placed in the Values mode of the vehicle debugging view, as indicated by the large green text at the bottom left of the screen. If you look across the bottom of the screen, you can see the other vehicle debugging views that are available to you, along with helpful hot-key shortcuts to access them.

> **TIP**
>
> If you ever want to access a specific vehicle debugging view directly from the in-game console, you can type the name of that view after `gsVehicleDebug`. For instance, if you want to jump straight to the Attributes view, you can type `gsVehicleDebug attributes`.

The views available for vehicle debugging are Values, Physics, Tuning, Transmission, Attributes, Attacher Joints, AI, Sounds, and Animations. Each of these views can give you specific information about your vehicle mod to help with ensuring that it behaves properly. The next few sub-sections cover some of the most commonly used of these views.

Attributes

One of the most frequently used debugging views is the Attributes view, accessed by pressing *Shift*+5 after you've already started `gsVehicleDebug` or by typing `gsVehicleDe-bug  attributes` in the in-game console. As shown in Figure 14.8, this view gives visualizations for your vehicle size area, foliage bending areas, work areas, and the license plate area. A common practice is to have this debugging view open to inspect the working area and vehicle size area to ensure that parts of your vehicle don't inadvertently clip with other vehicles. See Chapter 7 for more details on adjusting these work area attributes. Chapter 9 has details on the license plate area.

FIGURE 14.8   Use the Attributes view of gsVehicleDebug to check the general properties of your vehicle.

AI

In Chapter 7, you did a fair amount of work to define properties that your AI workers can use in-game to control your vehicle. If you switch to the AI view of `gsVehicleDebug` by using the *Shift*+7 hotkey combination, you get a visualization like what's shown in Figure 14.9.

FIGURE 14.9   The AI view of gsVehicleDebug lets you see collision boxes that are only defined in your vehicle-XML.

One particularly nice feature of this view is that it shows your `aiCollisionNode` box. Recall that this box is defined exclusively in your vehicle-XML file, with no visualization of it in Blender. Using the AI debugging view, you get a nice blue box that clearly shows the size and location of your collision node. Likewise, this view provides a visualization for the `agentAttachment` definition. And while the AI has the vehicle working on the field, there's additional debugging information displayed.

Animations

Like your AI settings, your vehicle animations are all defined in your vehicle-XML, as covered in Chapter 8. This means that you don't have an easy way of visualizing or checking your animations until you get into the game. Fortunately, once you're in the game the Animations view of gsVehicleDebug gives you a pretty nice interface that lists all of your animations and their current times, as shown in Figure 14.10.

FIGURE 14.10   Use the Animations view of `gsVehicleDebug` to check your animations in-game.

The visualization for animations in this view also includes the sounds, helping you visualize the timing of all your animation parts with more accuracy. You can toggle which animations get focused in this view by pressing *J* on your keyboard.

Physics

One other useful view of gsVehicleDebug is the Physics view, which you can switch to by pressing Shift+2. As shown in Figure 14.11, this view displays debug data for the physics components in your vehicle, like the motor and wheels. In particular, the numbers overlaying the left side of the screen are especially useful for setting up your motor power and fine tuning your vehicle's wheel suspension. Also, this view just looks cool as it responds in real-time to the actions you do in the game.

FIGURE 14.11   Use the Physics view of gsVehicleDebug to check the physics components of your vehicle like the motors and wheels.

gsVehicleDebugLOD

The `gsVehicleDebug` command is incredibly useful and powerful, but it doesn't give you all the information you need about everything. For instance, it can be pretty difficult to tell if your LODs are working (see Chapter 11 for more on what LODs are and how to set them up). In fact, if your LODs are done really well, it should be almost impossible to tell when they're being triggered.

Fortunately, the `gsVehicleDebugLOD` command exists specifically for this reason. Type that command in the in-game console and press *Enter*. Now, as you pull the game camera away from your vehicle, you should see a very clear indication of when your LOD levels are toggled. The vehicle actually maintains the same framing, but the camera lens changes as the camera moves farther away (kind of like a "dolly zoom" camera effect in horror movies). With this feature, you can see at what distance the LOD is triggered. Figure 14.12 shows what this visualization looks like.

FIGURE 14.12   Use the gsVehicleDebugLOD command to check when your LODs are triggered in-game.

TIP

If you press your mouse's middle button while moving the camera back in gsVehicleDebugLOD, you can see your vehicle at the actual camera distance with the standard lens size.

When you use gsVehicleDebugLOD, be sure that the game settings are set to 100% LOD distance, as covered in Chapter 11, so you can be sure that you're getting the correct results.

If everything is working as desired, you're good to go. If the distance value in your vehicle-XML could use a little tweaking, you can make that change, run gsVehicleReload, and check your LODs again with gsVehicleDebugLOD.

gsRenderingDebugMode

When testing your mod, you may sometimes find that there's a shading error that's difficult to track down just by looking at your mod in-game. To help with this problem, you can use the gsRenderingDebugMode command to isolate parts of the GIANTS Engine rendering pipeline so you can more easily see what's going on with the shader in your mod.

The gsRenderingDebugMode command has a long list of possible modes that you can type as possible choices. If you type the command without any parameters, the in-game console will list the full set of modes that are available to you.

As an example, you could view baked ambient occlusion on your mod's shader by typing this in the console:

```
gsRenderingDebugMode bakedAO
```

Likewise, other useful modes include alpha and normals, for seeing how the render engine handles alpha channels and mesh normals, respectively.

SUMMARY

In this chapter, you were exposed to a number of tips and tricks that you can use for testing your vehicle in-game. You started by setting up Farming Simulator so you can access the in-game console and run additional commands from it. Then you saw how to use gsFieldSetGround, gsFieldSetFruit, and gsTipAnywhereAdd to quickly populate the game environment so you can test your vehicle. Speaking of testing your vehicle, you also worked through a few commands that help you more quickly change the state of your vehicle so you can test effects that would take much longer to create in regular gameplay. After that, you saw how the gsVehicleReload command can be used to dynamically reload your vehicle mod after you've made changes to its vehicle-XML. And finally, you used gsVehicleDebug and gsVehicleDebugLOD to get real-time information about how your vehicle mod is working in-game. With these tools, you should be able to thoroughly tweak your mod until it's performing absolutely the way you want it to.

In the next chapter, we cover how to publish your mod to the Farming Simulator ModHub.

CHAPTER 15

Publishing Your Mod

CONGRATULATIONS! AT THIS POINT, if you've worked your way through the rest of this book, you officially have your very own mod for Farming Simulator. The only thing better than playing Farming Simulator with your own mod is having other players use your mod. If only there were a centralized place where people could go to download mods. Guess what? There is! The Farming Simulator ModHub is the official place to get mods for Farming Simulator that have been tested and reviewed by developers at GIANTS Software. As a mod creator (yes, that's what you are now!) that's the best place for you to share your mod with others.

This chapter is all about the process of getting your mod uploaded and ready to share. We start by showing a little bit about the basic publishing process and some of the resources available on the ModHub. After that, we review the process of getting your mod ready for publishing, including making a good description, capturing great in-game screenshots, and the steps to get your mod approved for use on console gaming systems. From there, we get into the actual upload process for getting your mod available on the ModHub. Next, we go over how you can actually get paid a small amount for your mod. And finally, since this is the last chapter of this book, we cover resources and events you can take advantage of to continue your modding journey beyond this book.

In this chapter:

- Discovering the ModHub

- Preparing your mod for publishing

- Publishing your mod to the ModHub

- Understanding monetization for mods

- Where to go from here

DOI: 10.1201/9781032659497-15

TECHNICAL REQUIREMENTS

The main requirement for this chapter is having a completed mod that works in Farming Simulator. You'll need a web browser to access the ModHub and an internet connection for doing the actual upload. Also, if you haven't already, go and create an account on the ModHub with the steps covered in Chapter 1. You'll need an active account to complete the publishing process.

DISCOVERING THE MODHUB

Although you need an account on the ModHub to publish your mod, players don't need an account to download any of the free mods that are available. However, once you have an account created, you can log in and have access to some additional resources that can help you on your modding journey. In particular, have a look at the Help section, as shown in Figure 15.1.

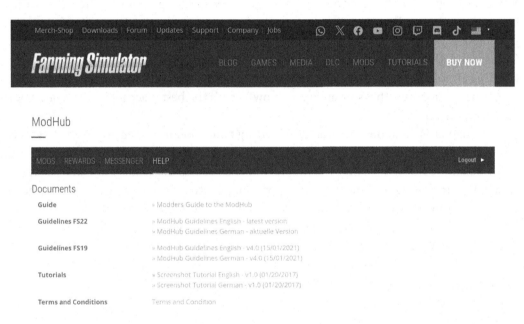

FIGURE 15.1 The Help section on the Farming Simulator ModHub gives you some additional resources for helping you refine your mod.

Of these resources, the Modder's Guide to the ModHub can be pretty helpful with guiding you on understanding what some of the most popular mods are for Farming Simulator. The other really useful document in this section is the ModHub Guidelines for Farming Simulator. These guidelines are available in English and German, and they have a lot of great technical information about the publishing process and things you can do to troubleshoot your mod so it gets accepted.

"Accepted?" Yes. GIANTS Software applies quality control procedures on your mod to ensure that it's properly made and won't break the game. So when you upload your mod to ModHub, it doesn't show up immediately. The team at GIANTS Software will test your mod according to the process described in that document. When they complete their testing, you receive a testing report that describes anything that needs to be adjusted or fixed in your mod prior to being published. Once you address all of these revisions, you can re-submit your mod, and, assuming everything works out, it is published on the ModHub so you can share with other players.

> **TIP**
>
> Read through the ModHub Guidelines document to make sure that you've addressed all of the requirements. In fact, you should go ahead and use their testing process on your mod yourself before publishing to ensure that it passes. The more you prepare ahead of time, the faster the turnaround on the testing and review process.

PREPARING YOUR MOD FOR PUBLISHING

You've gotten all of the most critical work done for completing your mod, but there are a few things left to handle before you can really get it uploaded to the ModHub and published for other players to use. For one, you need to ensure that you have a good description for your mod. Secondly, you need some fantastic images of your mod in-game. Your mod icon and screenshots are the first things players see, and they have the biggest influence on whether they download your mod. Third, if you want your mod to be published on gaming consoles, you'll need to go through a few checks and procedures to ensure that's possible. And finally, you should run a test on your mod folder to ensure that everything the mod needs is in there. Each of these steps is covered in this section.

Giving Your Mod a Description

In Chapter 6, we covered the parts of `modDesc.xml` where the general description of your mod is stored. However, now that you're ready to publish your mod, it's worth going back and being a bit more thoughtful about what you include in your mod's description. You really want to make sure that you're providing the most important specs on your mod. This way, players have an understanding of what is in your mod before they download it. That helps quite a bit when they're choosing.

The description for your mod lives in the `<description>` tag. You can find examples of other `<description>` tags in the ModHub Guidelines mentioned earlier. Those examples include attributes for machinery as well as descriptions for maps, placeables, and script mods. In our example cultivator, we include specs like the price, the required power, the working width, and the maximum working speed, as shown in the following code block:

```
<description>
    <en>
        <![CDATA[Price: $46.000
Required power: 190 hp
Working width: 6.0 m
```

```
Max. working speed: 18 kph
]]>
</en>
    <de>
        <![CDATA[Preis: 46.000 €
Benötigte Leistung: 190 PS
Arbeitsbreite: 6.0 m
Arbeitsgeschwindigkeit: 18 km/h
]]>
</de>
    <fr>
        <![CDATA[Prix: 46.000 €
Puissance requise: 190 ch
Largeur de travail: 6.0 m
Vitesse de travail: 18 km/h
]]>
</fr>
</description>
```

We also provide this description in three languages: English, German, and French. Of those languages, only English and German are required. If you don't happen to be fluent in all three languages, that's okay. You can use any of the many online translation websites to help you translate your description to those other languages.

When you upload your mod to the ModHub, this description from your modDesc. xml is automatically loaded in your ModHub description.

Capturing Good in-Game Screenshots

In order to publish your mod on ModHub, you need to have in-game screenshots of your mod in action. In fact, you need to have a minimum of three screenshots, or you won't be able to publish your mod at all.

Now, you can just hit the *Print Screen* button on your keyboard, but using that approach, you might not get the most attractive angles of your mod. Also, you have the game's HUD in the screenshot and that can obstruct the view of your mod. Fortunately, there's a process you can use to take really attractive screenshots. First and foremost, you need to enable Developer Mode in Farming Simulator. If you've worked through this book, you should already have Developer Mode activated, but if not, please review the section in Chapter 7.

With Developer Mode enabled, you're going to disable the in-game HUD and then enable Flight Mode for your player character so you can get the best possible view of your mod. Assuming that you're in Developer Mode, use the following steps in-game:

1. Access the in-game console by pressing *Tilde (~)* twice, as covered in Chapter 14.

2. From the in-game console, type gsHudVisibility and press *Enter*. You've now disabled the in-game HUD.

3. Enable Flight Mode by typing `gsPlayerFlightMode`. Congratulations! You're able to enable Flight Mode now (see the next paragraph for a description of the controls).

4. Press Tilde (~) a third time to hide the in-game console.

TIP

As you try to line up your shot in Flight Mode, you may want to try changing the field of view (FOV) for the player camera using the `gsCameraFovSet` command as covered in Chapter 14. Sometimes a more narrow field of view looks better and shows more detail on your mod.

At this point, you've given yourself the ability to toggle Flight Mode in the game by pressing *J* on your keyboard. With Flight Mode enabled, you can orbit around the level much like you can orbit around the 3D Scene in GIANTS Editor or Blender (though with game controls, not the hotkeys from those applications). Your standard *WASD* controls still work, but now you can use the *Q* and *E* keys to move your character up and down in space, respectively. With the HUD disabled and full control over your positioning, you can now get the cleanest possible in-game view of your mod.

NOTE

If you want to get your HUD back, you can bring up the in-game console and type `gsHud-Visibility` again. The HUD will reappear.

From here, you just need to move around your mod so it's framed nicely on-screen and press *Print Screen* on your keyboard. An image of your screenshot is saved to your hard drive in the Farming Simulator screenshots folder. That folder typically lives within your Documents folder at a path like this:

```
Documents/My Games/Farming Simulator/screenshots/
```

Your screenshot images are saved in PNG file format and are named with the date and time that they were captured. The required resolution for screenshots on ModHub is 1024×576 pixels. The ModHub uploaded will automatically convert for you, but if your image isn't using this same aspect ratio (16:9), the converted image will look stretched or squished.

Preparing Your Mod for Console Play

Farming Simulator is available on a wide variety of platforms, including PC and console gaming devices. Naturally, you may want to have your mod playable on as many devices as possible. The default support for a mod is, of course, on PCs. However, depending on the complexity of your mod, it may not be all that challenging to also have it work on consoles.

In fact, when the team at GIANTS Software tests your mod, one part of the testing process is always console testing. The key is doing the right things to ensure that your mod passes these tests. Here's a rough list of things to check for to help your mod get accepted for consoles (also referred to as *crossplay*). Your mod must do the following things:

- Pass all the base testing for PC release.

- **Not** use additional scripts for functionality.

- **Not** use custom shader variations.

- Use **only** brands that are licensed by GIANTS Software (fantasy brands are not permitted, so use the in-house Lizard brand if yours isn't one of the supported ones).

- **Not** require or have a dependency on another mod that is PC only.

NOTE

There's an exception to the branding requirement for maps. A map is permitted to show fantasy or "fake" brands in order to provide a consistent gaming experience.

Assuming that your mod matches all of these requirements, the GIANTS Software QA team will contact you to let you know that your mod is suitable for console publishing. Of course, if you still require some small changes to be compliant, they'll let you know that as well.

Pre-Verifying Your Mod with TestRunner

The publishing process that GIANTS Software has put together for testing and qualifying mods is pretty robust. However, it would be nice if you could make the QA group's life a little bit better by doing some automated testing on your mod prior to uploading it. Fortunately, GIANTS Software has created TestRunner. TestRunner is a piece of software used to help you by providing useful feedback on the most common issues and oversights found in mods before you upload. For example, it checks for duplicate files, verifies your textures are in compatible image formats, and validates your XML files. Plus, it does a few more checks that are a bit less interesting to talk about but still useful.

To download TestRunner, navigate to the Downloads page of the GDN and search for Test Runner.

There's no installer for TestRunner. Simply unzip it somewhere on your hard drive and move the `TestRunner _ public.exe` executable file into the folder that contains all of your mods. To test a specific mod, click and drag the mod folder for a single mod to the

TestRunner executable, as shown in Figure 15.2. When you drop the mod folder on the executable, TestRunner starts running tests on that folder.

FIGURE 15.2   You can run TestRunner on a mod by dragging and dropping the mod folder on the TestRunner executable.

NOTE

Your mod folder doesn't really need to be in the same folder as the TestRunner executable, but having it that way is often more convenient for quickly running tests.

When TestRunner is working, a command-line window opens, displaying the progress of the tool. If something goes wrong, TestRunner prints an error message with details on the issue. TestRunner saves all of its output to a log file named `TestRunner.log`, which lives in the same folder as the TestRunner executable. When TestRunner has completed running without errors, the results of the test are saved in the same folder as TestRunner as XML and HTML files with the same name as the folder of the tested mod. The HTML file only contains the errors for each module, whereas the XML file contains all errors as well as more detailed information about the tests. When TestRunner completes, the generated HTML report is automatically opened in your default web browser. Errors are outlined in red, explanations are in italics, and instructions for correcting the errors are colored green.

NOTE

It's worth noting that if an issue shows up in red, that's not necessarily a dealbreaker. Occasionally, you may see a warning listed in red, especially if you're still testing your mod. Warnings are often informational and don't necessarily prevent your mod from being published.

More information about TestRunner and troubleshooting can be seen in the announcement thread on the GIANTS Software forum, here:

https://forum.giants-software.com/viewtopic.php?t=187502

PUBLISHING YOUR MOD TO THE MODHUB

Assuming that you've sufficiently tested your mod on your own, you're ready to get it published on the ModHub. Before you start, make sure that you've generated your store and mod icons for your mod as described in Chapter 13. Also, compress your mod folder into a ZIP file so it's a single file to be uploaded. If you've never compressed a folder before, you can do this easily in Windows Explorer. Go into your mod's folder and select the necessary files for your mod (`modDesc.xml`, vehicle-XML, I3D files, textures, etc.). Then, just right-click and choose **Send to ▶ Compressed (zipped) folder**. Windows then creates a ZIP file. You should rename the resultant ZIP file so it matches your mod's folder name. The best practice is to prefix your file's name with the version of Farming Simulator that it was built for. So, for example, if your mod was built for Farming Simulator 22, you would prefix your file name with `FS22 _` .

IMPORTANT

When you build your compressed file, do *not* include any of your source files (PNG, GIM, `.blend`, `.ma`, and so on). They're not necessary for the mod to run in the game and only make your compressed file larger.

Uploading Your Mod

With your ZIP file created, you're now ready to start the publishing process. Log in to the ModHub and go to the Mods section. Assuming you have no published mods, the content of that page looks rather stark and empty. However, there's a large **Add New** button that you can use to add a new mod to your inventory. Click that button and your list of mods updates with a single mod named *Untitled Mod*, as shown in Figure 15.3.

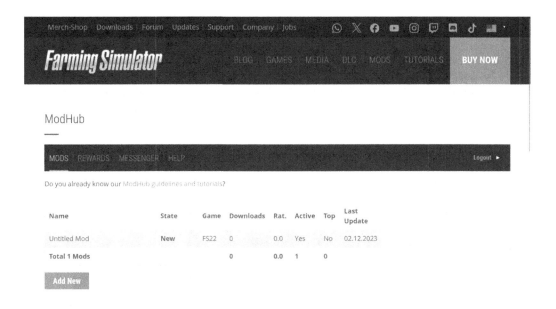

FIGURE 15.3   When you click the Add New button, the ModHub adds a new untitled mod to your inventory list.

The Untitled Mod item in the list is a placeholder for your new mod. At this point, there's not yet any specific information about your mod there. Click the name *Untitled Mod* in the list to start the process of getting your mod published. After you click the mod's name, the ModHub brings you to your mod's edit page. Right at the top of the page, it tells you the status of your mod and includes any text about anything missing. Since you haven't uploaded anything yet, the status tells you that your mod is in the Edit State. You have a lot of things to address.

Below the Status section is the Messenger section. This section is where you can create and track support tickets related to your mod. It's not the place to ask the staff at GIANTS Software how to make a mod or request features in Farming Simulator, so please don't try using it for that. This section is more for communicating about the testing results on your mod after it's been submitted or if you have troubles with the upload process.

The place where you really start the publishing process is in the next section, titled Data, as shown in Figure 15.4. You should see a red message in this section telling you that you need to upload your mod file and that it currently has a file name that's too short (which makes sense; you haven't specified a file, so currently the file name is zero characters long).

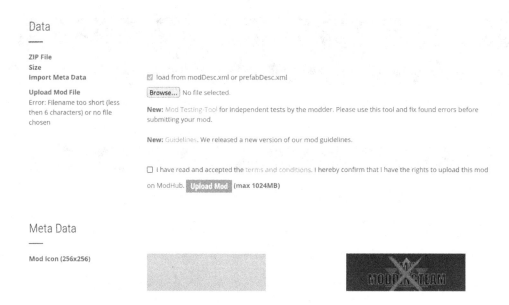

FIGURE 15.4   Upload your compressed mod file in the Data section.

Click the **Browse** button in the Data section to get a file browser where you can navigate to the location on your hard drive where your mod ZIP file is saved. Select your file and click **Open** from the file browser. It's important to note that when you click the **Open** button, it doesn't immediately begin to upload. You've just told the page where your mod file lives.

To actually upload your compressed mod file, you need to first enable the check box that indicates that you've read and understand the terms and conditions that GIANTS Software has set for the ModHub. If you haven't yet read those terms and conditions, you should click the link in that text and review them. Once you've done that, you can enable this check box and then click the **Upload Mod** button to upload your compressed file. Please ensure that your compressed file is less than 1024 MB (1 GB) in size; otherwise, the upload will fail. If the upload still fails, make sure that the ZIP file is correctly zipped and not corrupted. You should also check that the game can load your mod. If the game can load it, the ModHub should be able to as well.

If you've properly structured your mod folder with correct naming for your `modDesc.xml` file and vehicle-XML, the ModHub website automatically populates the information in the Meta Data section, including your icon image and description. Anything that's missing has its label highlighted in red. You can either go back into your mod folder and fix this meta data, or you can add that information right in the web interface. It's required that you include localization for English and German. If you don't happen to know both of those languages, you can use online translation tools to help.

One section that isn't automatically populated from your mod file is the next section, titled Screenshots. In order to be published on the ModHub, you need to include at least three in-game screenshots of your mod in action. See the preceding section on the process of capturing good screenshots in-game. Once you have your screenshots captured on your hard drive, click the **Browse** button in the Screenshots section to choose the first one. Like with your compressed mod file, after you choose your screenshot file, you need to click the **Upload Screenshot** button at the bottom of the section. After you have one screenshot uploaded, you have the ability to upload a second one. Repeat the process for each of the screenshots you've captured.

After you've gotten your mod file uploaded, your meta data properly completed, and your screenshots added, you're finally ready to submit your mod for review. Scroll back to the top of the page. You should notice that it no longer says *Untitled Mod* there and instead gives the name you have specified in your modDesc.xml. You should also see that in the Status section, the **Submit** button is no longer disabled. If it is, there's likely still something missing in the form, marked in red. But assuming that the **Submit** button is enabled, all you have to do now is click it to submit your mod to the GIANTS Software QA team for review.

All you have to do now is wait. Assuming that you've done all of the work to ensure that your mod works and meets the testing requirements, it shouldn't be long before you see your mod available to everyone on the ModHub!

Getting Feedback and Updating Your Mod

Once your mod is accepted and released by the ModHub team, anyone who plays Farming Simulator will be able to see and download your mod. That's millions of people! You're likely to get a lot of feedback from those players. Typically, feedback on mod shows up in a few different places, including the official GIANTS Software forum, Facebook, Discord, or other social platforms. At the very least, you should be available on the official forum. If you went through Chapter 1, you should already be registered there, but if not, you can find the English-speaking section of the forum at this address:

https://forum.giants-software.com/viewforum.php?f=478

One of the best ways to improve your mod is by listening to the feedback of people who have used it. Of course, you need to keep in mind that you may sometimes receive negative feedback. However, don't be discouraged by that kind of feedback. The trick is to only pay attention to constructive feedback. Feedback can be both constructive and negative, but when the feedback doesn't give you real, tangible issues to resolve (or suggestions on how to resolve them), your best course of action is to ignore it. After all, you're doing this for fun! There's no sense in letting a few bad comments take that fun away from you.

Of course, if you get constructive feedback, take it to heart. By updating your mod in response to that feedback, it's possible that you'll get more positive feedback from the community. People love when creators listen to them, and they'll be happy to see new content and their suggestions incorporated into the mod. This kind of responsiveness is a great way to build notoriety within the community. And of course, with more mods and consistent updates, your mod can become more popular, resulting in more downloads and additional rewards.

TIP

Mods that are updated have more visibility on the in-game ModHub as well as on the ModHub website.

UNDERSTANDING MONETIZATION FOR MODS

Your mod is now published. Congratulations! You put a lot of work into making that mod, and now you've shared it with the whole audience of Farming Simulator players. Assuming that you've created a great mod that people are interested in using (of course you did!), there are a lot of people who are going to enhance their gaming experience with your work.

The cool thing is that the folks at GIANTS Software understand the amount of effort involved with creating a mod and how much value mods bring to their gaming platform. Because of this understanding, they will actually pay modders a modest "thank you." There's nothing special that you need to do; you've already made your mod. You get paid a certain amount of money at the end of each month, depending on the type of mod, the number of downloads, and the rating it's given by players. Of course, you'll need to provide banking information so GIANTS Software can transfer that money to you.

As another option, you can choose to donate the money you get from your mod to one of the charities that GIANTS Software lists. If you choose that option, GIANTS Software will match your donation, effectively doubling it.

NOTE

Quality mods that receive the best reviews are more likely to appear in certain categories of the ModHub. When your mod is featured, more users are able to see it and download it, allowing you to earn more money from your mod.

Your mod can also earn awards. For example, if your mod is made compatible with consoles, you are eligible for the red *Console* award, as shown in Figure 15.5. Furthermore, there are also awards for how much your mod gets downloaded, separated into three tiers: *Bronze*, *Silver*, and *Gold*.

FIGURE 15.5   The red Console award is given if your mod gets 250,000 downloads on consoles.

WHERE TO GO FROM HERE

So your mod is published. Now what? More than likely, you can start making another mod! The process of making your first mod always exposes you to new questions and gives you ideas on how you can do even better on your next one. Of course, there are other ways you can improve your modding skills as well. This section goes over a few things you can do (and places you can go) to bring your mods to the next level.

Attending FarmCon

The GIANTS Software forums and the GDN are great ways to connect with the virtual community around Farming Simulator. However, sometimes you can get even more benefit by engaging the community in person. **FarmCon** is an annual convention where you can do exactly that. Members of the Farming Simulator community from around the world converge on a single location to hang out and cover all manner of things related to Farming Simulator. FarmCon is hands-down the best event to connect with other mod creators and community members.

When you attend FarmCon, you're typically the first to see new teasers, trailers, and announcements about the future of Farming Simulator. Also, there are a lot of talks by presenters focused on the best ways for players to build out their in-game farming ventures, as well as a wide variety of tips and tricks for mod creators like you (yes, you're a mod creator now!). Figure 15.6 shows a promotional image from FarmCon 22, which was held in Mannheim, Germany.

FIGURE 15.6   FarmCon is an annual convention for all things Farming Simulator.

FarmCon is an exciting event that's great for all levels of Farming Simulator enthusiasts. Of course, you may have some questions about what the experience of the convention is like. Here's a quick run-down:

- The event is typically held in the summer.

- A ticket is required for admission to the venue and in-person attendance.

- Although FarmCon is often where you get first-access to new information about Farming Simulator, none of that information is hidden. You can follow announcements on the Farming Simulator blog after the event.

- Most presentations at FarmCon in-person are given in German.

- Any additional questions you may have about FarmCon can be sent via email to farmcon@giants-software.com.

Mod Contests!

One of the really exciting things that GIANTS Software does from time to time are the mod contests. As a mod creator, you can join in on the contest and possibly win some pretty sweet prizes for your mod or your custom map. If you win a mod contest, it gets usually announced at FarmCon. In the past, mod creators have won computer accessories, cameras, graphics cards, and trips to the factories of select farm equipment manufacturers.

How does that sound to you? By working your way through this book, you should have the base skills necessary to be a part of the next mod contest. If you choose to be a part of the contest, here are a few things to keep in mind:

- Contest submissions can be made by teams or individuals.

- Submissions should be a new mod or map. Skins and prefabs are not allowed.

- You (or your team) need to be the only one who created your mod, including the 3D models, textures, or any programming. It has to be your work and no one else's.

- You or your team can only enter the contest once.

Scripting Farming Simulator with Lua

The content of this book focuses on the visual and functional parts of your mod, leveraging the capabilities that come in the Farming Simulator base game. However, there's even more customization that you can do that can extend your mod far beyond what's possible in the base game. All of that additional functionality comes from custom scripts written in a language called Lua. You write those scripts and publish them with your mod to extend what's possible in Farming Simulator.

Now, there's not enough space in this book to cover everything that you can do with scripting in your mods. In fact, to do so would require a whole book all by itself. And wouldn't you know it? That book exists. It's called *Scripting Farming Simulator with Lua*, written by Zander Brumbaugh and Manuel Leithner. Figure 15.7 shows an image of this book's cover.

FIGURE 15.7   The book Scripting Farming Simulator with Lua is an excellent way to up your modding game.

You don't need to have any previous coding or scripting experience for this book; it walks you all the way through, starting with an overview of the Lua language and working your way all the way up to extending base game features.

CG Cookie

Another way you can amplify your modding skills is by getting better with Blender. The Blender community is incredibly friendly and helpful, plus there are a ton of tutorials available all over the internet. However, if you really want to develop your skills and improve at modeling, texturing, animation, or any of the other bajillion things the Blender can do, the best place to go is CG Cookie. CG Cookie is an education platform that not only has incredible video courses to help you learn Blender; there's an incredible community there to help you as you progress. The instructors and instructor assistants will grade your exercises, provide feedback, answer your Blender questions, and serve as your guides as you improve with Blender (Full disclosure: I work with CG Cookie, but I said this stuff even before I started working with them).

You can get started with CG Cookie by going to this address: https://cgcookie.com/farmingsimulator or scanning the following QR code:

https://cgcookie.com/farmingsimulator

SUMMARY

And with that… you're a published modder. Great work! This chapter was all about that critical last step of publishing your mod to the Farming Simulator ModHub. You started by logging in to the ModHub and getting familiar with the resources that GIANTS Software has made available so you understand the publishing and testing process. After that, get your mod prepared for publishing with a helpful description, some really attractive screenshots, and refinements so your mod is suitable for use on gaming consoles. From there, you went through the process of packaging and uploading your mod to the ModHub so it can be reviewed by the GIANTS Software QA team. And, assuming that it passed the tests (I'm sure it did), your mod should now be freely available for other Farming Simulator players. Then, you saw a little bit about how your mod can be monetized. And finally, we covered where you can go to continue your modding journey beyond this book.

And with any luck, this is just the first of many mods that you'll be publishing. I look forward to seeing the great things you create. Have fun!

Appendix

Code/File Examples

THROUGHOUT THIS BOOK, I'VE referred to an example cultivator (actually a disc harrow) when illustrating how to build out your own mod. For your convenience, I'm including the full `modDesc.xml` and vehicle-XML files for that mod in this appendix. These files (and more) are available for you to download and inspect on your own from this book's page on the GDN (https://gdn.giants-software.com/blenderBook). However, if you're reading through this book without access to your computer, this appendix can serve as a quick and handy reference.

I've included both the `modDesc.xml` and vehicle-XML in their entirety. One difference is that the vehicle-XML you can download from GDN has a bunch of really helpful comments that describe each section of the file. In the interest of nice formatting (and to clearly indicate what's functional mark-up), those comments have been converted to regular text in this appendix.

In this appendix:

- `modDesc.xml` (Kverneland Qualidisc Pro)

- `qualidiscPro.xml`

MODDESC.XML (KVERNELAND QUALIDISC PRO)

What follows is the entirety of the modDesc.xml file for our example cultivator. This file is fairly short, especially when contrasted against the vehicle-XML later in the appendix, but the content of the file is essential for having a properly functioning mod.

```
<?xml version="1.0" encoding="utf-8" standalone="no" ?>
<modDesc descVersion="77">
    <author>GIANTS Software</author>
    <version>1.0.0.0</version>
    <title>
        <en>Kverneland Qualidisc Pro 6001T</en>
```

```
    </title>
    <description>
        <en>
            <![CDATA[Price: 46.000 €
Required power: 190 hp
Working width: 6.0 m
Max. working speed: 18 kph
]]>
        </en>
        <de>
            <![CDATA[Preis: 46.000 €
Benötigte Leistung: 190 PS
Arbeitsbreite: 6.0 m
Arbeitsgeschwindigkeit: 18 km/h
]]>
        </de>
        <fr>
            <![CDATA[Prix: 46.000 €
Puissance requise: 190 ch
Largeur de travail: 6.0 m
Vitesse de travail: 18 km/h
]]>
        </fr>
    </description>
    <iconFilename>icon_qualidiscPro.dds</iconFilename>
    <multiplayer supported="true" />
    <storeItems>
        <storeItem xmlFilename="qualidiscPro.xml" />
    </storeItems>
</modDesc>
```

QUALIDISCPRO.XML

This section has all of the functional mark-up in the vehicle-XML file for our example cultivator. All of the code parts of this file are included here, but I've extracted the comments from the file that you can download from the GDN and reformatted them to make the text more readable in book format.

What follows is the vehicle configuration file for our example cultivator. By having the <vehicle> tag include type="cultivator", it indicates that this file has all the functionality that is required for a cultivator. Also in the <vehicle> tag, the xmlns:xsi and xsi:noNamespaceSchemaLocation attributes link to the XML configuration schema files on the GDN. See https://validation.gdn.giants-software.com/vehicle.html to get the full vehicle xml documentation.

```
<?xml version="1.0" encoding="utf-8" standalone="no" ?>
<vehicle type="cultivator" xmlns:xsi="http://www.w3.org/2001/
XMLSchema-instance" xsi:noNamespaceSchemaLocation="https://
validation.gdn.giants-software.com/xml/fs22/vehicle.xsd">
```

```xml
<annotation>Copyright (C) GIANTS Software GmbH, All Rights
Reserved.</annotation>
  <storeData>
```

Name of the item:

```xml
<name>Qualidisc Pro 6001T</name>
```

Defines a list of specs that are displayed in the shop:

```xml
<specs>
  <neededPower>190</neededPower>
  <workingWidth>6</workingWidth>
</specs>
```

Defines a list of function texts that are displayed in the shop:

```xml
<functions>
  <function>$l10n_function_discHarrow</function>
</functions>
```

Defines the icon that is shown in the shop (path relative to mod base folder):

```xml
<image>store_qualidiscPro.png</image>
```

Defines the buying price:

```xml
<price>46000</price>
```

Defines the lifetime of an object; lifetime also affects the daily upkeep of a vehicle:

```xml
<lifetime>600</lifetime>
```

Spawn rotation at the shop area:

```xml
<rotation>0</rotation>
```

The vehicle's brand; there is a predefined brand enum list:

```xml
<brand>KVERNELAND</brand>
```

Defines the shop category of the vehicle:

```xml
<category>discHarrows</category>
```

Defines some offsets for the 3d shop preview and store icon. Use the gsVehicleDebug attributes command in-game and read the values in the bottom right corner of the screen:

```
<shopTranslationOffset>0 -0.185 0</shopTranslationOffset>
<shopRotationOffset>-0.817 0 0</shopRotationOffset>
```

Info needed for console modhub publishing will be added/changed during modhub submission process:

```
<vertexBufferMemoryUsage>0</vertexBufferMemoryUsage>
<indexBufferMemoryUsage>0</indexBufferMemoryUsage>
<textureMemoryUsage>0</textureMemoryUsage>
<instanceVertexBufferMemoryUsage>0</
instanceVertexBufferMemoryUsage>
<instanceIndexBufferMemoryUsage>0</
instanceIndexBufferMemoryUsage>
  </storeData>
```

Base settings of the tool:

```
<base>
```

The vehicle type is a disc harrow (text that is shown in the F1 help menu for example):

```
<typeDesc>$l10n_typeDesc_discHarrow</typeDesc>
```

The vehicle's I3D file to be loaded:

```
<filename>qualidiscPro.i3d</filename>
```

The size. Used for calculating the required store area when buying the tool:

```
<size width="4" length="9" height="4.6" lengthOffset="0.7" />
```

The speed limit while working:

```
<speedLimit value="18" />
```

The two physics components that are loaded from the I3D file:

- The main component
- The drawbar component

Additionally a joint is defined which connects the two components (componentJoint-Drawbar) the translation and rotation limit is set to 0, but is opened in the lockDrawbarLimit animation, so the drawbar can properly rotate:

```
<components>
    <component centerOfMass="0 0.4 0" solverIterationCount="10"
mass="4500" />
```

```
        <component centerOfMass="0 0 0" solverIterationCount="10"
mass="590" />
        <joint component1="1" component2="2"
node="componentJointDrawbar" rotLimit="0 0 0" transLimit="0 0 0" />
    </components>
```

The vehicle selection overlay in the input help HUD:

```
    <schemaOverlay attacherJointPosition="0 0" name="IMPLEMENT" />
```

Type of the tool on the ingame map:

```
    <mapHotspot type="TOOL_TRAILED" />
  </base>
  <wheels>
    <wheelConfigurations>
```

First wheel configuration which is used as base for further configurations:

```
        <wheelConfiguration name="$l10n_configuration_valueDefault"
brand="VREDESTEIN" saveId="VREDESTEIN_DEFAULT">
            <wheels>
```

The two main wheels of the tool. The left wheel has two wheel chocks defined which are placed in front and on the back of the wheel:

```
            <wheel filename="$data/shared/wheels/tires/vredestein/
flotationTrac/520_50R17.xml" isLeft="true" hasTireTracks="true"
hasParticles="true">
                <physics restLoad="1.5" repr="wheelLeft"
forcePointRatio="0.3" initialCompression="35" suspTravel="0.12"
spring="31" damper="20" yOffset="0.02" />
                <wheelChock parkingNode="wheelChock01"
filename="$data/shared/assets/wheelChocks/wheelChock02.i3d" />
                <wheelChock parkingNode="wheelChock02"
filename="$data/shared/assets/wheelChocks/wheelChock02.i3d"
isInverted="true" />
            </wheel>
            <wheel filename="$data/shared/wheels/tires/vredestein/
flotationTrac/520_50R17.xml" isLeft="false" hasTireTracks="true"
hasParticles="true">
                <physics restLoad="1.5" repr="wheelRight"
forcePointRatio="0.3" initialCompression="35" suspTravel="0.12"
spring="31" damper="20" yOffset="0.02" />
            </wheel>
```

The two wheels on the arms of the tool:

```
<wheel filename="$data/shared/wheels/tires/trelleborg/
AW305/340_55R16.xml" isLeft="true" hasTireTracks="true"
hasParticles="true">
        <physics restLoad="1.6" repr="wheelFrontLeft"
useReprDirection="true" forcePointRatio="0.15"
initialCompression="40" suspTravel="0.05" spring="75" damper="50"
rotationDamping="0.008" frictionScale="0.1" brakeFactor="0" />
        </wheel>
        <wheel filename="$data/shared/wheels/tires/trelleborg/
AW305/340_55R16.xml" isLeft="false" hasTireTracks="true"
hasParticles="true">
        <physics restLoad="1.6" repr="wheelFrontRight"
useReprDirection="true" forcePointRatio="0.15"
initialCompression="40" suspTravel="0.05" spring="75" damper="50"
rotationDamping="0.008" frictionScale="0.1" brakeFactor="0" />
        </wheel>
```

Two invisible physical wheels at the back in the center of the rolls. Those are used for a smooth ride on the field. Individual wheels for each roll would not make sense performance-wise, so we have one in the center and the rolls itself via speedRotatingParts (see below).

Important:

- brakeFactor is set to *0*, so the wheels do not brake the tool. This means that braking is only done by the two main wheels.

- supportsWheelSink is set to *false*, so the wheels do not sink too deep into the ground on the field.

```
<wheel>
        <physics restLoad="1.2" repr="rollLeftWheel" width="1"
radius="0.27" useReprDirection="true" forcePointRatio="0.1"
initialCompression="40" suspTravel="0.03" spring="90" damper="60"
rotationDamping="0.006" brakeFactor="0" supportsWheelSink="false" />
        </wheel>
        <wheel>
        <physics restLoad="1.2" repr="rollRightWheel"
width="1" radius="0.27" useReprDirection="true"
forcePointRatio="0.1" initialCompression="40" suspTravel="0.03"
spring="90" damper="60" rotationDamping="0.006" brakeFactor="0"
supportsWheelSink="false" />
        </wheel>
    </wheels>
</wheelConfiguration>
```

Trelleborg wheel configuration which is based on the Vredestein config. All attributes will be copied and just the filename is different compared to the first config. Empty tags are required for the wheels and wheelChocks, otherwise the corresponding wheel/wheelChock will be skipped

```
<wheelConfiguration name="$l10n_configuration_valueDefault"
brand="TRELLEBORG" saveId="TRELLEBORG_DEFAULT">
    <wheels baseConfig="VREDESTEIN_DEFAULT">
    <wheel filename="$data/shared/wheels/tires/trelleborg/
AW309/500_50R17.xml">
        <wheelChock />
        <wheelChock />
    </wheel>
    <wheel filename="$data/shared/wheels/tires/trelleborg/
AW309/500_50R17.xml" />
        <wheel />
        <wheel />
        <wheel />
        <wheel />
    </wheels>
</wheelConfiguration>
```

BKT wheel configuration which is based on the Vredestein config:

```
<wheelConfiguration name="$l10n_configuration_valueDefault"
brand="BKT" saveId="BKT_DEFAULT">
    <wheels baseConfig="VREDESTEIN_DEFAULT">
    <wheel filename="$data/shared/wheels/tires/bkt/
ridemaxFL693M/500_50R17.xml">
        <wheelChock />
        <wheelChock />
    </wheel>
    <wheel filename="$data/shared/wheels/tires/bkt/
ridemaxFL693M/500_50R17.xml" />
        <wheel />
        <wheel />
        <wheel />
        <wheel />
    </wheels>
</wheelConfiguration>
</wheelConfigurations>
```

Hubs that are linked to the defined nodes (list of available hubs can be found in the game directory at data/shared/wheels/hubs):

- color0: main color of the hub

- `color1`: color of the screws

```
<hubs>
  <color0>KVERNELAND_RED1</color0>
  <color1>SHARED_GREY3</color1>
  <hub linkNode="wheelLeft" filename="$data/shared/wheels/
hubs/hub_n8_6.xml" isLeft="true" scale="0.25 0.25 0.25" />
  <hub linkNode="wheelRight" filename="$data/shared/wheels/
hubs/hub_n8_6.xml" isLeft="false" scale="0.25 0.25 0.25" />
  <hub linkNode="wheelFrontLeft" filename="$data/shared/
wheels/hubs/hub_n6_1.xml" isLeft="true" scale="0.15 0.2 0.2" />
  <hub linkNode="wheelFrontRight" filename="$data/shared/
wheels/hubs/hub_n6_1.xml" isLeft="false" scale="0.15 0.2 0.2" />
  </hubs>
</wheels>
```

Dynamically loaded parts which are used for the wheelChock mountings on our disc harrow:

```
<dynamicallyLoadedParts>
  <dynamicallyLoadedPart node="0" linkNode="wheelChockSupport01"
filename="$data/shared/assets/wheelChocks/wheelChockSupport01.i3d"
/>
  <dynamicallyLoadedPart node="0" linkNode="wheelChockSupport02"
filename="$data/shared/assets/wheelChocks/wheelChockSupport01.i3d"
/>
  </dynamicallyLoadedParts>
```

Speed rotating parts which are rotating as soon as they have ground contact or the defined wheel is rotating. Used for the rolls at the back which are linked to the invisible wheels at the back (`rollLeftWheel`, `rollRightWheel`):

- Defined with a node which is then rotated (radius is used for speed calculations)
  Also used for the discs at the front which are rotated via shader parameter (`armLeftDiscs`, `armRightDiscs`)

- The ground reference node *1* is referred here, so they rotate as soon as the tool is lowered

- Negative radius results in an inverted rotation of the discs

```
<speedRotatingParts>
  <speedRotatingPart node="rollLeftFront" radius="0.27"
wheelIndex="5" />
  <speedRotatingPart node="rollLeftBack" radius="0.27"
wheelIndex="5" />
```

```
    <speedRotatingPart node="rollRightFront" radius="0.27"
wheelIndex="6" />
    <speedRotatingPart node="rollRightBack" radius="0.27"
wheelIndex="6" />
    <speedRotatingPart shaderNode="armLeftDiscs" radius="-0.30"
groundReferenceNodeIndex="1" />
    <speedRotatingPart shaderNode="armRightDiscs" radius="-0.30"
groundReferenceNodeIndex="1" />
  </speedRotatingParts>
  <attachable>
    <inputAttacherJoints>
```

Definition of the attacher joint on the drawbar.

Important: rootNode needs to be defined, as the attacher is not in the main component.

```
    <inputAttacherJoint node="attacherJoint"
rootNode="qualidiscPro_drawbar_component2" jointType="implement">
```

Defines the lowering and lifting state of the lower links (0.6m and 0.9m above the ground):

```
    <distanceToGround lower="0.6" upper="0.9" />
    </inputAttacherJoint>
    </inputAttacherJoints>
```

Two separate support animations to decouple the drawbar component joint rotation limit. Rotation limit is already unlocked as soon as the attacher process has started (otherwise is can happen that the tractor is negatively influenced).

```
    <support animationName="moveSupport" />
    <support animationName="lockDrawbarLimit"
delayedOnAttach="false" detachAfterAnimation="false" />
```

Defines how much brake force is applied on the wheels to brake the tool:

```
    <brakeForce force="1" />
  </attachable>
```

Definition of the connection hoses:

- Each connection hose has an adapterNode defined which is dynamically loaded into the connector node

- The detached version of the connection hose is defined in the objectChange, so it's hidden as soon as the dynamic hose is visible

- length and straighteningFactor influence how the hoses are hanging down

```
<connectionHoses>
    <hose inputAttacherJointIndices="1" type="hydraulicIn"
node="hydraulicIn01" adapterNode="hydraulicIn01_connector"
length="1.5" diameter="0.02" straighteningFactor="0.2">
        <objectChange node="hydraulicIn01_detached"
visibilityActive="false" visibilityInactive="true" />
    </hose>
    <hose inputAttacherJointIndices="1" type="hydraulicIn"
node="hydraulicOut01" adapterNode="hydraulicOut01_connector"
length="1.5" diameter="0.02" straighteningFactor="0.2">
        <objectChange node="hydraulicOut01_detached"
visibilityActive="false" visibilityInactive="true" />
    </hose>
    <hose inputAttacherJointIndices="1" type="hydraulicIn"
node="hydraulicIn02" adapterNode="hydraulicIn02_connector"
length="1.5" diameter="0.02" straighteningFactor="0.2">
        <objectChange node="hydraulicIn02_detached"
visibilityActive="false" visibilityInactive="true" />
    </hose>
    <hose inputAttacherJointIndices="1" type="hydraulicIn"
node="hydraulicOut02" adapterNode="hydraulicOut02_connector"
length="1.5" diameter="0.02" straighteningFactor="0.2">
        <objectChange node="hydraulicOut02_detached"
visibilityActive="false" visibilityInactive="true" />
    </hose>
```

Dynamically linked outgoing sockets for air hoses including dynamic outgoing adapters adapters:

```
    <hose inputAttacherJointIndices="1" type="airDoubleRed"
node="airDoubleRed" length="1.3" diameter="0.015"
outgoingAdapter="DEFAULT" socket="air_red" />
    <hose inputAttacherJointIndices="1" type="airDoubleYellow"
node="airDoubleYellow" length="1.3" diameter="0.015"
outgoingAdapter="DEFAULT" socket="air_yellow" />
</connectionHoses>
```

Power consumer definition which applies a force while working, so it's harder for the tractor to pull it:

```
<powerConsumer forceNode="qualidiscPro_main_component1"
maxForce="20" neededMaxPtoPower="0" />
<lights>
```

Definition of the shared lights:

- The full library of the shared lights can be found in the game directory: `data/shared/assets/lights`

- Light type of the shared lights can be overwritten (e.g. `rearLight23White` is used with light type *0*, so they are visible with the default light)

```
<sharedLight linkNode="rearLight05_01" filename="$data/shared/assets/lights/lizard/rearLight05_left.xml" />
<sharedLight linkNode="rearLight05_02" filename="$data/shared/assets/lights/lizard/rearLight05_right.xml" />
<sharedLight linkNode="redTriangle_02_01" filename="$data/shared/assets/reflectors/lizard/redTriangle_02.xml" />
<sharedLight linkNode="redTriangle_02_02" filename="$data/shared/assets/reflectors/lizard/redTriangle_02.xml" />
<sharedLight linkNode="yellowRound_02_01" filename="$data/shared/assets/reflectors/lizard/yellowRound_02.xml" />
<sharedLight linkNode="yellowRound_02_02" filename="$data/shared/assets/reflectors/lizard/yellowRound_02.xml" />
<sharedLight linkNode="rearLight23White_01" filename="$data/shared/assets/lights/lizard/rearLight23White.xml" lightTypes="0" />
<sharedLight linkNode="rearLight23White_02" filename="$data/shared/assets/lights/lizard/rearLight23White.xml" lightTypes="0" />
```

Light Types:

- 0: Default Light
- 1: Work Light Back
- 2: Work Light Front
- 3: High Beam
- 4: Pipe Light (optional)

Definition of real light sources:

- For back, brake and turn light we only have light sources in high profile (performance reasons)

- For regular front lights and work lights there can be real light sources on low profile as well (see tractors)

- If a light is used for regular light and brake light, it will light up brighter while both are active (backLightsHigh)

```
<realLights>
  <high>
    <light node="backLightsHigh" lightTypes="0" />
    <turnLightLeft node="turnLightLeft" />
    <turnLightRight node="turnLightRight" />
    <brakeLight node="backLightsHigh" />
  </high>
</realLights>
</lights>
```

Definition of the license plates:

- License plates can be either SQUARISH or ELONGATED

- Placement area defines the maximum used space (top, right, bottom, left)

```
<licensePlates>
  <licensePlate node="licensePlateBack" position="BACK"
preferedType="SQUARISH" placementArea="0.3 0.15 0.3 0.3" />
</licensePlates>
```

Ground reference node which is used for workArea activation and speedRotating-Part activation:

- If the node is below the terrain, it's active (threshold can be used to tweak it. In our case as soon as the node is lower than 5cm above the terrain

- Position/threshold should not be too tight for fields that are not flat

```
<groundReferenceNodes>
  <groundReferenceNode node="groundReferenceNode"
forceFactor="1" threshold="0.05" />
</groundReferenceNodes>
```

Definition of our work area:

- In this area the ground is cultivated

- The workArea is only active if the groundReferenceNode index 1 is below the terrain and the tool is lowered

```
<workAreas>
  <workArea type="cultivator" functionName="processCultivatorA
rea">
```

```
    <area startNode="workAreaStart" widthNode="workAreaWidth"
heightNode="workAreaHeight" />
      <groundReferenceNode index="1" />
      <onlyActiveWhenLowered value="true" />
    </workArea>
  </workAreas>
  <workParticles>
    <effect workAreaIndex="1">
```

Motion path effect for the discs (left and right side):

```
      <effectNode effectClass="CultivatorMotionPathEffect"
effectType="CULTIVATOR" linkNode="cultivatorEffectLeftNode">
        <motionPathEffect textureFilename="cultivatorEffectLeftAr
ray.dds" numRows="60" rowLength="18" minFade="0.07" />
      </effectNode>
      <effectNode effectClass="CultivatorMotionPathEffect"
effectType="CULTIVATOR" linkNode="cultivatorEffectRightNode">
        <motionPathEffect textureFilename="cultivatorEffectRightAr
ray.dds" numRows="60" rowLength="18" minFade="0.07" />
      </effectNode>
```

Motion path effects for the rollers at the back:

```
      <effectNode effectClass="CultivatorMotionPathEffect"
effectType="CULTIVATOR" linkNode="rollerEffectLeftNode">
        <motionPathEffect textureFilename="rollerEffectLeftArray.
dds" numRows="20" rowLength="18" minFade="0.07" density="0.75"
densityScale="0.35" />
      </effectNode>
      <effectNode effectClass="CultivatorMotionPathEffect"
effectType="CULTIVATOR" linkNode="rollerEffectRightNode">
        <motionPathEffect textureFilename="rollerEffectRightArray.
dds" numRows="20" rowLength="18" minFade="0.07" density="0.75"
densityScale="0.35" />
      </effectNode>
    </effect>
```

Dust particle effect:

```
    <particle>
      <node node="dustEmitter" refNodeIndex="1"
particleType="SOIL_SMOKE" />
    </particle>
  </workParticles>
  <foldable>
    <foldingConfigurations>
      <foldingConfiguration>
```

Definition of the foldable parts:

- Tool starts in folded state directly after purchase (`startMoveDirection`)

- The lifted state of the tool is at animation time 0.1 / 10% of the animation (as the "folding" animation is 10 seconds long, this is at 1 second)

```
        <foldingParts startMoveDirection="1"
foldMiddleAnimTime="0.1">
            <foldingPart animationName="folding" speedScale="1" />
        </foldingParts>
      </foldingConfiguration>
    </foldingConfigurations>
  </foldable>
  <animations>
    <animation name="folding">
```

Actual lowering of the tool by moving the back wheels up (3 point hitch is lowered automatically at the same time):

```
      <part node="backArm" startTime="0.0" endTime="1.0"
startRot="0 0 0" endRot="-25 0 0" />
```

Setting up of the working depth after the unfolded by adjusting the front wheel and back roller height:

```
      <part node="wheelArmLeft" startTime="1.0" endTime="1.5"
startRot="-16 0 0" endRot="0 0 0" />
      <part node="wheelArmRight" startTime="1.0" endTime="1.5"
startRot="-16 0 0" endRot="0 0 0" />
      <part node="armLeftBackArm" startTime="1.0" endTime="1.5"
startRot="4.7 0 0" endRot="0 0 0" />
      <part node="armLeftRollerArm" startTime="1.0" endTime="1.5"
startRot="-4.7 0 0" endRot="0 0 0" />
      <part node="armRightBackArm" startTime="1.0" endTime="1.5"
startRot="4.7 0 0" endRot="0 0 0" />
      <part node="armRightRollerArm" startTime="1.0" endTime="1.5"
startRot="-4.7 0 0" endRot="0 0 0" />
```

Folding up of the side arms:

```
      <part node="armLeft" startTime="2.0" endTime="9" startRot="0
0 0" endRot="0 0 90" />
      <part node="armRight" startTime="1.5" endTime="8.5"
startRot="0 0 0" endRot="0 0 -90" />
```

Lowering of the while tool after the arms have been folded up, so we reduce the transport height. The `upperdistanceToGround` of the attacher joint is animated here as well to lower the 3 point hitch of the tractor in parallel with the back wheels.

```
    <part node="backArm" startTime="9.0" endTime="10.0"
startRot="-25 0 0" endRot="-15 0 0" />
    <part inputAttacherJointIndex="1" startTime="9.0"
endTime="10.0" upperDistanceToGroundStart="0.9"
upperDistanceToGroundEnd="0.6" />
    <sound template="hydraulicLayerTone2" startTime="9"
endTime="9.99" direction="0" volumeScale="4" pitchScale="0.8"
fadeIn="0.1" fadeOut="0.1" />
    <sound template="hydraulicPiston01" startTime="2"
endTime="9" volumeScale="0.4" pitchScale="0.8" direction="-1"
fadeIn="0.1" fadeOut="0.1" />
    <sound template="hydraulicPiston01" startTime="1.5"
endTime="8.5" volumeScale="0.4" pitchScale="0.6" direction="-1"
fadeIn="0.1" fadeOut="0.1" />
    <sound template="hydraulicLayerTone" startTime="2"
endTime="9" volumeScale="1.7" pitchScale="0.4" direction="-1"
fadeIn="0.1" fadeOut="0.1" />
    <sound template="hydraulicLayerTone" startTime="1.5"
endTime="8.5" volumeScale="1.7" pitchScale="0.6" direction="-1"
fadeIn="0.1" fadeOut="0.1" />
    <sound template="hydraulicLayerTone2" startTime="1.01"
endTime="1.5" direction="0" volumeScale="2" pitchScale="1.4"
fadeIn="0.1" fadeOut="0.1" />
    <sound template="hydraulicLayerTone" startTime="2"
endTime="9" volumeScale="2" pitchScale="0.5" direction="1"
fadeIn="0.1" fadeOut="0.1" />
    <sound template="hydraulicLayerTone" startTime="1.5"
endTime="8.5" volumeScale="2" pitchScale="0.7" direction="1"
fadeIn="0.1" fadeOut="0.1" />
    <sound template="hydraulicLayerTone" startTime="0.01"
endTime="0.99" volumeScale="1.5" pitchScale="0.55" fadeIn="0.1"
fadeOut="0.1" />
    <sound template="metalImpHigh02" startTime="9" direction="0"
volumeScale="1" pitchScale="0.7" />
    <sound template="clackVar2" startTime="9" direction="0"
volumeScale="2" pitchScale="1.7" />
    <sound template="foldStartMed02" startTime="9" direction="0"
volumeScale="4" pitchScale="0.7" />
    <sound template="clackVar6" startTime="9" direction="0"
volumeScale="3" pitchScale="0.5" />
    <sound template="metalImpHigh01" startTime="8.5"
direction="0" volumeScale="1" pitchScale="0.7" />
```

```
    <sound template="clackVar4" startTime="8.5" direction="0"
volumeScale="2" pitchScale="0.7" />
    <sound template="foldStartMed02" startTime="8.5"
direction="0" volumeScale="3" pitchScale="0.9" />
    <sound template="clackVar6" startTime="8.5" direction="0"
volumeScale="2" pitchScale="0.3" />
    <sound template="clackVar4" startTime="9" direction="-1"
volumeScale="3" pitchScale="0.7" />
    <sound template="foldStartMed02" startTime="2"
direction="-1" volumeScale="4" pitchScale="0.6" />
    <sound template="sheetImp02" startTime="2" direction="-1"
volumeScale="4" pitchScale="0.7" />
    <sound template="metalImpHigh01" startTime="2"
direction="-1" volumeScale="1" pitchScale="0.8" />
    <sound template="clackVar6" startTime="2" direction="-1"
volumeScale="2" pitchScale="0.7" />
    <sound template="metalImpHigh02" startTime="1.5"
direction="-1" volumeScale="1" pitchScale="0.6" />
    <sound template="clackVar4" startTime="1.5" direction="-1"
volumeScale="2" pitchScale="0.6" />
    <sound template="sheetImp01" startTime="1.5" direction="-1"
volumeScale="2" pitchScale="0.6" />
    <sound template="foldStartMed02" startTime="1.01"
direction="-1" volumeScale="1.8" pitchScale="1.5" />
    <sound template="clackVar6" startTime="1.01" direction="-1"
volumeScale="2.0" pitchScale="0.7" />
    <sound template="sheetImp02" startTime="1.01" direction="-1"
volumeScale="2.5" pitchScale="0.7" />
    <sound template="foldStartMed02" startTime="0.99"
direction="1" volumeScale="4" pitchScale="0.7" />
    <sound template="sheetImp02" startTime="0.99" direction="1"
volumeScale="4" pitchScale="0.6" />
    <sound template="metalImpHigh01" startTime="0.99"
direction="1" volumeScale="1" pitchScale="0.7" />
    <sound template="clackVar6" startTime="0.99" direction="1"
volumeScale="2" pitchScale="0.7" />
    <sound template="metalImpHigh02" startTime="0.5"
direction="-1" volumeScale="1" pitchScale="0.7" />
    <sound template="clackVar2" startTime="0.5" direction="-1"
volumeScale="2" pitchScale="1.7" />
    <sound template="foldStartMed02" startTime="0.5"
direction="-1" volumeScale="4" pitchScale="0.7" />
    <sound template="clackVar6" startTime="0.5" direction="-1"
volumeScale="3" pitchScale="0.5" />
    <sound template="metalImpMechanic" startTime="9.7"
direction="1" volumeScale="1.2" pitchScale="0.8" />
    <sound template="foldStartMed02" startTime="9.99"
direction="1" volumeScale="5.5" pitchScale="0.8" />
```

```
    <sound template="metalImpHigh02" startTime="9.99"
direction="-1" volumeScale="0.7" pitchScale="0.7" />
    </animation>
    <animation name="moveSupport">
```

Movement of the support feet and hiding of the lock bolts while it's moving:

```
    <part node="supportFeet" startTime="0" endTime="0.75"
startTrans="0 0.88746 2.095" endTrans="0 0.5 2.095" />
    <part node="supportFeetLockBolts" startTime="0.00"
endTime="0.01" startVisibility="true" endVisibility="false" />
    <part node="supportFeetLockBolts" startTime="0.74"
endTime="0.75" startVisibility="false" endVisibility="true" />
    <sound template="slideOpen" startTime="0.01" endTime="0.74"
direction="0" volumeScale="3" pitchScale="2"
linkNode="supportFeet" />
    <sound template="metalClose" startTime="0.01" direction="-1"
volumeScale="3" pitchScale="2" linkNode="supportFeet" />
    </animation>
    <animation name="lockDrawbarLimit">
```

Drawbar limit which is opened as soon as the tool is attached:

```
    <part componentJointIndex="1" startTime="0.0" endTime="0.1"
startRotLimit="0 70 15" endRotLimit="0 0 0" />
    </animation>
   </animations>
   <cylindered>
    <movingTools>
```

backArm movement which updates the two wheel nodes that are inside of it plus the hydraulic moving part:

```
    <movingTool node="backArm" wheelNodes="wheelLeft
wheelRight">
        <dependentPart node="backArmHydraulic" />
    </movingTool>
armLeft/armRight movement which updates the front and roller wheel
nodes that are inside of them plus the hydraulic moving parts:
    <movingTool node="armLeft" wheelNodes="rollLeftWheel
wheelFrontLeft">
        <dependentPart node="armLeftHydraulic" />
    </movingTool>
    <movingTool node="armRight" wheelNodes="rollRightWheel
wheelFrontRight">
        <dependentPart node="armRightHydraulic" />
    </movingTool>
```

Movement of the back arms and roller arms which updates the roller wheel nodes that are inside of them plus the hydraulic moving parts:

```
    <movingTool node="armLeftBackArm"
wheelNodes="rollLeftWheel">
        <dependentPart node="armLeftBackArmHydraulic" />
    </movingTool>
    <movingTool node="armLeftRollerArm"
wheelNodes="rollLeftWheel" />
    <movingTool node="armRightBackArm"
wheelNodes="rollRightWheel">
        <dependentPart node="armRightBackArmHydraulic" />
    </movingTool>
    <movingTool node="armRightRollerArm"
wheelNodes="rollRightWheel" />
```

Movement of the front wheel arms which updates the front wheel nodes plus the hydraulic moving parts:

```
    <movingTool node="wheelArmLeft" wheelNodes="wheelFrontLeft">
        <dependentPart node="wheelArmLeftHydraulic" />
    </movingTool>
    <movingTool node="wheelArmRight"
wheelNodes="wheelFrontRight">
        <dependentPart node="wheelArmRightHydraulic" />
    </movingTool>
```

Update of the side ground-adjusted visual parts after the groundAdjustedNode has been changed (see groundAdjustedNodes section):

```
    <movingTool node="armLeftGroundAdjustNode">
        <dependentPart node="armLeftGroundAdjustArm01" />
    </movingTool>
    <movingTool node="armRightGroundAdjustNode">
        <dependentPart node="armRightGroundAdjustArm01" />
    </movingTool>
  </movingTools>
  <movingParts>
```

Hydraulic cylinders with translating parts as punch:

```
    <movingPart node="backArmHydraulic" referencePoint="backArmH
ydraulicRef" referenceFrame="backArmHydraulicRef">
        <translatingPart node="backArmHydraulicPunch" />
    </movingPart>
    <movingPart node="armLeftHydraulic" referencePoint="armLeftH
ydraulicRef" referenceFrame="armLeftHydraulicRef">
```

```xml
        <translatingPart node="armLeftHydraulicPunch" />
    </movingPart>
    <movingPart node="armRightHydraulic" referencePoint="armRigh
tHydraulicRef" referenceFrame="armRightHydraulicRef">
        <translatingPart node="armRightHydraulicPunch" />
    </movingPart>
    <movingPart node="armLeftBackArmHydraulic" referencePoint="a
rmLeftBackArmHydraulicRef" referenceFrame="armLeftBackArmHydraulic
Ref">
        <translatingPart node="armLeftBackArmHydraulicPunch" />
    </movingPart>
    <movingPart node="armRightBackArmHydraulic" referencePoint="
armRightBackArmHydraulicRef" referenceFrame="armRightBackArmHydrau
licRef">
        <translatingPart node="armRightBackArmHydraulicPunch" />
    </movingPart>
    <movingPart node="wheelArmLeftHydraulic" referencePoint="wh
eelArmLeftHydraulicRef" referenceFrame="wheelArmLeftHydraulic
Ref">
        <translatingPart node="wheelArmLeftHydraulicPunch" />
    </movingPart>
    <movingPart node="wheelArmRightHydraulic" referencePoint="wh
eelArmRightHydraulicRef" referenceFrame="wheelArmRightHydraulic
Ref">
        <translatingPart node="wheelArmRightHydraulicPunch" />
    </movingPart>
```

Alignment of the visual drawbar to the current component position/rotation

- movingParts are *active dirty*, so they are permanently updated as the component can also permanently move (maxUpdateDistance limits the update to 150m, so if the player is far away, we don't update it)

- drawbarYAlign for rotating around the Y-axis (limitedAxis definition to adjust only one axis)

- drawbarZAlign for rotating around the Z-axis (limitedAxis definition to adjust only one axis)

```xml
    <movingPart node="drawbarYAlign" referencePoint="drawbarYAli
gnRef" referenceFrame="drawbarYAlignRefFrame" limitedAxis="2"
isActiveDirty="true" maxUpdateDistance="150">
        <dependentPart node="drawbarZAlign" />
    </movingPart>
    <movingPart node="drawbarZAlign" referencePoint="drawbarZAl
ignRef" referenceFrame="drawbarZAlignRefFrame" limitedAxis="1" />
```

Visual alignment of the ground-adjusted parts on the side to the ground adjusted node (see groundAdjustedNodes section). Using an orientation line with start and end nodes to properly adjust the moving parts.

```
<movingPart node="armLeftGroundAdjustArm01" referenceFrame="
armLeftGroundAdjustArm01RefFrame" doLineAlignment="true"
doDirectionAlignment="false">
    <orientationLine partLength="0.395">
      <lineNode node="armLeftGroundAdjustArm01RefStart" />
      <lineNode node="armLeftGroundAdjustArm01RefEnd" />
    </orientationLine>
    <dependentPart node="armLeftGroundAdjustPlate" />
  </movingPart>
  <movingPart node="armLeftGroundAdjustPlate"
referenceFrame="armLeft">
    <dependentPart node="armLeftGroundAdjustArm02" />
  </movingPart>
  <movingPart node="armLeftGroundAdjustArm02" referencePoint="
armLeftGroundAdjustArm02Ref" referenceFrame="armLeftGroundAdjustAr
m02Ref" />
  <movingPart node="armRightGroundAdjustArm01" referenceFrame=
"armRightGroundAdjustArm01RefFrame" doLineAlignment="true"
doDirectionAlignment="false">
    <orientationLine partLength="0.395">
      <lineNode node="armRightGroundAdjustArm01RefStart" />
      <lineNode node="armRightGroundAdjustArm01RefEnd" />
    </orientationLine>
    <dependentPart node="armRightGroundAdjustPlate" />
  </movingPart>
  <movingPart node="armRightGroundAdjustPlate"
referenceFrame="armLeft">
    <dependentPart node="armRightGroundAdjustArm02" />
  </movingPart>
  <movingPart node="armRightGroundAdjustArm02" referencePoint=
"armRightGroundAdjustArm02Ref" referenceFrame="armRightGroundAdjus
tArm02Ref" />
  </movingParts>
</cylindered>
```

Definition of the ground-adjusted nodes. These nodes will be adjusted to the current terrain height below them:

- The raycast node defines the detection point
- The ground adjusted node itself is the translated to the current detected height (inside of that node you can define your reference nodes for movingParts for example)

```
<groundAdjustedNodes>
  <groundAdjustedNode node="armLeftGroundAdjustNode"
yOffset="0.3" minY="0" maxY="0.3" moveSpeed="0.5"
resetIfNotActive="true">
```

The raycast is 0.4m long and starting from the `raycastNode` plus the defined `yOffset`:

```
    <raycastNode distance="0.4" node="armLeftGroundRaycastNode" />
```

Only update the node while the tool is lowered:

```
    <foldable minLimit="0" maxLimit="0.09" />
  </groundAdjustedNode>
  <groundAdjustedNode node="armRightGroundAdjustNode"
yOffset="0.3" minY="0" maxY="0.3" moveSpeed="0.5"
resetIfNotActive="true">
    <raycastNode distance="0.4" node="armRightGroundRaycastNode"
/>
    <foldable minLimit="0" maxLimit="0.09" />
  </groundAdjustedNode>
</groundAdjustedNodes>
```

Definition of the cultivator settings:

- `useDeepMode` defines if the cultivator is a regular cultivator or disc harrow (we have a discs harrow, which is not going too deep)

- `isSubsoiler` defines if the cultivator is rewarding with the plow yield increase

- isPowerHarrow defines if the cultivator is a power harrow which can be used in combination with a seeder

```
<cultivator useDeepMode="false" isSubsoiler="false"
isPowerHarrow="false">
  <sounds>
    <work template="DEFAULT_CULTIVATOR_WORK"
linkNode="qualidiscPro_main_component1" volumeScale="1.2" />
  </sounds>
</cultivator>
<ai>
```

AI needs to lower the tool:

```
    <needsLowering value="true" />
```

Definition of the area markers. These are normally the same as the `workArea`:

```
<areaMarkers leftNode="aiMarkerLeft" rightNode="aiMarkerRight"
backNode="aiMarkerBack" />
```

Collision trigger node with size definition. As soon as a player or other vehicle is inside this trigger, the vehicle will stop:

```
<collisionTrigger node="aiCollisionNode" width="6.6"
height="2.4" />
```

AI cannot turn backward with this tool, as it has wheels:

```
<allowTurnBackward value="false" />
```

Used to calculate the turning radius of the tractor with the tool attached. This requires the `jointNode` and the regular wheels at the back:

```
<turningRadiusLimitation rotationJointNode="componentJointDraw
bar" wheelIndices="1 2" />
```

Node should be in the back center of the tool and helps the AI to reverse tools with wheels:

```
<toolReverserDirectionNode node="aiMarkerBack" />
```

AI agent definition which is used by the drivable AI on the street, so it can properly calculate the vehicle size and rotation points:

```
<agentAttachment jointNode="attacherJoint"
rotCenterWheelIndices="1 2" width="2.9" height="3.6" length="7.5"
lengthOffset="3.25" />
  </ai>
```

Nodes that are used to deform the foliage in a certain area, so the crops on the field are pushed away by the tool while driving through them:

```
<foliageBending>
  <bendingNode minX="-1.35" maxX="1.35" minZ="-3.3" maxZ="1.3"
yOffset="0.6" />
  <bendingNode minX="-0.3" maxX="0.3" minZ="1.3" maxZ="4.5"
yOffset="0.6" />
  <bendingNode minX="-0.3" maxX="2.95" minZ="-2.35" maxZ="1.0"
yOffset="-0.5" node="armLeft" />
  <bendingNode minX="-2.85" maxX="0.3" minZ="-2.35" maxZ="1.0"
yOffset="-0.5" node="armRight" />
</foliageBending>
```

Definition of the base materials. This helps to make sure to have the same color on all tools from Kverneland for example. The color KVERNELAND _ RED1 is part of our color library (data/shared/brandColors.xml).

```
<baseMaterial>
  <material name="qualidiscPro_mat" baseNode="qualidiscPro_vis">
    <shaderParameter name="colorMat0" value="KVERNELAND_RED1" />
  </material>
</baseMaterial>
```

Duration in which the tool gets dirty and worn. Duration is in hours and the multipliers are added on top if the tool is driving on a field or even actively working on the field

```
<wearable wearDuration="480" workMultiplier="5"
fieldMultiplier="2" />
  <washable dirtDuration="90" washDuration="1" workMultiplier="6"
fieldMultiplier="2" />
```

Automatic export of our i3d mapping into the vehicle-XML:

- Includes the defined names/IDs from Blender and adds the node index path to this certain object

- In the other parts of the vehicle xml we only have to use the ID

```
<i3dMappings>
  <i3dMapping id="qualidiscPro_main_component1" node="0>" />
  <i3dMapping id="aiCollisionNode" node="0>0|0|0" />
  <i3dMapping id="aiMarkerBack" node="0>0|0|1" />
  <i3dMapping id="aiMarkerLeft" node="0>0|0|2" />
  <i3dMapping id="aiMarkerRight" node="0>0|0|3" />
  <i3dMapping id="airDoubleRed" node="0>0|1|0|0" />
  <i3dMapping id="airDoubleYellow" node="0>0|1|0|1" />
  <i3dMapping id="hydraulicIn01" node="0>0|1|0|2" />
  <i3dMapping id="hydraulicIn01_detached" node="0>0|1|0|2|0" />
  <i3dMapping id="hydraulicIn01_connector" node="0>0|1|0|2|0|0" />
  <i3dMapping id="hydraulicIn02" node="0>0|1|0|3" />
  <i3dMapping id="hydraulicIn02_detached" node="0>0|1|0|3|0" />
  <i3dMapping id="hydraulicIn02_connector" node="0>0|1|0|3|0|0" />
  <i3dMapping id="hydraulicOut01" node="0>0|1|0|4" />
  <i3dMapping id="hydraulicOut01_detached" node="0>0|1|0|4|0" />
  <i3dMapping id="hydraulicOut01_connector"
node="0>0|1|0|4|0|0" />
  <i3dMapping id="hydraulicOut02" node="0>0|1|0|5" />
  <i3dMapping id="hydraulicOut02_detached" node="0>0|1|0|5|0" />
  <i3dMapping id="hydraulicOut02_connector"
node="0>0|1|0|5|0|0" />
```

```
    <i3dMapping id="supportFeet" node="0>0|1|1|0" />
    <i3dMapping id="supportFeetLockBolts" node="0>0|1|1|1" />
    <i3dMapping id="wheelChocks" node="0>0|1|2" />
    <i3dMapping id="wheelChockSupport01" node="0>0|1|2|0" />
    <i3dMapping id="wheelChock01" node="0>0|1|2|0|0" />
    <i3dMapping id="wheelChockSupport02" node="0>0|1|2|1" />
    <i3dMapping id="wheelChock02" node="0>0|1|2|1|0" />
    <i3dMapping id="componentJointDrawbar" node="0>0|2" />
    <i3dMapping id="dustEmitter" node="0>0|3|0" />
    <i3dMapping id="lights" node="0>0|4" />
    <i3dMapping id="rearLight23White_01" node="0>0|4|0|0" />
    <i3dMapping id="rearLight23White_02" node="0>0|4|0|1" />
    <i3dMapping id="movingParts" node="0>0|5" />
    <i3dMapping id="armLeft" node="0>0|5|0" />
    <i3dMapping id="armLeftBackArm" node="0>0|5|0|0" />
    <i3dMapping id="armLeftBackArmHydraulicRef"
node="0>0|5|0|0|1" />
    <i3dMapping id="armLeftRollerArm" node="0>0|5|0|0|3" />
    <i3dMapping id="rollLeftBack" node="0>0|5|0|0|3|2" />
    <i3dMapping id="rollLeftFront" node="0>0|5|0|0|3|3" />
    <i3dMapping id="rollLeftWheel" node="0>0|5|0|0|3|4" />
    <i3dMapping id="rollerEffectLeftNode" node="0>0|5|0|0|3|5" />
    <i3dMapping id="armLeftBackArmHydraulic" node="0>0|5|0|1" />
    <i3dMapping id="armLeftBackArmHydraulicPunch"
node="0>0|5|0|1|0" />
    <i3dMapping id="armLeftColPart" node="0>0|5|0|2" />
    <i3dMapping id="armLeftDiscs" node="0>0|5|0|3" />
    <i3dMapping id="armLeftGroundAdjustArm01RefFrame"
node="0>0|5|0|4|0" />
    <i3dMapping id="armLeftGroundAdjustArm01"
node="0>0|5|0|4|0|0" />
    <i3dMapping id="armLeftGroundAdjustPlate"
node="0>0|5|0|4|0|0|2" />
    <i3dMapping id="armLeftGroundAdjustArm02Ref"
node="0>0|5|0|4|0|0|2|0" />
    <i3dMapping id="armLeftGroundAdjustArm02" node="0>0|5|0|4|1" />
    <i3dMapping id="armLeftGroundAdjustNode" node="0>0|5|0|4|2" />
    <i3dMapping id="armLeftGroundAdjustArm01RefEnd"
node="0>0|5|0|4|2|0" />
    <i3dMapping id="armLeftGroundAdjustArm01RefStart"
node="0>0|5|0|4|2|1" />
    <i3dMapping id="armLeftGroundRaycastNode" node="0>0|5|0|4|3" />
    <i3dMapping id="armLeftHydraulicRef" node="0>0|5|0|5" />
    <i3dMapping id="cultivatorEffectLeftNode" node="0>0|5|0|7" />
    <i3dMapping id="wheelArmLeft" node="0>0|5|0|8" />
    <i3dMapping id="wheelArmLeftHydraulicRef" node="0>0|5|0|8|0" />
    <i3dMapping id="wheelFrontLeft" node="0>0|5|0|8|2" />
```

```
    <i3dMapping id="wheelArmLeftHydraulic" node="0>0|5|0|9" />
    <i3dMapping id="wheelArmLeftHydraulicPunch"
node="0>0|5|0|9|0" />
    <i3dMapping id="armLeftHydraulic" node="0>0|5|1" />
    <i3dMapping id="armLeftHydraulicPunch" node="0>0|5|1|0" />
    <i3dMapping id="armRight" node="0>0|5|2" />
    <i3dMapping id="armRightBackArm" node="0>0|5|2|0" />
    <i3dMapping id="armRightBackArmHydraulicRef"
node="0>0|5|2|0|1" />
    <i3dMapping id="armRightRollerArm" node="0>0|5|2|0|3" />
    <i3dMapping id="rollRightBack" node="0>0|5|2|0|3|2" />
    <i3dMapping id="rollRightFront" node="0>0|5|2|0|3|3" />
    <i3dMapping id="rollRightWheel" node="0>0|5|2|0|3|4" />
    <i3dMapping id="rollerEffectRightNode" node="0>0|5|2|0|3|5" />
    <i3dMapping id="armRightBackArmHydraulic" node="0>0|5|2|1" />
    <i3dMapping id="armRightBackArmHydraulicPunch"
node="0>0|5|2|1|0" />
    <i3dMapping id="armRightColPart" node="0>0|5|2|2" />
    <i3dMapping id="armRightDecals" node="0>0|5|2|3" />
    <i3dMapping id="armRightDiscs" node="0>0|5|2|4" />
    <i3dMapping id="armRightGroundAdjustArm01RefFrame"
node="0>0|5|2|5|0" />
    <i3dMapping id="armRightGroundAdjustArm01"
node="0>0|5|2|5|0|0" />
    <i3dMapping id="armRightGroundAdjustPlate"
node="0>0|5|2|5|0|0|1" />
    <i3dMapping id="armRightGroundAdjustArm02Ref"
node="0>0|5|2|5|0|0|1|0" />
    <i3dMapping id="armRightGroundAdjustArm02"
node="0>0|5|2|5|1" />
    <i3dMapping id="armRightGroundAdjustNode" node="0>0|5|2|5|2" />
    <i3dMapping id="armRightGroundAdjustArm01RefEnd"
node="0>0|5|2|5|2|0" />
    <i3dMapping id="armRightGroundAdjustArm01RefStart"
node="0>0|5|2|5|2|1" />
    <i3dMapping id="armRightGroundRaycastNode" node="0>0|5|2|5|3" />
    <i3dMapping id="armRightHydraulicRef" node="0>0|5|2|6" />
    <i3dMapping id="cultivatorEffectRightNode" node="0>0|5|2|8" />
    <i3dMapping id="wheelArmRight" node="0>0|5|2|9" />
    <i3dMapping id="wheelArmRightHydraulicRef" node="0>0|5|2|9|0" />
    <i3dMapping id="wheelFrontRight" node="0>0|5|2|9|2" />
    <i3dMapping id="wheelArmRightHydraulic" node="0>0|5|2|10" />
    <i3dMapping id="wheelArmRightHydraulicPunch"
node="0>0|5|2|10|0" />
    <i3dMapping id="armRightHydraulic" node="0>0|5|3" />
    <i3dMapping id="armRightHydraulicPunch" node="0>0|5|3|0" />
    <i3dMapping id="backArm" node="0>0|5|4" />
```

```
    <i3dMapping id="backArmHydraulicRef" node="0>0|5|4|2" />
    <i3dMapping id="rearLight05_01" node="0>0|5|4|3|0|0" />
    <i3dMapping id="rearLight05_02" node="0>0|5|4|3|0|1" />
    <i3dMapping id="redTriangle_02_01" node="0>0|5|4|3|0|2" />
    <i3dMapping id="redTriangle_02_02" node="0>0|5|4|3|0|3" />
    <i3dMapping id="yellowRound_02_01" node="0>0|5|4|3|0|4" />
    <i3dMapping id="yellowRound_02_02" node="0>0|5|4|3|0|5" />
    <i3dMapping id="backLightsHigh" node="0>0|5|4|3|1" />
    <i3dMapping id="turnLightLeft" node="0>0|5|4|3|2" />
    <i3dMapping id="turnLightRight" node="0>0|5|4|3|3" />
    <i3dMapping id="licensePlateBack" node="0>0|5|4|5" />
    <i3dMapping id="wheelLeft" node="0>0|5|4|6" />
    <i3dMapping id="wheelRight" node="0>0|5|4|7" />
    <i3dMapping id="backArmHydraulic" node="0>0|5|5" />
    <i3dMapping id="backArmHydraulicPunch" node="0>0|5|5|1" />
    <i3dMapping id="drawbarYAlignRefFrame" node="0>0|5|6" />
    <i3dMapping id="drawbarYAlign" node="0>0|5|6|0" />
    <i3dMapping id="drawbarZAlignRefFrame" node="0>0|5|6|0|2" />
    <i3dMapping id="drawbarZAlign" node="0>0|5|6|0|2|0" />
    <i3dMapping id="visuals" node="0>0|6" />
    <i3dMapping id="qualidiscPro_vis" node="0>0|6|1|0" />
    <i3dMapping id="workAreas" node="0>0|7" />
    <i3dMapping id="groundReferenceNode" node="0>0|7|0" />
    <i3dMapping id="workAreaHeight" node="0>0|7|1" />
    <i3dMapping id="workAreaStart" node="0>0|7|2" />
    <i3dMapping id="workAreaWidth" node="0>0|7|3" />
    <i3dMapping id="hoses" node="0>1|0|0" />
    <i3dMapping id="qualidiscPro_drawbar_component2" node="1>" />
    <i3dMapping id="attacherJoint" node="1>0" />
    <i3dMapping id="drawbarYAlignRef" node="1>1" />
    <i3dMapping id="drawbarZAlignRef" node="1>2" />
  </i3dMappings>
</vehicle>
```

Index

Note: **Bold** page numbers refer to tables and *italic* page numbers refer to figures.

adapterNode attribute 115, 259
additional scripts 106
Add-ons section of Preferences 29
Adobe Substance 3D Painter 16
agentAttachment definition 229
<agentAttachment> tag 140, 141
<agent> tag 141
AI
    areas 137–141
    gsVehicleDebug 228–229, *229*
    hierarchy 139
aiCollisionNode Empty 138, 229
ai Empty 137, 139
aiMarkerBack Empty 138, 140
<ai> tag 139–141
<allowTurnBackward> tag 139–140
alphaBlendingClipThreshold parameter 69
alpha mode 232
amount parameter 219, 221, 223
angle parameter 215, 217
animation, for vehicle 150
    in Blender 162–170
    folding process 153–156
    "moving parts," *see* "moving parts"
    setting up 151–153
    sounds with 161–162
    technical requirements 150–151
animationName attribute 151–152, 154
animations
    gsVehicleDebug 229, *229*
    for vehicle *see* animation, for vehicle
    workspace, Blender *164*, 163–164
<animations> tag 152, 154–156, 162
<annotation> tag 110
application programming interface (API) 4, 29
Apply Selected button 192
area markers 272
armature-based rig 79
armature bones 197–200
armature objects, in Blender 196–197

armLeftBone 199
armLeftDiscs Empty 131
armLeftHydraulic object 157
armLeftHydraulicPunch object 157
armLeftHydraulicRef object 157
armLeft mesh object 146
armLeft node 158
armLeft object 91, *161*, 190
armLeftPart01 object 160
armLeftPart02 object 160
armLeftPart02Ref attribute 160
armLeftPart01RefFrame attribute 160
armRightDecals 58
armRight object 91
attachable Empty 93–94
<attachable> tag 114, 151, 152
attacherJoint Empty 93–94
attachment points 114
    and connection hoses 93–97
Autodesk Maya 15, 16, 196; *see also* Blender
automatic export, of i3d mapping 273–276

backArm movement 267–268
backLightsHigh node 175
<bales> tag 108–109
baseConfig attribute 123
base information 112–114
base materials 47, 50, 60, 273
<base> tag 112–114
BKT wheel configuration 257
Blender 8–10, *9*, 12, 20
    animating in 168–170
    animation workspace *164*, 163–164
    armature objects in 196–197, 204
    built-in material system 55
    "clay" material 47
    as collision components 86, 93
    collision meshes in 88–89, *89*
    as DCC 13–15, *13–15*, 16
    Decimate modifier 190, *191*

Blender (*cont.*)
    and Farming Simulator 57
    File Browser 50
    GIANTS Editor 17
    GIANTS I3D Exporter add-on 48, 51, 70, 73, *73*, 77, 83, 86, 99, 116, 150, 171, 180, 187
    GIANTS I3D Exporter tab in *71*
    and I3D file 65
    interface 163, 165
    LTS version of 14
    materials in *see* materials, in Blender
    node graph in 56–57, 59
    normal map in 55
    object's name in 82
    object's origin 77
    Outliner 90, 182
    parenting operation 201
    render engine 49
    Repeat Last operator functionality 147
    rigging system 195, 199
    scene statistics 189
    snapping tools 61
    3D cursor 83
    3D model within 120
    transform tools 60
    UV coordinate box in 75
    UV Editor 53, 75
    UV maps in 60
    vehicle hierarchy within 120
    Weight Paint mode 201–202, 204
    working with *see* working, with Blender
Blender Basics course on CG Cookie 33
Blender Market 30
Blender's Interface, quick primer on 22–23, *23*
Blender's Preferences Editor
    Add-ons to Enable 29
    Auto Depth 27
    Button Mouse (Optional) 26
    GPU rendering 28–29
    Orbit around Selection 26–27
    Spacebar Action to Search 27–28
    Tab for Pie Menu 28
    Zoom to Mouse Position 27
.blend file 84, 115, 118, 130, 187, 209
Bone Constraints 199, *200*
Boolean modifier 33
Bounding Volume label 192
brackets 20
brakeFactor wheel 256
brake force 259
brand attribute 121
<brandColors> tag 106–107

<brands> tag 106–107, 111
buyField parameter 216, 218

<category> tag 111
CDATA syntax 103, 105
CG Cookie 8–10, *9*, *10*, 21, 33, *33*, 46, 249
-cheats 213, *213*
Child 1 Distance property 194
Child 2 Distance property 194
Child Of constraint 199–200, *200*
chocks, wheel 128–130
collision meshes 88–89, *89*
collision trigger node 272
color channel mappings 54–55
colorized material shaders 65
colorMask 53, 69
color materials 53–54, *54*
colorMat parameter 53
colorMat0 parameter 53, 54, 65
Color Space 55, 56
community
    Farming Simulator modding 13
    on GIANTS Software Community Forum 2, 10–11
complex farming equipment 150
componentJointIndex attribute 153
components 79, 82, 86
    animate components 166
    Blender, as collision components 86, 93
    GIANTS Engine 85
    physics components and function nodes *see* physics components and function nodes
    in 3D space 35
<components> tag 113
Compound Child check box 92
compound children 90, 91–92, *92*
computer-aided design (CAD) drawings 31
connection hoses 259–260
    attachment points and 93–97
    handling connection hoses 95–97
<connectionHoses> tag 96, 108, 114–115
Console award 245, *245*
console modhub publishing 254
constraints, armature bones 199
constructive feedback 244
<controls> tag 109
"convenience" keying sets 167, *168*
cratches_dirt_snow_wetness 69
Create Empty operator 39–40, 44, 96, 120–121, 125, 138, 146
crops, with foliage bending nodes 141–142
cultivatorEffectLeftArray.dds 148

cultivatorEffectLeftArray_ignore
    Empty 147
cultivatorEffectLeftNode Empty 146
cultivatorEffects.xml 147
cultivator mod 110
cultivator model 78, *78*, *81*
cultivator settings 271
<cultivators> tag 111
curvesLeft_ignore Empty 146
custom bounding volume 184–185, *185*
custom effect array textures 145–148
custom emissive map *74*
Custom Shader panel 67, *66*, *67*
custom UV map 75
Cycles Render Devices 28
<cylindered> tag 158–160

damper attribute 123
data/effects/cultivator/
    cultivatorEffects.xml 147
$dataS 106
Data section, compressed mod file in 241–242, *242*
data/shared/assets 130
data/shared folder 55
DDS format 47, 57
DDS texture animation file 145, 148
debugging, vehicle mod
   gsRenderingDebugMode command 231–232
   gsVehicleDebug command *see*
      gsVehicleDebug command
   gsVehicleDebugLOD command 230–231, *231*
decal mesh 60–62, *62*
Decal_normalThirdUV variation 60, 69
decals 57
   cleaning up 62–64
   positioning and unwrapping 60–62, *62*
   setting up 57–60, *59*
decals_diffuse.gim 68
Decal variation 69
Decimate modifier 190, 191, *191*
Decimation Type of Collapse 190
defaultHydraulicSmall sound
    template 162
default_normal.png 55
defaultPlacement attribute 176
default_vmask.png 55
deforming object 196
delimb parameter 222
<dependencies> tag 106
<dependentPart> tag 158, 160
<description> tag 110, 235
descVersion attribute 102

Developer Mode, in Farming Simulator 109, 116,
    212, *212*, 236
<development> tag 109
diameter attribute 115
diffuse(like decals_diffuse.png) 68
direction attribute 162
disableBackwards attribute 135
<distanceToGround> tag 114
Documents/My FS Mods/QualidiscPro 100
Documents/My Games/
    FarmingSimulator20XX/mods 116
Dope Sheet 168, 169
Dope Sheet Editor 164
drag-and-drop method 68
drawbar limit 267
drawbarYAlign, of visual drawbar 269
drawbarZAlign, of visual drawbar 269
driveNode attribute 122
dustEmitter plane 143, *143*
dust particle effect 263
dynamically loaded parts 130
<dynamicallyLoadedParts> tag 130

Edit mode 81, 83, 146, 198
Editor
   Blender's Preferences Editor *see* Blender's
      Preferences Editor
   Dope Sheet Editor 164
   GIANTS Editor *see* GIANTS Editor
   modern text editors 177
   text editor 18–20, 99, 102, 109, 119, 150, 171, 177,
    212
   Timeline editor 164, 170
   UV 53, 61
Eevee/Cycles render engines 48, 49, 76
<effectNode> tag 145
effects Empty 143, 144
<effect> tag 144, 145
ELONGATED type 176
emitCountScale attribute 144
EmitterShape attributes 143
empty tags 127, 257
endRot attribute 153
endRotLimit attribute 153
endScale attribute 153
endTime attribute 152, 162
endTrans attribute 152
endTransLimit attribute 153
endVisibility attribute 153
EXE file 16
Export Orientation check box 131
Export Position check box 131

eXtensible Markup Language (XML) 16, 18–19, 42, 68, 98, 102, 108, 177
<extraSourceFiles> tag 106

Face Count value 190
FaceNormalToOrigin 44
false attribute 130
FarmCon events 8, 10, 245–246, *246*
farming equipment 151
Farming Simulator 156
    Blender and 57
    custom shortcut for 213
    Developer Mode in 109, 116, 212, *212*, 236
    functional mod for 211
    game engine for 53, 187
    GIANTS Editor and 48
    GIANTS Engine for 76
    icon generator 206–207, *207*
    installation folder for 116
    with Lua 247, *248*, 249
    materials *see* surface materials
    modder 163
    modding *see* Farming Simulator modding
    and ModHub 101, 233
    rough-working mod for 118
    shared lights from 172, 261
    vehicle mod in 119
Farming Simulator 22 69, 70
Farming Simulator 25 60
    material system in *see* material system, in Farming Simulator 25
    new material system in *71*
Farming Simulator Debug 213
Farming Simulator modding 1–2
    Blender *see* Blender
    GDN *see* Giants Developer Network (GDN)
    Giants Software Forum, community on 10–11
    ModHub *see* ModHub
    technical requirements 2
    and 3D *see* 3D model
    tools for *see* tools, for modding
features, for vehicle 171
    license plate 176
    light sources *see* light sources
    technical requirements 171–172
    vehicle-XML 176–178
fertilizerState parameter 215, 218
F2 hotkey 93
fieldId parameter 217
fieldIndex parameter 214, 217
field of view (FOV) 225, *225*, 237
filename attribute 106, 122, 130
<filename> tag 113

File Path field 131
fillTypeName parameter 219, 223
fillType parameter 220
fillUnitIndex parameter 223
Flight Mode 236–237
foldable parts 264
<foldable> tag 137, 154, 156
<foldingConfiguration> tag 154
<foldingPart> tag 154
folding process 153–156
foldMiddleAniTime attribute 155
foliage bending nodes, crops with 141–142
<foliageBendingNodes> tag 142
forcePointRatio attribute 122
framerate 165
FreezeTranslation and FreezeRotation, in GIANTS I3D Exporter add-on 85
frontoffset attribute 141
fruitName parameter 217
FS25 materials 70
full-blown software development tool 20
functional nodes 93
functionName attribute 134
<functions> tag 111, 113

game-ready vehicle models 190
game.xml file 109, 212
GDN *see* GIANTS Developer Network (GDN)
GDN Community Forum 4
geometry, decals 60–62, *62*
Geometry Nodes 30–31
GIANTS Developer Network (GDN) 1, 3, *3*, 20, 251–252
    account 3
    available for modders 4, *4*
    familiar with 2–4
    forum 2, 12
    and ModHub 11
    Video Tutorials of 7–8, *8*
GIANTS Editor 4, *4*, 12, 15–18, *18*, 20, 38, 40, 43, 44, 47, 57, 64–66, *64*, 85, 89, 100–102, 113, 120, 152, 183, *183*, 187, 194, 210
    colorized material shaders 65
    exported file in 64, *64*
    and Farming Simulator 48
    mod and materials in 64–66, *64*, 76
    model in 65
    side panel of 65
    variable shader properties 65–67, *66*, *67*
GIANTS Editor Outliner 43
GIANTS Engine 1, 16, 53–55, 65, 72, 79, 85, 86, 90, 119, 122, 133, 150, 177, 183, 194, 203, 204
    Blender's material system 52

documentation 75
for Farming Simulator 76
integrated development environment (IDE) 19
physics system in 87, 89
rendering pipeline 231
GIANTS I3D Exporter 4, 12, 16–17, *17*, 20–22, 40,
    41, *43*, 49, 53, 54, *54*, 55, 60, 82, 118, 125,
    130, 144, 191
    attributes in 191
    in Blender 48, 77, 99, 116
    configuring 50–51
    merge group 186
    newer versions of 72
    placeholder material, in Blender 49, 50
    UV Vehicle Array with 65
    vehicle hierarchy and 185
    XML Config Files to *117*
GIANTS I3D Exporter add-on 48, 51, 52, 55, 64, 96,
    117, 121, 132, 138, 145, 157, 163, 171, 195
    for Blender 46, 70, 73, *73*, 83, 86, 150, 171,
        180, 187
    FreezeTranslation and FreezeRotation tools in 85
GIANTS I3D Exporter tab 82, 93, 131, 139, 143, 147,
    148, 157, 182, *182*
    in Blender *71*
    Export section of 194
    with node ID 82, *82*, 96
    Predefined panel within 88
    of 3D Viewport's SIdebar 74, 134, 174, 185
GIANTS Motion Path Tool 147, 148
GIANTS Software 1, 3, 4, 16, 21, 233, 249
    Community Forum 10–11
    FarmCon events 8, 10
    folks at 52, 244
    forum 239
    GIANTS I3D EXPORTER 42–44, *43*
    Lizard 107, 111
    ModHub *see* ModHub
    mod to 243
    publishing process 238
    QA team 238, 250
    quality control procedures 234
    staff at 241
    terms and conditions 242
    tests 238
    website 2, *2*, 7, 10, *11*, *39*, *48*, *78*, *87*, *100*, 120, *120*,
        151, *172*, *181*, *188*, *196*, *206*
GIANTS Studio/Debugger 4, *4*, 12, 18–20, *19*, 20,
    42, 99–100, 109, 150, 171, 177–178, *178*,
    212, 226
    vehicle-XML file in 116, 119, 143
GIANTS Texture Tool 47, 57, 67
    convert your image textures, to DDS format 76

with drag-and-drop method 68
getting and installing 68
handy helper scripts 69
using 68–69
.gim file 68
GIMP 31
ground adjusted nodes 135–137, *136*, 270
<groundAdjustedNodes> tag 135, 137, 268
<groundReferenceNodes> tag 135, 262
groundTypeName parameter 214–215, 217
grounReferenceNodeIndex attribute 132
growthState parameter 217, 222
gsBaleAdd command 220–222
gsCameraFovSet command 225, *225*, 237
gsFieldSetFruit command 217–219, *219*, 222,
    232
gsFieldSetGround command 214–217, *216*, 232
gsFillUnitAdd command 223
gsMoneyAdd command 222–223
gsPalletAdd command 220–222
gsPlayerFlightMode 237
gsRenderingDebugMode command 231–232
gsTipAnywhereAdd command 219–220,
    220, 232
gsTreeAdd command 222
gsVehicleAddDamage command 224
gsVehicleAddDirt command 224
gsVehicleAddWear command 224
gsVehicleDebug attributes command 112,
    141, 142, 209, 253
gsVehicleDebug command 226–227, *227*, 232
    AI view of 228–229, *229*
    animation view of 229, *229*
    attributes view of 227–228, *228*
    Physics view of 229, *230*
gsVehicleDebugLOD command 230–232, *231*
gsVehicleFuelSet command 225
gsVehicleReload command 116, 163, 212,
    226, 232
gsVehicleTemperatureSet command 225

handling connection hoses 95–97
handling ungrouped vertices 203
hard surface modeling, in Blender 30
hasParticles attribute 122
hasTireTracks attribute 122
height attribute 141
<high> tag 174, 175
hoseRig armature object 197–199, 201
hoses
    connection hoses *see* connection hoses
    hydraulic hoses, construction of *see* hydraulic
        hoses, construction of

`<hose>` tag 115

hotkeys *25*, 25–29, 45–46
    editing 45–46
    toolbar and *25*, 25–29
hydraulic cylinders 268–269
hydraulic hoses, construction of
    armature objects in Blender 196–197, *197*
    technical requirements 195
    vertex groups *see* vertex groups
`hydraulicIn01_connector` 115
`hydraulicIn01_detatched` node 115
`hydraulicIn01` node 115
hydraulic system 156–159

icon generator 205
    Farming Simulator 206–207, *207*
    for individual vehicles 208–209
    technical requirements 205–206
`<icon>` tag 209
IDE *see* integrated development environment (IDE)
I3D file 4, 15, 16, 38, *38*, 41, *41*, 43, *44*, 46, 53, 59, 64,
    82, 84, 93, 99, 101, 107, 113, 118, 119, 132,
    139, 152, 187, 191, 210, 254
    Blender and 65
    vehicle hierarchy in 154
    vehicle mod to 57
I3D mapping 82, 95, 117, 143, 273–276
`<i3dMappings>` tag 115–117
`<image>` tag 111
Image Texture node 58
in-game console *212*, 214
    command in 215–216, *216*
    gsVehicleDebug attributes in 227
    vehicle from 223–225
ingame map 255
in-game screenshots 236–237
`initialCompression` attribute 123
`<inputAttacherJoint>` tag 114
integrated development environment
    (IDE) 19
`isInverted` attribute 130
`isLeft` attribute 122
`isPowerHarrow` cultivator 271
`isSubsoiler` cultivator 271
`isSynchronized` attribute 123

`jointNode` attribute 140, 141, 272
`jointType` attribute 114
`<jointTypes>` tag 107

keyframe 164
keying set 166–168
Keymap section of Preferences 28

Kverneland Qualidisc Pro cultivator 77, 87,
    100, 110, 120, 251–252

Layout workspace 164
`lengthOffset` attribute 113, 141
`length` parameter 115, 141, 220, 222, 259
level of detail (LOD) meshes
    check box 193
    modeling 189–190
    setting up, merge group 191–192
    technical requirements 187
    understanding 188
    vehicle hierarchy 192–194, *193*
license plates 176, 197, 262
`<licensePlate>` tag 176
`<lifetime>` tag 111
lightControl parameter 69
light-Ids parameter 69
light sources
    real, working with 173–176
    shared lights from Farming Simulator 172
`<lights>` tag 172, 174, 175
`lightType` attribute 175
light types 261
`limeState` parameter 216, 218
`linkNode` attribute 145
Load Current button 192
Load Shader button 131
localization 104–105
`lockDrawbarLimit` animation 254
LOD meshes *see* level of detail (LOD) meshes
`log.txt`, in text editor 102
`<low>` tag 175
LTS version of Blender 14
Lua 247, *248*, 249

main collision component 86, 89–91, *91*
maps
    custom emissive map *74*
    custom UV map 75
    ingame map 255
    normal map in Blender 54–57, *56*, 64
    specular map 54
    UV maps in Blender 60
`mass` attribute 123
material assignments 77
`<materialHolders>` tag 107
materials, in Blender
    and Farming Simulator materials 48–49
    GIANTS I3D Exporter 50–51, *51*
    placeholder 49–50, *50*
material system, in Farming Simulator 25 and
    beyond

new staticlight shader variation, working with
74–75, *76*

shaders and materials, in new material system
70, *71*, 72–73

shader variations and parameters, names on
69, **70**

Merge Children check box 131

Merge Group Root check box 182, *182*, 183

merge groups 180

assigning objects to 182–183

custom bounding volume 184–185, *185*

GIANTS I3D Exporter 186

LOD mesh 191–192

technical requirements 180

understanding 181–182

mesh data 58

Meshroom 31

mod contest 247

Modder's Guide to the ModHub 234

mod description file (modDesc.xml) 68, 99,
101–102, 110, 118, 119, 210, 235–236, 243,
251–252

additional non-vehicle materials 107

additional scripts 106

attachment types 107

bales 108–109

brands and brand colors 106–107

connection hoses 108

essential parts of 102–104

localization 104–105

multiplayer support 104

naming additional contributors 104

naming dependencies 106

specializations 105–106

store packs 108

<brand> tag within 111

ModDesc Version: 77 102

modding 1

publishing process *see* publishing process,
modding

purposes of *see* purposes, of modding

and 3D *see* 3D model

tools for *see* tools, for modding

modeling

in Blender 30–34

LOD meshes 189–190

workspace 33

modern text editors 177

modes

alpha mode 232

Edit mode 81, 83, 146, 198

Flight Mode 237

normals mode 232

Object mode 146

Pose mode 199

Weight Paint mode 201, 202, 204

working, with Blender 24

ModHub 1, 4, 20, 188, 209

account 5–7, *6*

Farming Simulator and 101, 233

GDN and 11

and GIANTS Software 249

as Mod Research Tool 7

publishing process *see* publishing process,
modding

website 4, *5*

ModHub Guidelines for Farming Simulator
234, 235

Mod Icon 209–210

modifiers

Boolean 33

Decimate 190, *191*

stack, Blender 33

system, Blender 30

Mod Research Tool 7

monetization for mods 244–245

morphPosition parameter 69

motion path effects 263

<motionPathEffects> tag 145, 148

moveSupport attribute 151, 152

"moving parts" 156

hydraulic system 156–159

moving arms 159–161

movingParts Alignment, of visual drawbar 269

<movingParts> tag 158, 160

moving tools 156

<movingTools> tag 158, 160

mTrackArray 69, 131

My FS Mods 100

name attribute 121, 152

<name> tag 110

naming dependencies 106

navigating 3D space 23–24

<needsLowering> tag 139

new staticlight shader variation, working with
74–75, *76*

node attribute 128, 152, 153, 176

node ID 115, 125, 135, 139, 143, 152, 172, 174

in GIANTS I3D Exporter tab 82, *82*, 96

nodes

armLeft node 158

collision trigger node 272

crops, with foliage bending nodes 141–142

function nodes *see* physics components and
function nodes

nodes (*cont.*)
    Geometry Nodes 30–31
    graph, on Blender material 56–57, *56*, 59
    ground adjusted nodes 135–137, *136*, 270
    Image Texture node 58
    objectChange node 259
    Principled BSDF 58–59
    raycast node 136, *136*, 270
    rootNode 259
<node> tag 144
non-normalized vertex weight 204, **204**
non-physics components 86–88
Non Renderable check box 91
non-vehicle materials 107
normalized vertex weights 203–204, **204**
normal maps 54–57, *56*, 64
normals mode 232
Notepad++ 20
numRows variable 147
NURBS curve 146, *146*, 148
NVIDIA video card 28

objectChange node 259
<objectChange> tag 115
Object Data from Curve 147
Object Data tab of the Properties editor 173
Object mode 146
object's origin (pivot) 77, 83–84
    technical requirements 77
    vehicle hierarchy 84–85
    vehicle mesh 78–82, *80*
objects, to merge group 182–183
orthographic reference images 31

parameters, in new material system 69, **70**
parkingNode attribute 129
particle-based effects 144–145
particle system 142–144, *143*
particleType attribute 144
<part> tag 152
photogrammetry 31
Photoshop 31, 75, 202
physics components and function nodes 86, 184,
    229, *230*, 254
    attachment points and connection hoses 93–97
    collision meshes 88–89, *89*
    compound children 91–92, *92*
    main collision component 89–91, *91*
    nonphysics components 87–88
    technical requirements 87
physics system 86
    in GIANTS Engine 87, 89
<physics> tag 122

Physics view, of gsVehicleDebug 229, *230*
placeholder material, in Blender 49–51, *50*
placementArea attribute 176
plowingState parameter 215, 217, 218
PNG file format 68, 237
Pose mode 199
position attribute 176
power consumer 260
prefabricated materials 51–52
preferedType attribute 176
previsualizing animations, in blender 162–170
<price> tag 111
Principled BSDF
    node 58–59
    shader 56, *56*
Print Screen button 236–237
publishing process, modding 233
    CG Cookie 249
    console play 237–238
    description of mod 235–236
    FarmCon 245–246, *246*
    good in-game screenshots 236–237
    Lua 247, *248*, 249
    mod contest 247
    ModHub *234*, 234–235, 240–244
    monetization for mods 244–245
    technical requirements 234
    TestRunner 238–239, *239*
purposes, of modding 29–30
    modeling in Blender 30–34
    working with UVs 34–35, *35*
Python programming language 29

QualidiscPro folder 101
qualidiscPro_lod Empty 193
qualidiscPro_lod2 Empty 194
qualidiscPro_main_component1 object
    90, 91
qualidiscPro_vis works 182, 184
qualidiscPro.xml 252–276
quality mods 244

radius attribute 122–123, 128, 226
Random button 80
raycast node 136, *136*, 270
<raycastNode> tag 137
RDT parameter 66, 69
real light sources 261–262
    working with 173–175
<realLights> tag 174
rearLight05_01 172
referenceFrame attribute 158–160, *159*,
referencePoint attribute 158, 160

removeFoliage parameter 216
repr attribute 122
reset parameter 226
restLoad attribute 122
rigging system, Blender 195
Rigid Body panel 90–91
rollLeftBack object 82
rootBone 197, 201
root, merge group 182, *182*, 183
rootNode 259
rotationAngle parameter 67
rotationJointNode attribute 140
rotation limit 254, 259
<rotation> tag 111
rotCenterPosition attribute 141
rotCenterWheelIndices attribute 141
rowLength attribute 148
rowLength variable 147
rows parameter 220

saveId attribute 121, 123
<schemaOverlay> tag 113
Scripting Farming Simulator, with Lua 105, 247, *248*, 249
scrollPosition parameter 69
SelectedToOrigin 83
setSpray parameter 218
shader folder 50
shaders and materials, in new material system 50, 69, 70, **70**, *71*, 72–73, *73*
shared lights, from Farming Simulator 172, 261
<sharedLight> tag 172
<shopFoldingState> tag 112
<shopRotationOffset> tag 112, 209
<shopTranslationOffset> tag 112, 209
single Blender object 78, *78*
sizeMarkerBack Empty 138
<size> tag 113
skinnedMeshes Empty 197
skinning process 195, 204
Smart UV Project unwrapping 36, *37*
soil effects
    custom effect array textures 145–148
    particle-based effects 144–145
solverIterationCount attribute 113
sounds, animation for vehicle 161–162
<SourceFile> tag 106
spacing parameter 220
<specializations> tag 105–106
specialized CDATA syntax 103
<specs> tag 110, 111
specular map 54
<speedLimit> tag 113

speedRotatingPart activation 256, 262
<speedRotatingParts> tag 124–128, 132, 135
speedScale attribute 154
sprayTypeState parameter 215, 217–218
spring attribute 123
SQUARISH type 176
sRGB 53
    spectrum 106
    values 65
startAnimTime attribute 154
startMoveDirection attribute 154, 155
startRot attribute 153
startRotLimit attribute 153
startScale attribute 153
startTime attribute 152, 162
startTrans attribute 152
startTransLimit attribute 153
startVisibility attribute 153
static light compounds 75, *76*
<staticLightCompounds> tag 75
<storeData> tag 108, 110–113, 209
store icon 112, 205, 206
    for individual vehicles 208–209
    for mod 209–210
    3d shop preview and 253
<storeItems> tag 109
<storePacks> tag 108
straighteningFactor 259
stubbleState parameter 216, 218
Sublime Text 20
supportCollisionLeft object 152
supportsWheelSink 256
<support> tag 151, 152, 154
surface materials 47
    in Blender *see* materials, in Blender
    decals *see* decals
    Farming Simulator 25 *see* Farming Simulator 25
    GIANTS Editor *see* GIANTS Editor
    technical requirements 48
    Textures to DDS, converting *see* Textures to DDS, converting
    vehicle *see* vehicle
suspTravel attribute 123
sweepEffectNode01 Empty 144
System section of Preferences 28

tangentType attribute 153
<template> tag 161
testing, vehicle in-game 211
    debugging *see* debugging, vehicle mod
    modification 223–225
    populating fields 214–223
    reloading 226

testing, vehicle in-game (*cont.*)
    setting up Farming Simulator for 212–213, *213*
    technical requirements 212
testing vehicle-XML (and your mod), in Farming
    Simulator 116
TestRunner 238–239, *239*
TestRunner.log 239
TestRunner_public.exe 238, *239*
text editor 18–20, 99, 102, 109, 119, 150, 171, 177, 212
textures
    custom effect array textures 145–148
    DDS texture animation file 145, 148
    GIANTS Texture Tool *see* GIANTS Texture Tool
    Image Texture node 58
    in new material system 69, **70**
    UDIM textures 52, 75
Textures to DDS, converting 67
    GIANTS Texture Tool, getting and installing
    68–69
textureTool.exe 68
textureToolInfo.cmd 69
textureToolLowQuality.cmd 69
textureToolRecursive.cmd 69
thing attribute 178
third-party add-ons 30
3D model 7, 21, 31, 52, 77
    Assets, with GIANTS I3D Exporter 16–17, *17*
    with Blender 8–10, *9*
    cursor 83, 196, 198
    digital content creation (DCC) tool 8, 12, 13–15,
    13–15, 21
    Video Tutorials, on GDN 7–8, *8*
3D Scene in GIANTS Editor 237
3D Viewport 17, 23–25, *25*, 31, *32*, 33, 39, 42, *43*, 44,
    49, 51, 53, 63, 64, 74, 82, 84, 89, 96, 125,
    134, 138, 148, 164, 168, 169, 174, 185, 189,
    190, 196, 201
Tilde (~) key 212, 236
Timeline editor 164, 170
<title> tag 110
<toolReverseDirectionNode> tag 140
tools, for modding 12–13
    Blender, as DCC 13–15, *13–15*
    GIANTS Editor 17–18, *18*
    GIANTS I3D exporter 16–17, *17*
    GIANTS Studio/Debugger 18–20, *19*
topReferenceNode attribute 93–94, 114
trackArray 69
tractorBody object 49
tractorDecal_mat 58

tractor_mat placeholder material 50, *50*, 53, 55,
    56, 64–65, *64*
traditional armature-based character rig 198
traditional UV unwrapping 35–36
trailer attribute 114
transform group 38
<translatingPart> tag 159
trelleborg wheel configuration 257
true attribute 130
turnOnFoldDirection attribute 155
<turnRadiusLimitation> tag 140
type attribute 110, 134, 178
typeDesc_steelPipe 104, 105
<typeDesc> tag 113
type parameter 222

UDIM textures 52, 75
unified 3D model 85
Untitled Mod 240–241, 243
unwrapping
    with Project from View 37–38
    with Smart UV Project 36, *37*
    traditional UV 35–36
upperdistanceToGround 265
useDeepMode cultivator 271
UV
    coordinate box, in Blender 75
    coordinate system 52
    custom UV map 75
    Editing workspace 58, 61
    Editor 53, 61
    maps 52, 58–61, 77
    shifting mechanism 72
    slots 75
    Smart UV Project unwrapping 36, *37*
    space 53
    square 52
    traditional UV unwrapping 35–36
    unwrapping 55
    Vehicle Array 52, 53, 64–65, 72, 76
    working with 34–35, *35*
uvRotate variation 69
uvScale variation 69
uvScroll variation 69
uvTransform variation 69

"vanilla" Blender 64, 83
vehicle
    animation for *see* animation, for vehicle
    features *see* features, for vehicle

functions *see* vehicle functions
hierarchy *see* vehicle hierarchy
I3D file 254
materials to *see* vehicle, materials to
mesh 78–82, *80*
testing *see* testing, vehicle in-game
visual effects for *see* vehicle, visual effects for
Vehicle—Compound preset 90, 91, *91*
vehicle functions 119
    technical requirements 119–120
    wheels *see* wheels
    work areas *see* work areas
vehicle hierarchy 77, 84–85, 135, 143, *143*
    within Blender 120
    in Blender's Outliner 136
    and GIANTS I3D Exporter 185
    in I3D format 154
Vehicle.lua script 106
Vehicle Masks (vmasks) 54–57, *56*, 64
vehicle, materials to
    colors with color materials 53–54
    GIANTS I3D Exporter 54, *54*
    prefabricated materials 51–52
    vmasks and normal maps 54–57, *56*
vehicleShader 50
vehicleShader.xml 51, 60
<vehicle> tag 110, 177–178, 252
<vehicleTypes> tag 105–106, 110
vehicle, visual effects for
    particle system 142–144, *143*
    soil effects *see* soil effects
vehicle.xml 109
vehicle-XML file 75, 76, 82, 85, 93, 95, 99, 104, 108, 121, 177–178, 251
    attachment points 114
    automatic export, of i3d mapping 273–276
    base information 112–114
    connection hoses 114–115
    Developer Mode for Farming Simulator 109
    in GIANTS Studio 119, 143
    help with 116
    I3D mappings 115–116
    modDesc.xml and 119
    store data 110–112
    <wheels> tag 126
    testing 116
    understanding 110
    XSD for 178, *178*
vertex groups 197, 200–202
visual effects, for vehicle

particle system 142–144, *143*
    soil effects *see* soil effects
visuals Empty 193
Visual Studio Code 20
vmasks *see* Vehicle Masks (vmasks)
vmaskUV2_normalUV3 variation 69
vmaskUV2 variation 69
Vredestein brand 122
Vredestein config 257
vtxRotate shader variation 67

WASD controls 237
weedState parameter 215–216, 218
Weight Paint mode 201, 202, 204
wheelChockSupport01 Empty 130
wheelChockSupport02 Empty 130
<wheelChock> tag 128–130, 257
wheel configuration 121, 122, 124, 255, 257
<wheelConfiguration> tag 121–124, 127, 130
wheelIndex attribute 127, 128, 132
wheels 120
    chocks 128–130
    configuration 120–124
    crops with foliage bending nodes 141–142
    performance with merge children 130–132
    <speedRotatingParts> tag 124–128
    visual effects for vehicle *see* visual effects, for vehicle
<wheels> tag 122, 123, 126–128, 130, 257
width attribute 123, 141
workArea activation 262, 272
workAreaHeight Empty 133
workAreaIndex attribute 145
work areas
    AI areas and collision node 137–141
    configuration 133–135
    ground adjusted nodes 135–137, *136*
    groundReferenceNode 135
workAreas Empty 133–135
workAreaStart Empty 133
<workArea> tag 134–135
workAreaWidth Empty 133
<workingWidth> tag 111
working, with Blender 21–22
    Blender's Interface, quick primer on 22–23, *23*
    GIANTS I3D EXPORTER 42–44, *43*
    modes 24
    navigating 3D space 23–24
    purposes of modding *see* purposes, of modding
    Smart UV Project, unwrapping with 36–42, *37*

working, with Blender (*cont.*)
    technical requirements 22
    tips and tricks for 44–46
    Toolbar and Hotkeys *25*, 25–29
    unwrapping *see* unwrapping
<workParticles> tag 143–145, 148
worldx parameter 221
worldz parameter 221

xmlFilename attribute 104
xmlns:xsi attribute 252
XML Schema Definition (XSD) 177,
    178, *178*
xsi:noNamespaceSchemaLocation
    attribute 252

ZIP file 16, 68, 206, 221, 240, 242

Printed in the United States
by Baker & Taylor Publisher Services